D1576866

The
singing
of
the travels

Other books
by the same author

FOLKLORE

English Folk Dances
The Traditional Dance (with Rodney Gallop)
Pyrenean Festivals
Introduction to English Folklore

NOVELS

The Blue Dress
Wind from the South

*In search
of dance and drama*

The singing of
the travels

VIOLET ALFORD

*With
10 illustrations in half-tone
and 17 line drawings
by the author*

MAX PARRISH
London

First published
1956

MAX PARRISH AND CO LTD
55 Queen Anne Street
*London W*1

The author's thanks are due to the following
for permission to reproduce photographs in this book:

Photo Georges, Arles (pl. I); E.N.A.Ltd. (pl.II); Mrs Ross
Smith (pl. V); Swiss National Tourist Office and Swiss Federal
Railways (pl. VI); Decurtins, Disentis (pl. VII); Musée
Nationale des Arts et Traditions Populaires (pl. IX); G. Augier,
Carpentras (pl. X)

Printed and bound in Great Britain by
THE CAMPFIELD PRESS
St Albans

Contents

Illustrations in half-tone

Illustrations in line

(A map to illustrate the author's travels appears overleaf)

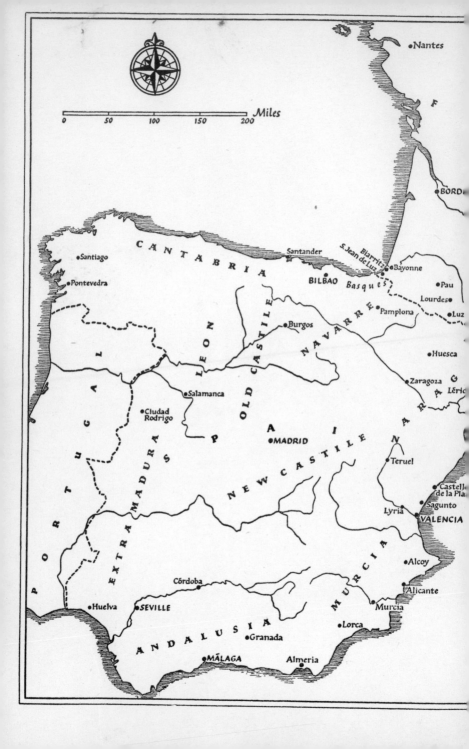

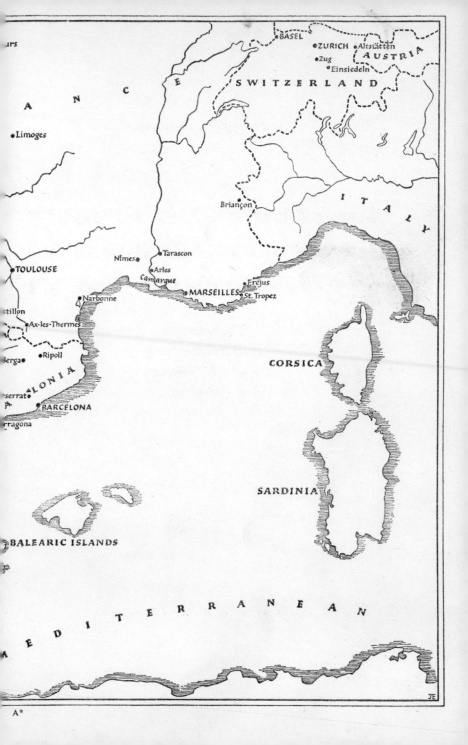

'The singing of the travels'

*This is the title
of the traditional song
sung by the Mummers
of Symondsbury
Dorset*

by permission of Peter Kennedy

Prologue

The opening verses of the Basque Pastoral Plays and the man
who sings them are both called Prologue. He begins

| *Egun houn souhetatzen deiziet* | *I wish you good day* |
| *Coumpagna ouhouratia* | *All the honourable company* |

and goes on to say

> *I begin by setting out the subject of our play.*
> *If you do not listen now, later on*
> *You will understand nothing.*

I too begin by setting out the subject of this book. It is to
follow some of my travels in search of folklore, and as that
lore presently began to mean to me one particularised branch
it will be quite true to say, like the Basque Prologue, 'the
subject of our play'. Moreover, if you do not listen now,
later on you will understand nothing.

My travels started with the sound of Morris bells, for I
came to folklore and anthropology by way of dance. In the
very early days of England's folk dance revival an invitation
took me to see some children dancing the then unknown
Morris. They were much too small for a virile men's dance;
their little hands could not clap, their little feet could not
stamp. But the jingling bells and the waving handkerchiefs,
above all the unknown, yet perfectly familiar, English tunes
so excited me that I said to myself, 'Nothing shall keep me
from learning more about this.' The programme, explaining
that the handkerchiefs 'represented the waving turbans of the
Moors' and the bells their horse bells, struck so false a note
that then and there my researches began. They have continued ever since. One thing at least I have mastered and

that is the relative place of our British dance and drama in the great whole which is the European Rite of the Renouveau.

As the travels proceed, different aspects of 'the subject of our play' will be seen. The plays will range from those in a group of Greek villages, to that of the Wild Man in the Grisons, and from characters who have broken loose from their Schembart play in other parts of Switzerland, to Sword dances in their stylised form in which dance overrides drama. The first group may be regarded as the fulfilment of the European pattern. As my serious travels began in the Basque countries I was quickly led to a confused and complex play; and when like the Doctor in one of our own plays, after travels in

> *Italy, France and in Spain*
> *Now I've comed back to England again,*

our other example, the Lincolnshire Plough Play, assumes its place as one of the most remarkable examples living and the one most plainly showing relationship to the prototypic Greek plays.

All across Europe, here and there, relics of this drama are annually performed, one region supplying what another has lost, so that by patient comparison and piecing together a reasonable view of the whole has emerged. The value of dance and drama to anthropology is now generally acknowledged (which was not the case some years ago) and some of my material has been accepted as 'new evidence' for the study of comparative religions.*

All sorts of other subjects which were and are being gathered will be 'set out' here and there, yet will be but a hare to the dance-drama fox, for a book must hold to its main theme or it will end in the disillusioned Spanish manner with *nada*, 'nothing', denoting the speaker's uninterest or blankness of mind. Just occasionally a travel has ended like

* Dr A.C. Bouquet, *Comparative Religion*. Penguin Books, reprinted 1954.

that – *nada*, a tiresome journey, a boring time of waiting and no rewarding plum. Sometimes, on the contrary, such a flow of material comes in without being looked for that unremitting work hardly garners it. I think of a week at Huesca in Alto Aragón, when I worked all day and lay awake half the night listening to a captive quail; ♩. ♪♪ |♩. ♪♪   it said from dusk till dawn; and again of Midsummer in Portugal, where celebrations began on Midsummer Eve and went on till the middle of the next night.

It will be quite impossible to avoid the first person singular and therefore not the slightest attempt will be made to do so. When the first person plural is used it will almost always mean myself and S. B. with me, the friend with a sailor hat on the back of her head, who at our first meeting told me with superiority that she learnt 'tonic Sol-Fa'; which I immediately countered with the news that I learned proper notation on a modulator with a moveable Do. None of your lettered Sol-Fa for me. Or it may mean S. B.-C. who most usefully accompanied me on two travels and who also wrote tonic Sol-Fa. Both these gifted people have therefore a pull over my staff notations, which take longer to write. Heredity perhaps helps to square things up. My father, who taught me to read music on the modulator, was a good amateur musician whose mother belonged to a family which produced the founder of the Church of England Sunday School Institute, Mr John Fleet, and three members of the D'Oyly Carte Opera Company. The most notable of these was Rutland Barrington (Fleet), who created Pooh Bah and other baritone characters as they flowed from the Gilbert and Sullivan brains. His sister-in-law, in the fashion of her time, took the romantic stage name of Geraldine St Maur and her lively old age must have reflected her young gaiety as one of the Three Little Maids. Amongst her stories was one of a scandalised diplomat home from Japan, who rushed round to re-tie the three little maids' three sashes. The bows, as they first appeared, were tied as only Geisha girls wear them.

The first part of this book is about Spanish travels. I have been going to Spain for so many years that the post-war fashion for that country still takes me by surprise. When the most surprising people lightly tell me they are 'going to Spain for a fortnight' it is all I can do to refrain from saying 'Don't'. Yet we too must follow the fashion and that entails a special Prologue to Spain.

Travel and travellers have changed out of all knowledge. Quiet people from the English Universities botanising at Zermatt to not at all quiet people sun-bathing on the Costa Brava; poor intelligentsia viewing ruins in Rome to rich persons seeking night-life in Madrid. But Spain remains the individualist, the unwelcomer, the looker-on at her surprising guests. The great blue and white coaches from Sweden, saloons as long as a railway coach spilling Swiss and Belgian francs; more practical coaches from Wupperthal (of dam memories) spilling clacking Germans after their enforced absence; these are the tourists in Spain today. A Swede sits shoulder to shoulder with a Swede, a Swiss with a Swiss, hour after hour, day after day. No contact is made with their Spanish hosts, no word exchanged, even if they could do so.

A rising lift in a Valencia hotel once took me within sound of a well-known accent.

'I want a hanger.'

A landing came into view, an awe-inspiring Momma confronting a little Iberian chambermaid. The one looked down, suspiciously, the other looked up, timorously. No mime was employed, no encouraging inflection of the strident voice.

'I want a hanger. I – want – a – hanger.'

The picture telescoped together, the lift rose above it, the voice went on.

Coaching tourists only see some small, prescribed part of this unmoved land through glass windows which protect them from contiguity. The proprietor of a china shop, where

last year we were looking for Hispano-Arabic pottery, said
in a charming idiomatic phrase:

'You are the used-to-be ladies who came before the war.
Now foreigners cannot say what they want so we cannot
serve them as we would like.'

For neither he nor any other Spaniard is going to take the
trouble to learn a strange tongue. That it rests with them the
coaching gentry cannot believe, nor do they believe that
some pains might be taken to conform, be it ever so slightly,
to the manners around them. Offended Britons have told me
how beach inspectors stopped them from, or fined them for,
undressing on the shore. The head waiter of that same
Valencian hotel was so outraged by the table manners of a
party just left that, the dining room being empty, he came to
unburden himself to us. He had the constipated face of a
Ribalta martyr – the dark saucers under his eyes, the selfsame tortured expression. It seemed to be caused at the
moment, not by the wheel, but by his late *Americanos*.

'*Los Ingleses*,' he said. '*Mucho protocol*. Excellent manners.
Children taught to sit up properly. *Los Americanos* –' and the
Ribalta character mimed a diner crossing his legs, pushing
out his chair from the table, shovelling in food. His young
waiters crowded round to see.

The luxury coaches roll from one luxury hotel to another,
which is one of the reasons for the painfully long stages so
much complained of. For the parties inside them cannot
believe there is no comfortable Swiss-like hotel erected for
their convenience every hundred kilometres along the roads
of Spain. This and the language are the main reasons, one
supposes, for the unbridled coach-travelling now infesting
the country. When the new traveller learns, if he wishes to
learn, that he but sees through a glass darkly, he will acquire
enough Spanish to ask for what is necessary ('I want a
hanger'); he will take to the railway or to the little, bad,
second-class roads in his own car and all Spain will be open

to him. He will find himself in a small town hotel with *Exquisito Confort* emblazoned on it, the exquisiteness consisting of a bathroom. He turns the tap. '*Agua? No hay, señor.*' 'Water? There isn't any.' Or in a pension where the friendliness is such that his table will be surrounded by affable fellow guests; or seated at late, late dinners consisting largely of fish. He will find politeness, amiability and presently true friendliness, peculiarly contrived on the top of an ineradicable enmity. Some effects of such amiability on my work will appear as they occur.

'Now you are our *señora*,' said the married couple in charge of the great eighteenth-century house in Andalusia lent me by a friend, in which I wandered alone.

'By yourself?' said a young man on hearing I was going up the hill to hear the Granada nightingales. 'No, *señora*, no. I shall come with you.'

If you ask the way somebody, man, woman or child, will immediately leave what he is doing to accompany you. The *touriste libre* will find the bread delicious, but apt to stick in his throat at the thought of how few can buy it. Never must one forget that hunger is common, a post-war hunger touching innumerable people who would get no relief even if they deigned to apply for it at – one knows not where. '*Come bien,*' you will eat well, they say, joined finger and thumb approaching their lips, on learning where you are going. Then '*Aqui no se come,*' here there is not much to eat. This is a truth which disagreeably affects a working day out if one expects to find a meal when needed.

I realise that some of the above remarks contradict my epithets of Spain, 'the unwelcomer', 'the looker-on' who could not care less. Everything is in fact contradictory and *on se trompe toujours sur l'Espagne*. Théophile Gautier wrote a good deal of nonsense about her on his famous long-ago journey, but that sentence holds a truth. So once the traveller has left the Basque Provinces and climbed to the endless

Castilian plateau he must cultivate a special state of mind, a shutting-away of all haste, all insistence, and adopt receptiveness, enjoying with pleasure the kindnesses given, ignoring the xenophobia he knows lies beneath. Xenophobia nurtured, I believe, by the fact that one comes from that go-ahead, despised Europe north of the Pyrenees, to which Spain has always refused to belong.

1

Cantabria

Cantos y sonos montañeses,   *Songs and mountain airs,*
melodías de Cantabria.   *Cantabrian melodies.*

Cantabrian Song

Not many foreigners go to Cantabria, that edge of Old Castile, shut off from the rest of the province by the great Picos de Europa to the south, gazing over the rollers of the restless Bay to the north. I went there in March and the cold was terrible. Yet eucalyptus trees grow there and as spring came on the sun shone warmly enough to bring out primroses.

We went to stay, the S.B.-C. of my collected airs and I, in an old country house belonging to an ardent regionalist in the village of Cabazón de la Sal. This gifted woman had literally saved the dance, song, instruments and costume of her native Montañas de Santander. She directed a choir of three hundred voices singing the lovely songs, she had had local costumes remade and had prevailed on the girls to learn to play the *pandereta*, their large tambourine, from the three old *pandereteras* still living. Do not imagine a Cantabrian tambourine can be played by banging it with the knuckles or shaking it to make the bells ring. It must be held flat like a tray, while the fingers slide over the skin face, which is held downwards, never breaking the gentle thrumming. This quiet throbbing with singing is the traditional accompaniment to dancing when one gets west of the shrilling *txistu* music of the Basques, but not so far west as the bagpipes.

Every evening the house was filled with the youth of Cabazón who poured in to visit the '*señoras de Londres*'.

Sibella Bonham-Carter and I had rival groups pressing upon us for hours, singing, humming, whistling everything they knew into our ears. Never have I worked so frantically, never have I had such riches poured out without even asking. When complete exhaustion overcame us we withdrew in turns to fall upon our respective beds for a space. On one occasion I came upon Sibella prone on the stairs, just out of sight round the bend. *La Folia de la Barquera* had temporarily knocked her out.

We noticed the young men bunched together at the door and thought they were talking bulls or *futbol*. But after two evenings of this segregation of the sexes our hostess came to us with a worried face, to ask if the boys too might not talk to us. They had been modestly holding back, waiting our pleasure. So the sexes changed places and one brawny young man, the blacksmith's apprentice, with short, tight curls like a young bull himself, presented me with a bunch of Parma violets – which must have been a rarity on that coast – scraping his foot like an English country lad and saying, 'Señora Violeta'. He had already brought two such bunches, but not being invited, as he thought, to the steps of the throne, had hidden them from sight.

Sadness overcasts what should be delightful memories of all those girls and boys. We heard from the other side of the chasm of war that every one of the young men had been killed. Their leader, with all her local activities, had been an aspiring politician and one of the first women delegates in the Republican Cortes. I fear she sailed too near the wind which filled red sails, for she disappeared when the war turned against the Government and, like hundreds of disappointed politicians before her, managed to get across to the New World, never to return to her Picos de Europa.

The famous cave of Altamira, not far from Cabazón, was my first introduction to prehistoric art *in situ*. There are no difficulties of entry; the authorities have even cut sunk pathways so that one walks on a lower level than the original floor and can look up at the ceiling paintings without too much craning of the neck. Here are the large – so much larger than I had expected – red bison we all know, the apogee of Magdalenian art. Without fanciful thinking it really does appear as though the old Cantabrians never moved from their ancient dwelling ground. Their Franco-Cantabrian culture lived on from Palaeolithic to Neolithic times and passed to the Bronze and Iron Age peoples. It stretched, like those who practised it, from these Cantabrian mountains into the Pyrenees and beyond them into the plains of France, where the painted and engraved animals and the strange, disguised humans of the Vézère caves are of the same school and often of the same majesty as those of Altamira.

The men who drew them were probably of earliest Euskarian blood, now represented by the Basques. This indigenous race, shrinking in the course of ages into its modern centre, yet left a deep substratum beneath the incoming Celtic tide with its later top wash of Visigothic military lords. The Cantabrian population quite certainly contains Euskarian affinities. Basque types are easily recognisable though of course these need not always be of ancient date. Love of their own traditions reminds one of their Basque neighbours, together with their agile lightness in the dance. Here the bloodcurdling *irrintzina* of the Basque has moderated to the *relincho* and the *i-xuxu*, when dance and drink excite the men to cry their mountain cry. Their folk tales, too, have strong Basque affinities, their habit of going a-wassailing and, of course, their sea-going propensities.

Their music is simple and melodious, untouched by the ever-spreading Andalusian influence except perhaps for a few singing mannerisms. A little further west, in Asturias, we hear the amusing regional style which imitates the bagpipe. The instrument lets out a groaning last breath. So does the singer. The instrument pumps in wind and blows it out again in a volume of sound. So does the singer. And all with the utmost simplicity, no striving to be humorous.

Some mediaeval romances live on in Cantabria, one forming the accompaniment to the beautiful *Danza del Romance*. The young men in their white shirts and trousers, clacking beribboned castanets, leap and flutter before their partners; the girls, singing and tambourining, receive this choreographical homage with eyes on the ground. Then a sudden sweep of skirts and a wide three-quarter turn takes them away from their adorers, and it is all to do again. The men, following round an arc, are disappointed a dozen times. The manoeuvre continues till the long, long romance is sung to its end when, on the last beat, feminine contrariness gives way and the kneeling follower is rewarded by a hand placed on his head. It is a lovely thing to see – adoration, denial, acceptance, gracefully mimed, while the old romance works itself out with no bearing whatsoever on the choreography. Here the Celt must be uppermost for no Basque man would deign to bend a knee, no Basque girl would dare place a hand on a male head.

Putting aside the drum and the primitive conch shell which accompany the Sword dance of Ibio, the music and traditions of this unique part of Spain belong to the general European concept, beginning with New Year mumming, then lovely Wassail songs lasting from Twelfth Night to Easter but all called *las Marzas*; even a verb, *marcear*, has been invented to describe the March night songs and visits. Men and boys, ringing a bell to mark the time and carrying lanterns, modestly announce themselves:

> *We do not come from Holland*
> *Nor from England,*
> *God sent us from Heaven*
> *To the earth.*

One lovely tune sung to me by the Cabazón young men runs

The Sword dance just mentioned belongs to the European hilt-and-point family, which was never martial but drew its content from magico-religious forces. It is hardly necessary to describe the formation, the never-broken circle of men, each holding his own sword in his right hand and the point of his neighbour's in his left – a circle not adapted for fighting. Here we get a first glimpse of the ritual dance-drama which is the recurring theme of this book. The young men of Ibio no longer remember the correct day on which they should perform their dance. They appear at various festivities but not on a day ruled by the calendar. There are no words; mime is sufficient. A man, a leader, is raised up for all to see before he meets his symbolic death. The swords of Ibio have degenerated into longish sticks painted in red and white spirals. Nevertheless a 'lock' is made. It is not woven in the usual way but the sticks are cleverly piled up like spillikins and on this insecure 'shield', as it is called, the Captain still more cleverly climbs. Standing erect upon it he is shown to the people like his long-ago predecessor, Pelayo, on his election as first King of Asturias. That thrilling moment was the beginning of the Reconquest and the turn of the Moorish tide. So the Ibio Captain conforms to an historic as well as to a dance usage. This seems significant, as though both sprang from the same traditional custom; and if the representation of the Divine King (who, when old age came to him or at midwinter or at the end of a cycle of years, died for the good of the people) has descended to a ritual dance leader this may well be so.

Well-known folk characters go with the Sword dance, at Ibio the man in woman's clothes, called the *Zorromoco*, doubling the part with that of the Fool. For an attempted explanation of this name we must turn to the relics of the Euskarian language left scattered about Spain. As with the lettering on Iberian pottery, only by this means can sense be made of this ancient word. It would then have no affinity with the Spanish *zorro*, a fox, but would read *zorro*, a fool, *moko*, a beak. And 'beaked Fools', with appropriate masks, are well-known spring-time guisers.

The tension of the never-ceasing drum-roll broken by the sudden booming of the conch shell ≡≡≡≡≡ adds to the mysticism of this rite. It is not by any means the farthest west of the shining chain of Sword dances, each linked in its magic circle man to man, each linked to the next in the chain by its adherence to tradition. Jovellanos (1790) tells of a Sword dance in Asturias, now extinct; and in Galicia it still circles at Pontevedra and Bayona. To the student of comparative folklore not only does this immense chain of Sword dances seem an almost miraculous exemplar of continuity, but so also does the invariable announcement by the dancers that theirs is the only Sword dance in their region or country or in Europe or the world. One asks, how is the tradition so closely carried on if they know no other but their own?

This Danza de Ibio has never been overrun by Moors and Christians, as has happened in too many Sword dances. The fervour of the Reconquest brought Moors into fashion to such an extent that they managed to push into seasonal rites both popular and ecclesiastic. In the passion of victory ancient ritualists, almost forgetting their own *raison d'être*, dressed themselves in the costume of the vanquished and of the Christian knights who vanquished them, and added a battle-drama to their real business. Sword dances have been particularly affected by this irruption of quasi-historical fashion, and when the travels take us to Aragon we shall see the results and must pause to discuss the phenomenon. Ibio seems to have been saved from the *Morisca* infection because at some date, unknown now, a real *Morisca* came into being in the same village. They ride out on Shrove Tuesday, do these later Moors and Christians, one party with blackened faces, the other with white. As they ride a girl wrapped in a cloak comes between the parties, whereupon they fight for the cloak and tear it in two. This evidently superseded a fight for the girl herself, such as occurs in the *Morisca* on Korčula in the Adriatic. I write in the present tense, but so far as the cloak goes it should be the past. Nowadays the Cavalcade, as it is called, consists of one party only, all with blackened faces, and the Christian girl is forgotten.

As firmly linked to European custom as the Sword dance are the *Viejeneros*, literally the 'Old Yearers', who come out on Twelfth Night to magic in the New Year. There is Madama, the man-woman in skirts and frills, the Galán, covered with small bells, who escorts her, a 'bear' shambling and dancing, led by his master, and two apparitions which might have stepped down from the walls of the cave of Altamira straight from the Old Stone Age. Goat skins turn them into beasts, and over this shaggy disguise hang huge cow-bells, as many and as big as possible. Their every movement makes a sonorous clanging. They station themselves at the entrances to their village to levy contributions on people coming in to see the fun, and there they jump for hours on end. The sound of the bells fills the valley. These too are *Zorromocos*. Neither the rite nor the ritualists are peculiar to the Cantabrian mountains. We are again looking at the folk drama, this time in its Midwinter form, bridging the darkest days to the earliest 'turn of the year'. Such characters invariably appear at their appointed season and if it includes the Twelve Days they are likely to be frightening in their behaviour, for that is one of the periods when spirits may roam on earth. The goat-skin men are amongst the most primitive of these guisers. Although we are almost within sight of the Roman 'end of the Earth' which was Galicia, we can look back as far east as Greece and there find their counterparts in the skin-clad leapers who appear in the Thracian plays to which we have called such serious attention – the *Callicant-zari*, creatures wearing so many bells that they can hardly walk. But, like the Cantabrian *Zorromocos*, they can jump, coming down to earth with a formid-able crash to awaken reluctant spring. Thus in the single province of Mon-tañas de Santander we find two forms of the seasonal play, both moreover in fairly good condition.

*Zorromoco
the Belled Fool*

Church festivals bring out the *Pica-yos*, young men who accompany their Patron Saint on his annual procession. They dance backwards before his statue, using the light, fluttering step we noticed in the *Danza del Romance* while they were courting the line of tambourine-playing girls. These same girls pace along on either side the roadway, their fingers as agile as the men's feet, sliding over their sonorous tambourines. Their red skirts with black velvet borders and their folded white head kerchiefs contrast well with the dancers' gala white and with the grey, storm-worn village streets.

A famous festival is that at San Vincente de la Barquera when the statue of their Virgin is taken down to the sea and aboard a fishing boat, many more boats following out into the waves. One verse of the *Folia* recalls a long-ago accident when many people, fishermen and boatmen, were drowned in the very procession itself.

Oye, Marinero, sacame del agua!	*Listen, O Boatman, take me from the sea!*
no muera yo de muerte tan amarga.	*I would not die a death so bitter.*

The word '*Folia*' shows some confusion, for a *Folia* is in reality a wild, somewhat Bacchic dance done in the excitement of village fairs. This dance before the Virgin of the Barquera is airy, but orderly and sincere.

At Comillas, on the coast a few miles to the east, when their much venerated statue of St Peter is safely in the church again, the dancing *Picayos* drop on their knees three times, then immediately turn their attention to the 'Old Woman's Dance', a speciality of this village. A row of old village ladies in their best headkerchiefs and Manilla shawls – Manilla shawls come round to the north-west by sea, especially to Vigo; they are not confined to Andalusian shoulders – are sitting in the little square. They are tambourining vigorously and singing in their sharp voices, but they keep a lively eye on the *Picayos* who now approach. One, clacking his castanets, presents himself before the old lady of his choice, who coolly remains seated until her young gallant kneels before her. Up she then gets and, more elegantly by far than her grand-daughters, begins to step to and fro, her gentle style contrasting finely with the leaps and twirls of her partner. Presently all the old ladies are up and at it and a charming compliment it is, for it is they who are the repositories of tune and verse and the best tambourine players in the place.

Pujayo, up in the mountains above the Besaya river, boasts a maypole at its feast, though not in May, which seems to have kept some relics of its pagan nature. When fair and pilgrimage are over, people crowd round it at dusk and bow with uncovered heads before throwing it down. A lovely mimed dance, now done only for fun but once in earnest, is that of the *Maya de la Copa*, the Girl with the Cup. It must once have been a pre-wedding ceremony, but the girls of the Montañas, becoming modernised like everyone else, probably consider it humiliating to ask for public contributions to their dowries, so that it has lost its real intention. I saw it in the hall of the house at Cabazón de la Sal and the Bride was

a child, not more than thirteen years old, with red-gold
hair and lovely blue eyes. She was still childish enough to go
through the rôle as a game, paying no attention to the
attendant young men, who paid a good deal to her. An
improvised procession of girls walked two and two round
the room, then seated the Bride in a chair where she remained
motionless like some lovely image, clasping in both hands a
large, stemmed cup. Her maidens marched round her thrumming and singing, then divided into two files, one each side
of her.

> *This year we must marry our Maya.*
> *We will go beg a dowry for her*
> *From the boys of the village.*

Then warningly they sang:

> *A boy who wears a sword like a gallant*
> *Seems a lord of the town,*
> *And a town lady he will marry.*

> *Look well at the husband you take,*
> *Don't seek him with the sword*
> *Nor him with the cape,*
> *For he will make love to another girl.*

> *Don't take a man with a degree,*
> *Nor the Sacristan of the Church either,*
> *Look for the handsome rose*
> *In this rose garden!*

Off they go to collect the dowry, holding out their tambourines as receptacles. The young men crowd near the door
as usual, but this time they are not talking *futbol* nor bulls.
The pence pour into the cup but the golden-headed little
Maya thinks it but a scant amount. Up she rises, the cup high
above her shining head. She shuffles up and down with tiny
steps which seem to have been borrowed from Africa, with

sudden spins on her own axis. Then saying to herself, 'I will go and get some more', off she goes into the crowd and gets not only the dowry but the husband. Throwing her arms round his neck she draws after her the sheepish, highly gratified blacksmith's apprentice.

> *A pink in his hat*
> *A rose over his ear*

sing the girls as he stands stiff and grinning behind the Maya in her chair, where she reseats herself, sure now of husband and money.

> *Choose the lordly boy*
> *Who knows how to plough!*

Reverting to Spanish duenna memories the first woman member of the Cortes informs us, 'Her mother knows I am always here'.

Lovely Cantabria has received and conserved an epitome of Indo-European folk culture. I came to her by sea to the port of Santander and still think this is one of the most beautiful parts of Spain, lying green as an emerald at the foot of her Picos de Europa. But her pale, northern spell has not made me return, for the south calls and we must leave for that great province which, although on the European side of the straits, is not entirely Europe.

2

Andalusia

*Mudar costumbre a par de   To change a custom is as bad
Muerte.   as death.*

                                      Spanish proverb

On se trompe toujours sur l'Espagne.
                  Théophile Gautier

This travel may seem as though folklore had been cast aside.
The fundamental Indo-European culture which the folklorist expects and finds all across Europe cannot be trusted
to show itself in Andalusia. This Mediterranean-Atlantic
population, the nearest to Africa, reared from Phœnician,
Punic, Tartessian, Romanised-Iberian ancestry, has developed an immensely long tradition. Two thousand years
have led to such stylisation of music and dance that they
must be studied on the stage and in the dancing school
rather than in the village. Rarely does one see country people
enjoying a dance; when one does it will be in the patio or in
a room. The dances are in reality indoor dances, needing
small space, floor boards to sound the 'heel and shoe' work,
and walls to contain the frail sound of guitar music – though
the clapping and castanets are, on the contrary, too noisy for
indoors. Moreover what country tradition there is seems, on
account of theatre work, to be failing. On enquiring in
Andalusian villages as to occasions for dancing I have been
told 'At the Patronal feast, only at the Patronal feast'. This
was supplemented by the news that the girls then dressed
'as Gypsies'. Thus they now assign their own regional costume to the Gypsies who show themselves off in it to dance
and beg.

Like all northerners I looked forward to Andalusia the exotic; I ought to add 'the intoxicating', 'the luscious', but she has never yet appeared thus to me. We first went to the south in the February before the Civil War, when not only was every man's hand turned against his neighbour but Spain's latent xenophobia was let loose. Nature was also let loose, an icy wind whistled down Madrid's 'pneumonia streets', rain poured down south of the Sierra Morena as snow had fallen north of it. The Guadalquivir rose in turgid masses until it came up the pipes, all yellow and frothing, into the bath, and washed the population from the lower parts of Seville and Triana.

These poor people were unwillingly housed in the palaces of the exhibition once held in the Maria Luisa park, amongst the orange trees and the fountains with their painted tiles. What a lesson in ethnology and social conditions it was to see the police forcibly depositing them in their marble halls, unfolding mattresses and blankets, which those who were to lie on them disdained to touch, or directing a decrepit caravan into the gates, the Gypsy owners immediately setting up camp on the marble steps outside the great doors they refused to enter and tethering their horse on the adjacent flowerbed. Girls paraded in their new surroundings, so poor that a cotton frock seemed their sole garment. Yet the first thing they did on arrival was, each in turn, to help herself to a camellia to wear in her hair. I could not tear myself from the railings – beyond which the public was not admitted – and was earnestly begged by solicitous Civil Guards to put more space between myself and the flood refugees, on account, said they only too truly, of vermin, begging and thieving.

Passing Sevillanos showed no spark of pity. Revulsion at the invasion was stamped upon them; the frilled, beribboned nurses with their charges fled the park. Nevertheless organised charity took a hand and was the means of showing us the young Carmen Amaya in her early days, dancing her terrific *zapateado*, dressed in her tight, grey riding habit, half killing her gasping, stonily-concentrated guitarists; and Pastora Imperio in her later days, majestically draped in her Manilla shawl while a nimble young partner did all the stepping for her. A film of local life, *La Hija de Juan Simón*, was shown at this performance, depicting real Sierra scenes, and people as far removed as it could be from the Fiestas and such-like 'Spanish' films of today. I have often enquired for it, hoping to see it again. Last summer I was urged to see a 'true' Spanish film – of cocaine addicts in the Barcelona *Barrio Chino*.

When the rains ceased the elections began, those 1936 elections which led to Civil War. 'If the Socialists get in you can stay a while,' said my professor of Spanish. 'If the Reds get in, pack up and go to Gibraltar.'

While things warmed up life went on. We heard a *cuadro flamenco* in a theatre to which señoras might go unescorted because it was a charity show given by generous-hearted Gypsies. It was the first I had heard and it stunned me soul and body. How useless an effort is that of Pilar Lopez or the young Antonio to turn *flamenco* song and dance into ballet. Succeed as they may with other parts of the Spanish heritage – I do not think they succeed – this flaming exotic should not be touched. All the fiery elements are already there and of such dramatic intensity that they need no scenic handling.

Andalusian dancing cannot be picked up like an English Country dance. It needs learning and practice and is a School rather than a style. I was able, between downpours, to take some lessons in *Seguidillas* and other dances on the roof of the hotel. I imagined the parapet hid the *gaucheries* of the beginner so it was embarrassing to hear loud clapping and cries of '*Olé, olé*' from the street but my *professora* was highly pleased. She was a lovely girl, daughter of a German business man and an Andalusian mother, whose Spanish side entirely overpowered the Teutonic blood. She paid visits to

She danced
Alegrías for them

relatives in Berlin and having donned her trained dress, her comb and castanets, she danced *Alegrías* for them, turning the heads of the German young men and – so it appeared from her conversation – having her own turned as well. With mournful, dark eyes she told me her father had forbidden her to dance.

'But you may teach?'

'No, nor teach. But he is out all day and Mama won't say anything.'

Poor Teutonic father.

So she turned me into an *aficionada* and explained the classification of Andalusian dances: the classical stage style, the *flamenco* and the real folk dance of the people – which interested her not at all. This last, as has been said, is hard to find and unless one may count the work of the girls of the much criticised *Sección Feminina* of the Falange movement I have never been fortunate enough to see any. The *Sección Feminina* seems to use the dances of Spain wholly and solely for social work, to occupy its members. Sometimes this treatment succeeds pretty well, especially when true village musicians are brought to play their traditional instruments, but the leadership is concerned with the girls, not with the popular art they practise. Up to now – realisation of their mistaken road is perhaps beginning at last – leadership has not treated their great heritage (one of the greatest in Europe) with sufficient reverence nor has it followed tradition. One can only suppose that the movement, beginning during or immediately after the Civil War, swung along without counsel from established folklorists, whom Spain does not lack. The confirmed habit of giving public performances by girls only has bereft their dances of their most striking characteristics; courting dances such as the *Jota* mean nothing when the man to mime the pursuit is absent. The very essence of Andalusian pair dances is the presence of the man behind his flashing partner. He is there to show her off. When I asked some of the ladies of the movement if they were not afraid that after a few more years of undiluted feminism the young men of the country would believe dancing was for women only, they sweetly agreed it might be so. '*Puede ser.*'

The worst piece of ill judgment is not perhaps to thrust away men partners but to teach these young women to take the place of men, in men's ritual dances. Sword dances, for instance, are known all across Europe as man's prerogative, yet a girls' team once came to the great International Eisteddfod at Llangollen to display a particularly virile Sword dance. In the Basque provinces women have very little place in the dance. There is for instance their own Chain dance, the *Auresku*, which requires the Head man to perform frenzied show-off steps before his partner, who stands with downcast eyes. There is also a dance-duel between the Head and Tail man. Could anything bring a historic, traditional dance into more ridicule than to see two stout young women bulging with petticoats, carrying out this male challenge in front of a third girl?

To give these girls their due, their manless activities have had one excellent result. They have undoubtedly saved many of their magnificent regional costumes from a slow death. They wear their grandmothers' costumes with ease and they remake hundreds of new ones to traditional patterns.

Maruja gave me a *Fandanguillo* tune from Almería and told me of the old Fandango still existing in Andalusia. I have since seen a stage version of a magnificent one from Huelva. From thence, as the travel in Aragon will show us, it started on its journeys all round the Iberian peninsula. She laid down firmly that *Bulerías* were vulgar – a young Englishman once

B

told me to my delight that this denoted 'the tune played as the bulls ran into the arena' – and that *Soleares* were the oldest form of *cante jondo* and as a dance are considered too gypsy-fied and therefore low. In spite of her turned head Maruja was but a drawing-room dancer; to her the only polite dances were the *Seguidillas* and the *Alegrías*, but she did know something about her complicated subject and I suspect her half-foreign parentage allowed her a less prejudiced understanding than most 'fan' Spaniards. I have always felt grateful to this disobedient daughter.

I was amazed on turning over S.B.'s diary the other day to find that Realito had deigned to give me a few lessons. It must have been before he reached the height of his fame. We spent two long evenings also at Otero's celebrated dancing school, deafened by the thumping on a miserable piano, the rattle of castanets and the *taconeado*. The Maestro was growing old but danced as in a frenzy in front of any pupil needing attention, teaching by example as he could not make his voice heard, his own castanets adding to the din. In his day he had trained many a dancer, and interesting it was to see his raw material gathered there. Little girls of five or six in worn frocks, a few *centisimos* clutched in their hands, the price of *their* lesson, for Señor Otero was generous. Beautiful girls in dance dresses arrived with their Mamas, and the finished *bailaoras*, just ready for a cabaret engagement, scowled with correctly fierce faces as they crossed each other in the interminable *Seguiryas*. Except for the Maestro and his nephew there was not a man in the place. Where the male dancers were trained I never knew.

Maruja, of course, held the general opinion that *cante jondo* means deep song, *jondo* being a dialect form of *hondo*. This would properly explain the strongly aspirated *j* instead of the silent *h*. But new research brings a new theory. A writer, calling himself a Sefardim Jew, finds strong affinities between deep song and Hebrew festal music, so strong that he

describes himself in the synagogue singing religious words to *Seguidillas* and *Soleares*, tears streaming down his face. In the *Saetas* of Holy Week he finds the strongest similarity.[1]*
The same theory is put forward by Medina Azara – a Moorish pseudonym one supposes – in almost the same words, and in his turn Professor Torner, reviewing the work of this last writer, gives his less prejudiced opinion that the one does not derive from the other but that both *cante jondo* and the Hebrew religious music spring from a common source. He does not venture to tell us what that source may be. He further remarks, quite truly, that the 'folk' do not call their creations by such psychological names as 'deep', and that some of the dances and songs in the *cante jondo* category are anything but deep.[2] Nevertheless enquirers will still be assured that Maruja's opinion is the correct one, and that deep song is the expression of the tragic depths of humanity in prison, the slums and the brothel.

It was not Maruja, disdainful as she was of the *flamenco* style, who enlightened me as to how a *cuadro flamenco* knows which of its artists, after a prolonged wait filled with pistol-shot handclaps, will spring to his feet and break into dance. The secret is four yet more incisive claps before the self-appointed executant leaps up and on a fifth clap begins – very likely with closed eyes and a shudder from head to foot. He has been waiting for his *duende*, 'which comes up through the soles of the feet'[3] and which, for want of a better word, must be translated 'inspiration'. But with true gypsy adroitness this magical impulsion can be used to explain unwillingness to dance, or pure laziness. '*No tengo duende*' is an excuse which cannot be gainsaid for refusing a lesson to a *gorgio* pupil.

Cante jondo is not a possession of the Gypsies, though only they can rend one's soul so profoundly with the opening 'Ay . . . ay . . . ay . . . ' (*aficionados* in Seville went in their

* Numbers refer to short bibliographies at the end of each chapter.

pitiless way to a cabaret where a phthisic Gypsy was singing, 'to hear him suffer'). It must be remembered that in Andalusia one of the early western Mediterranean civilisations flowered in the Kingdom of Tartessos. The cyclopean building of Tarragona and Sagunto is repeated at Niebla and round Cadiz; the Iberian sculptor's art and that of the bronze figurines are of this soil too, while music and dance were so renowned that, as we are often reminded, no Roman banquet was complete without the *improbæ Gaditanæ* as dancing girls.

The violent coming of the Moors interrupted the consolidation of an Ibero-Roman civilisation with its quickening of Visigothic overlords, but is it probable that these long ages of culture were entirely and immediately lost? It would have been swamped by the Moorish flood but time brought it up again, and the Andalusian Moors, when highly educated as they later were, would have appreciated the ancient indigenous music, which continued its life though strongly influenced by their own art. Add to this a Jewish liturgical influence and a far backwash from Byzantium. The Gypsies, wandering into Spain in the fifteenth century, annexed the music and dance they found there as they do wherever they journey, stamping it always with their Romany stamp. It is over-simplification to set down Andalusian music as Moorish. I think this tendency to ignore the continued activities of conquered underlying populations is only too common. When as a child I learnt about the coming of the Romans or the Normans my ignorant mind pictured an army sweeping through an entirely empty land. It really seems as though many people nurture this fantasy today.

Again, *flamenco* is not necessarily gypsy. Andalusians often take to this style and used – not so much now – to be thought 'low' for doing so. Gypsies kept it to themselves but can do so no longer. It has become popular. I find a note on *cantes flamenco* written in 1871 which says: 'I introduce them for the *first time*, low and humble cradle of song. Born often in the inn, the result of contacts between the low population Andaluz with the Gypsies.'[4] It is difficult for a foreigner to decide whether *cante jondo* is sung in the *flamenco* style or not and I practically despair of hearing true Andalusian folk songs, *cantes cantores*. They are a return to the general European style of simple melody and cannot be sung in the *flamenco* manner.

I will not enter into the quite bitterly disputed origin of the word. For myself I do not see why the straightforward 'Fleming' solution should not be accepted. There was continual intercourse between the two countries under Charles V and his successors, and when he arrived from 'Europe', a stranger from Flanders, he began to give the highest Court positions to the *Flamencos* who accompanied him. They considered themselves infinitely superior to the Spaniards; 'he and his Flemings spoke Spanish badly and in return were badly spoken of'. Here, I think, lay sufficient grounds for the first disparaging meaning of the words.

Spanish influence, not always in the spirit of the *Kermesse Héroïque*, is still quite recognisable in Belgium, for example women going to Mass in 'the Spanish cloak'; *Op Sinjoorke* (Up, little Señor), the often-stolen puppet passing between Malines and Antwerp Universities, which is own brother to Goya's mannikin tossed in a blanket by exuberant *Mayos* and *Mayas*; Baroque sculptures in stone and wood which breathe of Spain and a hundred small details.

The flow was not through a one-way street. Flanders sent waves southwards – witness the 'Dutch' houses on the quay at Ciboure, the Valona (Walloon) dance which went to South America, and, of course, the long procession of Flemish Masters who profoundly influenced Spanish painting before Italian fashions came in. The name of the swashbuckling, flashy Flemish followers might easily have been transferred to swashbuckling, flashy dance and song.

Just as *cantes cantores*, not belonging to typical southern

culture, do yet exist, so also do a few Sword dances unknown
amid the concretion of what is now Andalusian dance. These
are of the Indo-European culture, which I began by saying
cannot be trusted to show itself in Andalusia. They are found
chiefly in a geographical pocket near the Portuguese frontier
in Huelva. Pueblo de Guzman is a hill town behind which,
on a remarkably shaped higher hill, is a chapel of a *Señora de
la Roca*. On a day in May her statue is carried up from the
church to the chapel; everyone turns out on mule or horseback; the girls, riding pillion, are in local costume and some
time ago used to exchange hats with the men. (This was also
a holiday fashion in England, notably on Hampstead Heath,
and may have a buried sexual significance.) Five men or
more, always from the same families, go before the statue
performing at intervals their Sword dance. It is in hilt-and-
point formation, a chain, a circle and a Single Under called
puente, the bridge. A rival Virgin from another village
appears, when both statues are set down and their bearers
enjoy a little hand-to-hand fighting for the honour of their
own Lady, accompanied by all manner of curses and
epithets thrown at the rival. El Cerro de Andévalo is another
of these villages where the same truncated dance is performed, the dancers nowadays accompanied by three women
acting as *Majordomos* – a character well known in western
Spain.

Far away from these, at Obejo in the Sierra Morena above
Córdoba, lives an exceedingly interesting example. The
dancers, who have lost their costume – as have those of
Huelva – belong to a confraternity which is known to have
been in existence in 1600. They are divided into *Orantes*, who
give money, and *Danzantes* who give their dance. They lead
a pilgrimage on the Day of San Benito, March 22nd, and
again in July, when crops are in danger and when a calamity
threatens or has occurred. The music is supplied by guitarists and players of the tambourine, and contains passages,

so I am told, from *The Geisha*. The dance is more developed than that of the Huelva villages – a hilt-and-point chain, a circle, Single Under working up to a lock of swords round the neck of the senior brother. This lock is called the Gallows but the figure is *el Deguëllo*, the Beheading. The brother sinks down under the lock and the chain starts on its way again. That agricultural rites attached themselves to the cyclic death of a Chief is here well demonstrated, for they say or sing a prayer for the most precious element in their region, without which no crops could grow.

Agua, Padre Eterno,	*Rain, eternal Father,*
agua Padre mio,	*Rain, O my Father,*
que se van las nubes	*Don't let the clouds pass*
sin haber llovido![5]	*Without dropping rain.*

I shall mention these Andalusian Sword dances again. A proposition as to their possible history will be more in place amongst the Sword dances of Aragon than here, in the midst of a travel in Andalusia.

That first journey showed us, quite unexpectedly owing to our own ignorance, the celebrated Seises issuing from their little golden doors each side of the High Altar in the Cathedral of Seville, to dance their traditional religious dance. This was performed to the accompaniment of their own castanets and a suite of delicate, unsuitable eighteenth-century airs played by an orchestra. But this survival – often believed to be the only one – of Church dancing has been so often described[6] that I must travel on to when, having been cut off by wars and the results of wars for something like eighteen years, I went again to Andalusia.

This journey was concerned with Holy Week, Saetas and processions, which come into another chapter. So I will end this travel in travel-book style with a glance at the scenery and at present-day Gypsies, both of which are what tourists go to Andalusia to see.

You can fly from Madrid to Málaga in a miniature plane which sometimes leaves your luggage behind, and which alights like a fly on its landing-ground amongst the sugar canes. I am a convinced train-traveller and enjoy the dawn over the great chasm of the Chorro, and the descent into the subtropical vegetation of the coast. The sugar fields form an immense, inland green bay between the sea and the sierras, where one can walk on open ground sloping up to the Mijas. It is seldom one can walk in the country in Spain, so this came as a delightful surprise amongst the rosemary, cistus and yellow daisies. One can pick out the bends of the road to Granada, loop upon loop, to the right the Sierra Nevada like a white cloud above a dark blue sea.

The first time I went to Granada it was a never-ending journey from Seville, beggars boarding the train in pestilential swarms at Bobadilla, where one might have expected sighing Moors. The second time was up the loops from Málaga, over the mountains and across the Vega, richly green. The country people on the heights are very different from the too ancient, not-quite-European population of the coast. The mountain girls strode along strongly, their heads wrapped in white kerchiefs, their eyes pale in their brown faces. Workers in olive orchards were raking up those piles of loose stones they keep heaped round the trees, and the rakes they used were as primitive as the Basque *laya*, the hand ploughing-fork. Some were nothing more than three-pronged branches, others had prongs bound to a long stick; one marvels that neither Republic nor Dictatorship can manage to put modern implements into the hands of the agricultural workers. These men had grey eyes like the girls, hard brown skins and appeared much better fed than many a townsman. These mountain folk must represent the Ibero-Roman population which, but for the coming of the Moors, might have made and managed a very different Spain.

Granada does not display its Gypsy population much

except in their own suburbs. The first time I was there the shocking weather which flooded the Guadalquivir must have followed us, for snow lay everywhere. Yet the Gypsy girls, decked in their frills and finery, sat like a row of gaudy birds on the low wall of the Generalife to be looked at – a peseta a look. The second visit showed only two displaying themselves in the Alhambra. I presume only two were entrusted with hawkers' licences to inveigle the tourist; they were both stout matrons draped in flowery shawls, a rose standing absolutely upright on their well-oiled heads, and they sold every trumpery article imaginable. The moment a coach arrived the occupants made a bee-line for the two gaudy figures, who clacked castanets, flattered and cajoled.

I have never been to see the dancing in the caves of the Sacro Monte arranged for tourists. Every great dancer is supposed to have been born there but this is by now a traditional tale. Carmen Amaya, for one, is a Barcelona Gypsy. They send away their best dancers for training and then abroad, so there is little likelihood of seeing anything outstanding in the caves. An American friend who went there with her guide told me the price last year was 300 pesetas for her alone; she was not in the least interested in dance or music yet she paid it.

The tourist flood rises to its height in May, and when several coaches arrive at the Alhambra together it is well to flee before them. The best time for the palace is in the warmth and quiet of midday, when one has space to think disagreeably about Charles V and his palace amongst the delicate beauties he could not leave alone; of Washington Irving – I prefer him to the orthodox Sultanas lurking in their screened apartments – clearing a few rooms in his free American way in which to lodge gratis; and most of all of Manuel de Falla organising his *cante jondo* competition in the little *plaza* on the hill. This stimulating effort, made with the great Basque painter Zuloaga, Lorca, poet of tragic memory,

B*

and other artists, brought to the Alhambra hill Gypsies and countryfolk who came miles on foot. As Washington Irving brought about the rebirth of the despoiled Alhambra so did these ardent regionalist artists bring about the rebirth of the Deep Song of Andalusia.

On the way back to Málaga on one of the sharpest of the hairpin bends a caravan was drawn up beside a fountain, no Gypsy van, all spotless and shining. A couple of young women were at the fountain and working on the engine was a young man naked but for the shortest of shorts and a pair of sun glasses. It was early May, we were about 2,000 feet above sea-level, and a wind was blowing off the snowy sierra. A sort of growl rose from our busload. Our driver, within a foot of the precipitous edge, took both hands from the wheel in order to accompany a few telling words with appropriate mime.

'*Extranjero*,' said everyone – forgivingly I thought.

Extranjero, indeed . . . I had a sinking feeling that the letters on that caravan were G.B.

BIBLIOGRAPHY

1 J.M. ESTRUGO, *El Retorno al Sefard* (Madrid, 1933). I have not been able to see this book.
2 'Cante Jondo y Cante Flamenco: Resumen', in *Las Conferencias* (London), 16 June 1954.
3 Dr WALTER STARKIE, *In Sara's Tents* (London, Murray, 1953).
4 Alvarez, *Folk-lore Español* (1884).
5 A. CARBONELL, *Boletin de la Real Academia de Ciencias de Córdoba*, April–June 1930, and other later sources.
6 The latest account I know is in LUIS ORTIZ MUÑOZ, *Sevilla en Fiestas* (Madrid, 1948). See also ALFORD and GALLOP *The Traditional Dance* (London, 1935).

3

Aragon

*The intense emotion towards the weather which breaks out into
these magical* agones . . . *is not very easy to realize.*
Jane Harrison, *Ancient Art and Ritua*

O, 'tis the Moorish dance I see a-coming.
A Madrigal

All my travels to Aragon have begun through the Somport,
the *Summus Portus* of the Romans who, following the prehistoric track, made this pass or port their main route from
Romanised Iberia to Romanised Aquitaine. When they
pushed westward from the Fabled Shore they followed the
river way, more or less ignoring the people to the north of
it. Salduba, ancient Iberian city, was renamed Caesar
Augusta, from which came Zaragoza. Ebro, Ibero, is an
explanation not to be despised of the river name; the shepherds' customs, food and garments, the cloaks, the wide
breeches, the footgear, have not moved far even now from
their Iberian originals. Maladetta, the Accursed Mountain,
rears its huge mass between Aragon and Catalonia, and
Mont Perdu can occasionally be seen.

I shall not easily forget my first view of the Lost Mountain.
With a party of friends, one lovely summer evening, I drove
up the long valley past Eaux Chaudes and up again, round
the flank of the soaring Pic du Midi d'Ossau, or Jean-Pierre
as the disrespectful Béarnais nickname their giant. We were
making for the Portalet, the pass between the French Val
d'Ossau and the Spanish valley of the Gallego river. An unknown mountain surged into view, a great silver moon

43

coming up over its snowy shoulder. In the twilight snow and moon glimmered in a ghostly radiance. We stood in acres of deep-blue iris flowers and the tranquil splendour was such that one of the children came to put her hand in mine.

Another climate, spiritual and physical, reigns south of the Ebro. This part of the province is of African texture, altogether lacking the green *huertas* of Valencia lying between Aragon and the sea. The Moorish occupants of four hundred years have visibly left their mark on the population, which seems to me more Moorish than the heterogeneous peoples of Andalusia. Music and dance, to foreigners, may appear of the South, but they are, in fact, Aragonese and as different from those of Andalusia as the song and dance of north Italy are from those of Naples. The Aragonese themselves are convinced that the *Jota* is their prerogative and that

> *Calatayud was its cradle*
> *On the banks of the Jalón.*

They are encouraged in their claim by the whole of Spain as well as by traditional *Jota* verses, telling the story of the legendary Aben-Jot.

> *Desde la orilla del Turia*
> *a la orilla del Jalón,*
> *vino cantando la Jota*
> *el desterrado Aben-Jot.*

> *From the banks of the Turia*
> *To the banks of the Jalón,*
> *Singing the Jota came*
> *The exiled Aben-Jot.*

> *La Jota nacio morisca*
> *y despues se hizo cristiana,*
> *y cristiana ha de morir*
> *la Jota bilbiltana.*

> *The Jota was Moorish born*
> *And then turned Christian,*
> *And Christian it will die*
> *The Jota from Bilbilis.*

This Moorish musician-poet was exiled by rigid Mohammedans from his native Valencia, as the composer of the new and therefore improper musical form. Singing his cherished invention he sadly followed the Turia to Teruel in Aragon, from whence it spread to west and north. Thus we find a curiously exotic influence to within sight of the Pyrenees, while the southern parts of Catalonia have repelled it. The truth seems to be in what Professor Eduardo Torner wrote in his massive contribution to a great compilation.[1] Torner considers, with very good reason, that the *Jota* song arose from Andalusian songs of the *Fandango* type. Since I saw the *Fandango* from Huelva, albeit a stage version, I consider the *Jota* dance had the same origin. *Jota* music and dance seem to make a basic form exactly suited to the Spanish temperament, a form which can be manipulated to suit the taste of every region and climate and which, for these reasons, travelled from Andalusia through Murcia to Valencia, up the Turia with or without Aben-Jot, to Aragon. There it has a flowering peculiar to that region. I have never seen it at its most passionate, at Zaragoza for instance at the fiesta of Our Lady of the Pillar. I have danced it outside Huesca and found it shorn of excitement, for the true *Jota* does not mean Pyrenees but, as the popular verse says, 'it means love and the Virgin of the Pillar' – that is, Zaragoza.

La Jota no dice Jota	*The Jota does not mean Jota*
cuando en Aragón se canta;	*When sung in Aragon;*
*dice amor y la Pilarica,**	*It means love and la Pilarica*
dice Madre y Patria,	*It means Mother and Fatherland,*
dice amor y Patria,	*It means love and Fatherland,*
la Jota no dice Jota.	*The Jota does not mean just Jota.*

The *Jota* of the Navarrese plain is not far behind that of Lower Aragon, but when it reaches the French frontier it changes its character, reverts to its original *Fandango* name and, under the lamplit trees on the *place* at St Jean de Luz, becomes languorous and slightly erotic. This is strange, for French Basques delight in brisk movement. It journeys west-

* The dialect name for the Virgin of the Pillar.

wards – the Cantabrians have it under its *Jota* name –
right into Portugal where two men *vis-à-vis*, holding the
lapels of their coats, eyes on their feet, lugubriously step a
Fandango.

Back in Aragon the singer is as important as the dancers.
His *copla* or verse pierces the air, so strident is his *Jota* voice;
then comes the stereotyped phrase of dance music, another
of dance and then a second sung verse. One grows weary of
the strained voice, the modern pretentious words, but the
guitar ensemble, sometimes up to six or eight players, is
inspiriting and the snatches of dance are exciting if somewhat
rough.

The stage version so often seen does not reflect the spirit
of the popular form. This is a large musical and choreographical subject, has had much attention and for a long time was
believed to be the only expression of Aragonese music.[2] But
the province possesses a wealth of simple folk songs akin to
those on the other side of the Pyrenees.

Our best *Jotas* were obtained in little Andorra, curiously
enough. At the odd little bath place of Escaldes, a couple of
miles from Andorra la Vella, was, very usefully for us, a bath
attendant from Zaragoza. A great stalwart girl was she, well
built for plunging patients into the primitive wooden baths
scooped out of a tree trunk. When, after heavy meals, the
patients were sleeping Pilar Morales would come upstairs
and start her *Jota coplas* in the true *Jota* voice. Very soon the
whole staff came too, slinking in one after another to stand
round the walls, enrapt. We had the cook and the kitchen
hands, the aged waiter and the whole hotel family, whose
father was an honourable Andorran Parliament Councillor
and wore a three-cornered hat and a cloak at Council meetings. As each ringing verse ended Pilar would lay a hand on
her breast, modestly remarking, 'Very good, isn't it?'

Whenever folk drama is in question the *Morisca* will crop
up and here, in Aragon, is the very ground for a study of

this, to me, vexing subject. Even as the Moorish warriors came within sight of the Pyrenean barrier Aragon began its heroic struggle. Round about Monte Oroel the people who had barely seen Romans began to throw off Islam, as soon as or sooner than the Asturians at Covadonga. As a result the mountain race remained free of taint. Here can be seen grand examples of the ancient Sword dance and here can be studied the insidious infiltration of the *Morisca*. The earliest *Morisca* known to me was at the betrothal ceremony of Ramon Berenguer of Barcelona and the young Petronilla, Queen of Aragon, at Lérida in 1150. 'A choir of minstrels and many dancers, amongst which mention is made of Moors and Christians who gave a feigned combat.'[3] It is likely to have been the first *Morisca* invented, for the Moors had retreated from Lérida only one year previously, but Aragonese nobles, bred to battle, thought nothing of turning a dreaded enemy into a Court dancer. One can almost follow the rise of *Moriscas* by following the advancing line of the Christian–Moorish frontier. The victorious tide swept down the coast more quickly than inland, thus the *Moros y Cristianos* round Valencia may have come into being a century before those in Lower Aragon.

I had had news of a Sword dance at Sena, a village about 60 kilometres from Huesca, and we drove there one midsummer morning through scrub-land where tall Pyrenean sheep wrenched a living from rosemary, lavender and cistus bushes. We had an introduction to two Sena worthies, one the Notary, the other a somewhat mysterious person in a soiled cassock who, we were insistently told, was not the parish priest. Eventually we gathered that he was an unfrocked priest, ordered to keep out of harm's way at little Sena. He had employed his time there well, for he had faithfully collected every spoken word, every sung and played note of music of *El Dance*, the dramatic dance of the village. In the usual incredibly generous manner of Spaniards, Don

A. gave his notebooks into my hands and allowed me to carry them off to our lunch place in the desert.

'Where can we find some shade?' we asked the Notary.

'Under the trees,' was his proud reply. Our eyes searched the landscape but he had to point out three small trees swaying before a furious wind, growing in a bunch by a dry stream. In its bed we sheltered and there I absorbed the treasures of Don A.'s notebook.

Afterwards the Notary took us to visit a great convent rising a good deal higher than the trees from the desert. This had been founded by Alfonso II's Queen, who became the first Prioress of one of the two women's communities of St John of Jerusalem. The dress worn was the same as at the time of the foundation, the cross of St John conspicuous on the habit. The poor ladies had had their life work and most of their livelihood taken from them by the Republican Government, who had closed their superior boarding school. At the sight of two foreign visitors creeping into their Chapel they were devoured by longing for conversation. Their Chaplain suffered the same pangs. Never have I heard an Office finished so quickly, never did officiant unrobe and appear at his vestry door in so few minutes. He bore off the visitors to see the famous alabaster sculptured panels in the Cloisters, leaving the Sisters still grappling with a community Rosary. Presently a lay Sister brought us white wine, begging us to await the Prioress. But the afternoon went on and so did the Rosary and the road to Huesca lay ahead. We were heart-broken for the disappointment of those poor ladies left singing in the wilderness.

This is what Don A.'s notebook and 'the mouth of the folk' at Sena told me. *El Dance* is performed twice yearly, in full for the Patronal Feast, October 2nd, and a shortened version on another day. The ceremony opens on the Eve with the lighting of a fire in the church porch late at night, and the singing of the 'Romance of the Guardian Angel'.

The bagpiper accompanies on the biggest bagpipe I know. Before dawn of the great day everybody meets again at the church to go round the village 'singing in' the festival – but now they sing *Jota* verses. Later, church bells clamour their own festal dance as they turn right over on their beams in the manner of southern bells, the bagpiper and the dancers marching in front, stick-tapping and singing as they process. Later again they come out with swords in their hands. Some of the men are now Turks – synonymous with Moors – some are Christians, and these pass between the drawn-up Sword dancers who later dance in the church itself. The Patron Saint's statue on its *chasse* is placed on a table – such is the simple arrangement – in the Square, the priest and village authorities standing round. The headman, called the *Mayoral* or chief flock-owner (his second being the *Rabadan* or head shepherd), orders the dancers to begin. Each man whips off his headgear, cries, '*Viva nuestro Angel Custodio*', and spins round in front of the statue. Only the Turkish and Christian generals are costumed, one with a turban ornamented with a crescent, the other in a fireman's helmet. They shout challenges and a dialogue, the theme of which is Christianity versus 'Mahoma' (everywhere in Spanish folk ebullitions the Prophet is thought to be the Moslems' God), the Turks are converted before a crucifix held aloft by an Angel, and the inevitable Devil-Fool rushes out with exploding fireworks in his tail.

The dance contains both stick and sword figures; the hilt-and-point circle is called the Wheel and the whole finishes with a Tower. This is most impressive as four boys, called Flyers, climb on the dancers' shoulders to make a second storey, while on to their shoulders climbs the little Angel to make a third. The men wear regional dress – the wide, black breeches, broad waist-sashes and the string-soled *alpargatas* with dancers' bell-pads on their legs. The *Volantes* wear their sisters' white frocks and frilly drawers, with bells on their legs. Before they make their acrobatic climb their frocks are thoughtfully pinned up round their waists. The Angel wears a white frock, white gloves and a star on his little head.

This is one of the most rustic dance-dramas I know. We will briefly analyse it, extracting the mediaeval *Morisca* from the pre-Christian residue and, when that is done, adding the ecclesiastical stamp which seals it today. It will not be time lost for practically all *Moriscas* are made up in the same way.

Sena is not mentioned in recorded history so far as I can find, but we can properly suppose it to have been freed about the same time as Huesca, which was in 1101. News of the Reconquest of Zaragoza (1118) would have been trumpeted through the 'New Aragon' but in none of these places do we hear of a *Morisca* in the victory celebrations.

Lérida remains historically the first city to stage a Moors-versus-Christians battle and it might well have been tales of this performance which led to similar characters appearing at little Sena. Nobles were often as illiterate as their men; travelling troubadours or *Jutglars* sang to lords and ladies, men and maids alike and the nobility sometimes conde-scended to attend village feasts to dance with the people. (When Don Quixote attended Don Camacho's wedding there were villagers, labourers and students, while in England King and people alike went out 'to fetch in the May'.) So when the new *Morisca* found itself amongst country drama and dance it easily amalgamated with them. It had never known a real stage, we must remember; the *Morisca* of Lérida took place in the Cathedral, so a street or a *plaza* did not come amiss.

But at Sena lived still one of those traditional seasonal rites, here in the form of the hilt-and-point Sword dance with a 'raising' of the leader. An important character is this man, carrying his magic wand topped with a bunch of magic basil, taking over from village authority and saying his say, at which no one takes offence *on that day*. Often he doubles his rôle with that of the ritual Fool and at Sena, as we have seen, he is the *Mayoral*, the chief flock-owner. He is mightily concerned with the weather, which rules the lives of mountain shepherds. Flocks, meaning food, clothing and merchandise, are as dependent on the weather as were the herds which fed Pyrenean hunters of the Old Stone Age. On the first day of the feast the *Mayoral*, after verses on local scandals and the supposedly hidden doings of the notables, improvises on the weather from October to March, recounting the terrible snows, the raging winds, ending thus:

Mañana, Dios mediante,	*Tomorrow, God willing,*
esplicaré el otro tiempo	*I will explain the rest of the year*

and the villagers eagerly look forward to the morrow when they will all recall the torrents of rain, floods, drought and winds – always winds – from April to September. They listen absorbed, these men who have chiefly weather in their long folk memory, and who perhaps still have hopes that their sunwise circling Sword dance, duly performed, may in some mysterious way temper the wind to the shorn sheep.

On these two quite different elements – Sword dance and *Morisca* – the Church, as always in Spain, has laid her hand. The first amalgam has welcomed Church influence in its music; the festal fire is lit in the church porch, the chief performance is in honour of the Patron Saint and under his very eye, the whole is dependent on a Church festival – thus the third ingredient is added.

The hoisting of the Captain – turned for the sake of ecclesiastical acrobatics into an Angel – may have been influenced by the spectacular *Torres*, the towers, rising to four or five storeys of men standing on one another's shoulders, which occur in Castile and Catalonia, but the *Torres* – always called a dance and done to music – may themselves be an exaggerated raising – now separated from their Sword dance. The original date is now lost in the Saint's day. The masculine form *El Dance* instead of the usual *La Danza* is interesting, denoting something of greater importance and virility than a mere dance. All these Aragonese dance-dramas are thus called, for there are many of similar pattern containing sword and stick figures, a Devil, *Mayoral* and *Rabadan*. Nowhere are they more thickly congregated nor better preserved than between the Ebro and the Pyrenean wall.

In Alto Aragón there are also *Moriscas* which appear to have come into being on their own account, not having found an ancient ceremony with which to amalgamate. One of these is the *Morisma* (meaning a multitude of Moors) at the village of Ainsa, with Mont Perdu as a backcloth soaring into the sky. This drama is considered to be Gospel Truth and the first victory of the Reconquest in A.D. 724. But it is quite uncertain whether Moors ever reached the little kingdom of Sobrarbe in which Ainsa then lay, and the story is of legendary wonders, a red Cross surrounded by shining splendour conducting the Christians to victory. An ancient Cross was erected on the supposed spot, a new one replaced it in the seventeenth century, and the present one was erected by Carlos III. The drama was supported by 10 *libres Jaquesas* voted annually by the Cortes of Zaragoza from 1678 onwards.

The *Morisma* takes two days to perform, the whole village the stage. It begins with an immensely long prologue on the morning of September 14th, the Day of the Holy Cross; the two armies meet, the Infidels mocking the Christians as they leave the church. The Moors then withdraw 150 metres – so tradition ordains – while Mass is said before the Cross of Sobrarbe. In other villages, as here, there is often difficulty in recruiting sufficient Moors, the men considering this role blasphemous. The folk-devil rushes about shouting, the

Moor and Christian from Alto Aragón

Head Shepherd says his speech or *dicho*, and battle is joined till dinner-time, when all go home.

In these villages the men eat largely of what, farther south, is considered unappetising food. The shepherds' confraternities feast on mutton broth and easily polish off a pound of mutton for their communal breakfast and three pounds for their dinner, per man. High on the side of the Pic d'Anie, after the historical handing over of three heifers by a French valley to a Spanish one for grazing rights,* I was presented with a wooden ladle full of greasy broth from a sheep cooking in the open, so I know the taste and smell of this delicacy. I had just surreptitiously been mountain-sick, so the moment seemed ill-chosen. However *noblesse obligeait*. Some of the *Morisma* 'pieces' echo the alimentary ideas of the speakers: for instance,

> *Now I shall go to drink*
> *At the house of Sr Antonio,*
> *Where very good wine is sold . . .*

and

> *Make sure nobody gives me* migas;
> *Give me good cutlets instead.*

* Known as the *Tres Vacas*. The heifers are given by the Béarnais valley of Barétous to the Navarrese valley of Roncal, a 'tribute' paid since before 1373 at a frontier stone, in the presence of two hundred people or more who climb up from either side and hold a fête.

Migas is boiled bread often eaten by the shepherds but I am glad to say never offered to me.

In the afternoon, as soon as digestion allows, the Moorish King is taken prisoner and beheaded then and there by the Christian Ambassador. The Christians sing a hymn of thanksgiving so fervently that Moors fall dead around them. The Infidel Queen then steps out to order her remaining men to accept baptism. With eating still in their minds this calls forth

> *Our Queen is right.*
> *We will all become Christians*
> *And then we can eat bacon.*

Next day the play reopens with the mass baptism, and headed by their Kings – the Royal Moor has returned to life – both armies prostrate themselves before the famous Cross.

When travelling down the Fabled Shore we shall see *Moriscas* more true to history than Ainsa's battle, which have neither need nor opportunity to lean upon an ancient country ritual, but here, although it is away on the other side of the Pyrenees, I will cite one from Martres near Toulouse which illustrates an interesting amalgamation. It rests on something quite different from a Sword dance. Like the *Morisca* at Ibio in Cantabria it is merely called the *Cavalcade* or *La Procession des Cavaliers*.

On Trinity Sunday a men's society, existing for the purpose, goes to mass, half of them dressed as Saracens in baggy trousers and turbans, half as Christians whose helmets are marked with the Maltese Cross. In 1947 they were well dressed and their Kings mounted on good horses. The Christians escort the relics of their Patron, St Vidian, who they suppose was slain by the Moors. (One must remember that for every happening misunderstood or nearly forgotten, 'the Moors' are responsible in these regions. The impact of news of incursions on a terrified population must have been terrific, and the terror is remembered if not the event.) St Vidian is a hero-saint, inheriting something from the Paladin Roland who, in his turn, inherited from a folk-hero who has left gigantic foot-prints and horseshoe prints all along the chain. St Vidian's bed is an immense depression on the mountainside, his horse's manger another; his fountain is still red with his blood and there devotees go to drink and bathe their eyes.

After a battle by horse and foot the Saracens take flight, but during the *Te Deum* sung in the church they gather outside, heads and lances low. This is the most northern battle-*Morisca* I know and its connection with a sacred well, gigantic landmarks and a miracle-working saint show it to have annexed very ancient foundations indeed.

When the *Morisca* reached England the battle did not cross the Channel. The fashion came chiefly in name, *Morysse* meaning something 'in the Moorish style'.* This name, I believe, fastened, in the same manner as did the battle, on to a very ancient indigenous men's rite. To carry the discussion to great house and Court Masques, where *Moriscas*, *Mauresques* and Morris were at one period an expected part of the entertainment, would take us into another branch of the subject which began by being historical and became 'folk', in which guise it is still full of life.

We have considered the dance-drama by itself, the *Morisca* by itself and the amalgamation of the two. We now have to consider the drama as distinct from a choreographical form. It is seen in its clearest shape in a few Greek villages and in our own Plough Play, but as neither Greece nor England come into the travels travelled in this book this examination must be a mere outline in spite of the importance of these examples.

* Such as 'Morysse and Damashin very profitable to goldsmiths and embroderers' in the first English pattern book for craftsmen, 1543. (*Folk-Lore* Vol. XLIII. p. 142.)

The Greek plays occur in Thrace and Thessaly in the New Year, Carnival or May. The characters are men in goat-skins carrying wooden phalloi, masked or with blackened faces, covered with bells both great and small to clang as they leap. There are a Bride and a Bridegroom who perform too realistic fecundity scenes; there is an old woman carrying a baby – child of an unknown father. The baby grows up rapidly, demands a wife, undergoes a mock marriage with crowning as in the Greek rite, is killed and brought to life by a Doctor.[4] There are many lesser links with western plays, gypsies who are smiths, a plough, a man with a whip (the Whiffler), ritual stealing of eggs or children, and finally the highly significant throwing into the air of the agricultural implements with the cry 'Next year also!'[5]

Our Lincolnshire Plough Play repeats these characters: the old woman with the baby, child of an unknown father (for the supposed father repudiates it), Bride, Bridegroom, Doctor, farm men and the more modern Recruiting Sergeant and his 'Ribboner'. Both plays suffer from intrusions, ours from St George who comes from our other Mummers' Play, the Greek one from an 'Arab' – so that even this remarkable example cannot be said to be entirely free from the *Morisca* taint.

I called the *Morisca* a vexing subject on account of it drawing its life from some far more valuable pre-Christian rite, on to which it has fastened like a leech. It has spoiled for us many a description which should have been of untold value. Always writers and travellers have made the mistake of taking the part for the whole. Unable to explain the circling Sword dance they have called it (and still do) a 'war dance' – 'Pyrrhic' is the usual name given it – pretending to see in it a battle, because swords are in the men's hands. But this is really impossible to see in a formation where each man clasps the point of his neighbour's weapon. The Provençal Sword dance, *Les Olivettes*, has through this sort of thinking been turned into a romantic scene of men fighting pirates – and this in spite of an impressive raising of the Captain (p. 239). In the Piedmont mountains the Fenestrelle dancers must needs wear turbans, but just across that frontier the French Sword dance in Dauphiné shows no Moorish taint at all (p. 239). Happily there are several examples in Spain similarly immune. In the north, Burgos carries out its dance on Corpus Day guided by Fools with bells and thongs. Galicia boasts one at Pontevedra and another at Bayona. At the last the dancers are 'pilgrims' using staves instead of swords, no doubt under the influence of the great pilgrimage place near by, Santiago de Compostella. Nor must we forget the *Danza de Ibio*, saved from the *Morisca* taint by the appearance of a *Morisca* Cavalcade in the same village (p. 23), nor the very rustic dances in the Huelva district (p. 38) and that at Obejo in the Sierra Morena with its typical beheading and no Moors (p. 38). I picture those of Andalusia as continuing their seasonal appearance throughout the centuries of Moorish occupation and very likely throughout the ebb and flow of the Reconquest, ignored by the conquerors of either side, never connected with either Islam or Christianity. The physical situation of these dances, close to the prehistoric mines of the Rio Tinto, may explain their primitive state, coming even from the Metal Age which brought into being the magical metal sword and its magical protective dance.

In the following of traditional ways Aragon is one of the provinces *par excellence*. The *ronda de la villa*, a guitar band of men, regularly comes out on festal nights, singing personal *Jota* verses to those they wish to honour. So flattered were they at the visit from 'the lady from London' that I was once thus complimented. About 2 a.m. a motor lorry – a sad downcome from a bullock cart – covered with green boughs stopped with a jerk under my window and the guitars and the *Jota* voices began. I had been coached as to the proper procedure, so stood at my window with one hand holding back the curtain; one visible hand is all that is allowed, to show the recipient is awake and listening.

There are special Aragonese sports, such as throwing the bar, and there is a queer little Midsummer pilgrimage to Cillas where you shut yourself into a chest, say a Paternoster and rap on the lid to be let out again. This Midsummer magic procures good health. And there is the distasteful Feast of Santa Orosia and the *Endemoniados*, who are epileptics hoping for a cure by creeping under the saint's *chasse* in procession, by tearing off their clothes as the relics are unveiled, veil after veil, and by working themselves and the congregation into shrieking hysterics. The study of the *Morisca* was, however, our subject in this great and diverse province which we now leave, turning our right shoulders to the brimming Ebro, our left to the towering Pyrenees, the Fabled Shore before our eyes.

BIBLIOGRAPHY

1 CARRERAS and CANDI (ed.), *Folklore y Costumbres de España* (Barcelona, 1931), Vol. II.
2 VIOLET ALFORD, 'The Valencian Cross-Roads', in *The Musical Quarterly* (New York, 1937), Vol. XXIII, No. 3.
3 M. SORIANO FUERTES, *Historia de la Musica Española* (1855).
4 *Journal of Hellenic Studies*, Vol. XXVI, Part 2.
5 *Ibid.*, Vol. XVI, p. 232.

4

The fabled shore

The Massiliots, so the 5th century B.C. rhyming geographer
Scymnus tells us, founded first Emporion, then Rhode. . . .
The Greeks may have traded Greek wine and olive oil, commo-
dities till their arrival apparently unknown in Spain.

Pierson Dixon, *The Iberians of Spain*

And so we reach the Fabled Shore, magnet for a thousand
years of Eastern Mediterranean enterprise. I have not yet
seen the first Emporium, now Ampurias, set up by the Greek
merchant venturers who, about 550 B.C., came in their ships
from their colony at Massilia (Marseilles). It still lies by the
sea, temples and streets of houses protected on the land side
by walls against any ill will from the Iberian countryfolk, for
whom the wares were displayed. I usually come by the
Cerbères–Port Bou frontier, but the railway runs inland from
the Emporium and one cannot see it. My longest sojourn on
the Fabled Shore was given up to reading in the Biblioteca
de Catalunya in Barcelona, so field work was limited to one
country *festa*, which has been described elsewhere[1] in some
detail, and small folklore items which came my way.

But the going to this up-country town was itself full of
live Catalan lore. And here I will say, for the sake of the new
tourist, that he would do well to realise that a bathing holiday
on the Costa Brava is not equivalent to a visit to Spain. One
might as well say one had visited England after a sojourn at
Caernarvon. The language is Catalan, not Castilian; customs
are different, the ethnic type is different and at that time, two
years before the Civil War, politics were alarmingly different.

After the departure of Alfonso XIII his palace at Pedralbes, a little way outside the city, was converted into a museum and its top floor into a hostel for Catalan women students at Barcelona University. Through an introduction from one of the professors I was able to live in the hostel. The gardens were exquisite; ponds covered with waterlilies, from pale yellow to deep red, swimming on clear, dark water; tall resinous trees after hot sunshine giving out unforgettable savours in the evening; and roses over every arch and wall. The Republican spirit had not swept away the old Catalan Guards from the Palacio. Rather had it fostered them as part of Catalonia's national renewal, for their uniform was the traditional regional dress – scarlet *barretina*, brown breeches, white cotton stockings and smartly laced-up coloured ties on jute-soled *alpargatas*. These were elderly men, sober guardians of the sprightly *senyoretas* who had taken the place of the Royal family, and they felt their responsibility strongly, closing the gates on the last of the home-going public with proprietary clangs, and reopening them with disapproval to admit students with late passes. The numberless rooms on the top floor had been those of the King's suite. There were marble floors and not a single plug in the marble bathrooms. To keep the water in, the bather had to sit on the escape hole. Everything was Catalan during that exciting but aborted wave of nationalism. The very few foreign students were amazed and annoyed when they found no Spanish conversation in the hostel and the greater number of courses at the University in Catalan.

From the flat roof of the Palacio on Midsummer Eve thirty-two Midsummer fires were visible, many actually in the streets of the city. One was enriched by a bomb – a not unusual occurrence there – which wrecked a near-by school and injured a few fire-leapers. The students spent most of the night on the roof, dancing and playing elaborate Singing Games which must have descended from mediaeval romances.

It is significant that the words were in Castilian. One I remember built up a beautiful pattern of girls to represent a lady imprisoned in a Moorish castle. A lovely girl, whose name was Montserrat after the Black Virgin of the Mountain, stood on a chair placed against the wall; two joined her kneeling, one on either side, to represent her pages. The next verse introduced two Moors whose raised arms made a window through which the captive gazed towards her home. Each verse brought in other characters up to ten or twelve, everyone assuming their correct position and attitude, so that a symmetrical group grew before one's eyes rather like a *Château d'Amour* carved in ivory. Finally several Christian Knights rode up on imaginary horses, attacked the castle and delivered the lady. It was too dark even on that Midsummer night to write, but the whole is photographed in my memory. This game, descended from a ballad or *romance* in Spanish, corroborates Pidal's comment, '*le romance Moresque se développa dans le Romancero comme une mauvaise herbe*',[2] and is one more example of the *Morisca* taint.

One very hot summer night I wandered out of the gardens to sit on the edge of a fountain in the flowery Avenue outside. Away from our trees one could sense the shore with the waves breaking on it, and the air was fresher. I had yellow hair then (which was always a great nuisance to me in Spain) and almost immediately up came a gentleman who, raising his hat with great courtesy, began a conversation. He was an interesting talker and I enjoyed a change from the *senyoretas*.

Needless to say, very shortly proposals for further meetings were made and declined. The courteous señor took the refusal like a grandee, went to the public flowerbeds and under the eyes of the Guards picked a well-selected bouquet which he presented to me, still sitting on the fountain's edge. The Guards were delighted.

'*Precioso*,' said they. '*Que situación preciosa!*'

This little tale, though of no folklore significance, shows the Spaniard strongly in the Catalan.

Now the *senyoretas* have left the marble precincts. Barcelona University is no longer for them. The place for a good Franquist woman is at home. Even the park is closed to the public.

My way to the Berga *festa* revealed other than library folklore. Only two days after my arrival at the hostel I was told of this feast and urged not to miss it. My chief concern, not knowing my way about, was 'Could one get back the same night?' A new acquaintance in the hostel knew of an Englishwoman who was going, so she there and then rang up this compatriot of mine and passed me the receiver. A rather reluctant 'Yes, do come' changed to an urgent 'But you must please promise not to speak about it to any of the Barcelona English'.

Wondering what the Berga feast contained so antipathetic to English tastes, and the promise duly given, arrangements were made to meet that afternoon. Exactly at the hour a young woman emerged from the Metro in the Plaza de Catalunya, slight, fair and pale. Recognising a fellow northerner she seized me by the hand; together we plunged back down the steps and into a train which immediately pulled out of the station, for this proved to be the terminus of a regional line as well as a Metro stop.

At one end of the carriage sat a silent young man who was introduced as my guide's husband. I vaguely wondered what was the matter with him. Opposite sat a young Catalan who was introduced as one of the dancers going to the feast. He began at once to eat – a latish lunch, I imagined, the hour being about 5 p.m. Minding my Spanish manners I politely offered some fresh hazel nuts, first fruits of that year. Then I wondered what was the matter with *him*. Some time afterwards I learned that the silent husband was silent because, supposing the intruding Englishwoman to be a sight-seeing tourist, he, an ardent regionalist, found her a nuisance; and that a nut, being a popular erotic symbol, was hardly a well-chosen gift to a young man in a railway carriage.

The Barcelona group to which the man belonged called themselves with pride *Esbart Fol-clore*, 'esbart' meaning a society, 'fol-clore' meaning something grand, they were not quite sure what. The silent young man turned out to be Richard Armstrong, proprietor and Headmaster of the well-known English School at Barcelona. My fair guide, Lucile Armstrong, his wife, turned out to be one of the star dancers of the Esbart and also of a Spanish dance school, an adept in the exacting precisions of Andalusian dance. This of course would never do for the wife of the Head of the English School. So silence as to her private recreations was duly observed in English company, even when a cruiser-load of tourists were entertained by the dance school. In came the dancers for a *Sevillana*, their wide, frilled skirts billowing, their castanets clacking, their black hair plastered and shining.

'Oh,' exclaimed the tourists, 'look at that fair one! How beautifully she bends back! We did not know there were such fair Spaniards.'

We wound up the valley of the Llobregat beneath one of the most magical heights in Catalonia, its magic well in hand however, organised by the monastery long established there. The magic lives in Montserrat (Christianised into Montsa-grat), supposed home of the Holy Grail and towering shrine of La Morena, an ancient Black Virgin who seems to have superseded a still more ancient Mother Goddess, once enthroned upon her rocky seat and suitably surrounded by gigantic natural phallic columns. Like many another Mother-image, the Virgin was found by shepherds in an enveloping cave, the womb of the earth, a cave being both the symbol and the dwelling-place of her pagan predecessor. The mystery of fecundity still broods over this terrific upspringing of calcareous rock. Newly wedded couples from city and countryside make a visit to La Morena their first duty and religious tourism increases each summer; while awe is shewn plainly enough by the countryfolk who live below the terrifying mass.

Berga lies at the foot of a lower range, where another life-giving Virgin is seated in a high shrine, Our Lady of Queralt. The town I barely visited, for my time was filled firstly by meeting and making friends with the Esbart and afterwards by observing and listening to the pandemonium of *La Patum*. This is the name of the feast. It was impossible to find a room in the town but a charming Esbart girl without a murmur gave me her bed and herself joined two more in a double one. When I woke next morning they had all three vanished, giving me yet another lesson in living tradition. They had left their bed to climb to the shrine of *Nostra Senyora de Queralt*, to usher in the festal day. Pure piety was not perhaps the mainspring of this dawn pilgrimage, for though the visit would bring fecundity the first step towards this end is a *novio*.

Catalan Esbarts, for there are many all over the province, break clean away from the foreign idea of what is Spanish. The Barcelona men wear the city costume, not the country one of the Palace Guards; scarlet *barretinas* on their heads, but their hair in the black net of Goya's day which hangs baglike down their backs. The girls' rich dresses are more Pyrenean than southern – silk aprons, flowered silks and black lace, their flat white *manteletas* in complete contrast to the Andalusian mantilla raised over the comb. In mountain villages these give place to the real Pyrenean *capulet*, often of white cloth, which keeps its wearer's head and shoulders warm.

The Barcelona society had been invited to lend interest to Berga's own traditional doings, which are of a different nature. They are in fact left-overs from mediaeval Corpus

Christi processions, which still come out on that great day and on the Sunday following. On the Sunday they give a performance in the *plaça*, announced by the thundering of the biggest drum my eyes have ever seen. It is called the *tabal* and the drummership is hereditary in a good old Berga family. The onomatopœic name of *Patum* seems to come from the deep reverberating beats of this majestic instrument.

Just before midday the hereditary drummer got to work and set the little city vibrating from end to end. The first *Entremès* or Interlude – here is a word straight from the mediaeval procession – to answer the call was that of the Turks and Little Horses, who fought each other, clashing shields against scimitars, the crowd marking each clash by a traditional yell. Odd and dull it was, the same monotonous clash, the same monotonous yell. Turks should probably be Moors, but on this coast they have confused piratical Turks with occupying Moors. The Little Horses represent the Christian cavalry.

A more exciting company then invaded the scene, devils carrying poles with giant squibs fizzling on the top. They rushed about like all folk devils, and when the squib exploded each devil fell down to await the coming of St Michael, the Archangel. In he came, accompanied by a little angel, to finish off the devils with his spear. The *Aguila* or *Aliga* (for the Catalan language loves metatheses) gives the crowd a good time. The man beneath the immense, brown 'hobby' bird dances very well with his human legs, then spins round and round knocking over the men and boys who love to stand in the path of his heavy tail. This character from the procession symbolises St John the Evangelist and is of long standing, for at Barcelona in 1424 we are told he danced *tota sola* in the streets.

Thus far we can understand mediaeval Church teaching and the enlivening of illiterate people with simple shows, but the monstrous beast next lumbering on the scene can

C

hardly claim that he comes, like the others, to the glory of *Cristo Sagramentat*. An immense black creature with a giraffe's neck, fireworks blazing and smoking out of his mouth, two men leading him, several more staggering under his coverings – what does he teach? His head reaches to the balconies, smoke breathes into the faces gazing down, off go the squibs till his victims, their balconies and their houses are lost in smoke. This is the Wild Mule, said to be descended from the dragon formerly slain by the Archangel, but to my mind more closely related to the monstrous secular, ceremonial beasts of Languedoc in France, more especially to the Poulain de Pezenas, a fearsome colt which comes out at Carnival.

When the smoke and the uproar ceased (or lessened, for noise never ceases on this side of the Pyrenees), the Esbart displayed its *fol-clore*, dancing beautifully in many traditional dances from the Catalan countryside. One in particular was worth seeing – *Les Gitanes* of ceremonial Carnival origin, connected with a plough and ritual characters. *Colles*, as the troupes are called, carry out the traditional collection at farms, where they dance on the threshing floor. They appear also in big villages, when many troupes will meet. The rival devils rush about to stake out their claims to dancing places, whipping their antagonists about the legs. Sometimes a plough will go right round the ground ploughing up a furrow, and an Old Man and Old Woman appear, he with straw with which he brushes people's hair to leave it full of grain; she (a man of course) with the usual baby in her arms; and sometimes an intruding Moor. The opposite numbers to the Old Couple are the Bride and Bridegroom, who lead the dance. All these characters abound along the Indo-European paths across Europe. The dance itself has some fine figures, and the music is from either the national Cobla band or from the local *graelles*, woodwind instruments of strident tone.

The Esbart invited me several times to visit them after the Berga outing. They danced in a room down one of those questionable-looking streets off the Ramblas. It was quite a respectable little street in reality, unlike those of the Barrio Chino, to which some of the dancers begged to escort me to show me those famous and infamous, wretchedly gay young men, with their wreaths and their rouge. When I explained that I found no interest in them they still urged me to see them dancing together.

'*Muy tipico*,' said the Esbart with complete detachment.

Coming out of the Liceo theatre at two in the morning one closely follows the crowd, lest the Barrio Chino insidiously beckon one into a short cut. But that is the theatre where the *Zarzuelas*, those entirely Spanish light operas as they might be called, the best dance, song and the cleverest Spanish comics (with a *genre* all their own) were to be seen. Since the war they have scattered themselves, Pilar Lopez dancing in a theatre in the Paseo de Gracia, while a stray Amaya, detached from the tribe, was dancing the other day near the Diagonal. A Barcelona audience, Catalan though it mainly is, is composed of *aficionados* of the Andalusian School. Therefore to appear in this northern city is to run the gauntlet of informed criticism, and here a young dancer can be made – or made to disappear. Barcelona opinion by no means coincides with that of London. There Carmen Amaya is *esta gitana despeinada*, this uncombed gypsy, and her trick of shaking her hair right over her face is viewed with distaste. Indeed that amazing young girl of pre-war days, wrenching the most powerful *taconeado* out of her slender feet, came back from South America another woman. Her fury and abandon, her childishly conceived ballets leave her aunt, the majestic Faraona, still the classic prima donna of the company.

In Diaghilev's days his ballet had the lack of perception to put on *The Three Cornered Hat* in Barcelona. This condensation of Spanish dance is a chef d'œuvre for Europe and America, but not for Barcelona. The celebrated Picasso décor seems to portray a glimpse of Castile, which is where the best known *Molinera romance* belongs; the Miller's Wife, with maddeningly flaccid handclaps (which would be hissed off any Seville cabaret stage) gives a composite dance more reminiscent of Andalusia than anywhere else; the Miller, when he is Massine, gives a passionately inspired stage imitation, not version, of an Andalusian *Farruca*; finally the corps de ballet, some of whom wear Galician costume, with devilish energy introduce an Aragonese *Jota*. That long-ago Barcelona audience took it all with supreme enjoyment, rocking with laughter. This reception – not, it seems, fully perceived by the company – was recounted to me by some habitual theatre fans.

Amongst all the regional treasures practised by the Esbart – the *Crespelles*, in which young men slip rings of bread on their girls' arms, the showy dance from Villanova de Geltru of one man with two girls, the dance with lighted candles outside the church from Castelltersol, and many more – there was never a *Sardana*. When I enquired about this, the best known of all Catalan dances, they replied with disdain, 'Popular'. They had satisfactorily settled a question which continually presses on folklorists – what is the difference between folk and popular?

During a disturbed period when Catalonia revolted against the Government in Castile (I always think they would not take the Government so hardly if the capital were, say, in Extremadura), *Sardanas* were frowned upon, especially one called *La Espina Sagrada*, the Sacred Thorn. This tune was supposed to excite regionalistic passions and had indeed a symbolism prejudicial to law and order. During the early days of the present régime the same anti-regional spirit prevailed and *Sardanas* were again frowned on, never seen, never heard.

What, then, was my delight in 1950 to see men pushing a familiar wooden platform into position in a paved cul-de-sac off the Plaza de Catalunya. As University students were leaving their lectures, as offices were closing and people beginning to hang on the platforms of trams like swarms of bees, the *Cobla* arrived. They too looked familiar. They might have been the very men I had heard playing in those other days. Up they climbed to their raised seats, out came the familiar instruments, the tiny pipe and drum, the ear-splitting prima and tenor, the brass, and the double bass so oddly added to the ensemble. The familiar rhythm began to throb.

Instantly the paved space was flooded with students, older schoolboys and girls, married couples going home, a taxi driver, respectable elderly people. Rings formed as though by magic. On to the paving-flags in the middle of them went University library books, women's handbags, the door key and the baby. Late-comers pushed in, for partners are neither needed nor desired. The rings widened, almost imperceptibly began to move, two steps to the right, one to the left, so that gradually they moved round. Very quickly each ring projects its leader, someone with a musical or just a human ascendancy over the rest. The rhythm becomes monotonous, hypnotic. You would think they were wound up for ever. Every now and then the pace brightens, the *llargs* (longs) take the place of the *curts* (shorts), the men begin to spring, there is a trifle of show-off, then flat down again. You think they will never run down.

But they do, suddenly. The *Cobla* ceases to play, the rings break up, bags and babies are retrieved and with barely a smile and no farewell the participants make off tramwards. Participants is the correct word, for this is a communal rite. The soul of Catalonia, artistic, political or spiritual, or whatever you choose to see in this phenomenon, becomes visible for a brief space, turns and turns in sudden liberty and again goes underground. The year after the place of ritual had shifted to one side of the Ronda de la Universidad and the hour to Sunday morning.

A great deal has been written about the *Sardana*, linking it to the *Farandole* of the Greek merchants who brought commerce to the Iberian shore. But it appears to have been moulded into its present form by a local musician or dancing master, in the town of Figueras. He probably took an old *Contrapás*, which is a *Farandole*-like chain though more static, closed it into a circle and gave it a new rhythm. There is nothing unique about it; open and closed chains are popular from Provence to the Atlantic, which fact shows them to be indigenous and not of Greek descent.

Much of the wonderful sub-Pyrenean country north of Barcelona is still unknown to me but I know the great white rampart of Nuria, on which young Barcelona goes ski-ing in the latest thing in trousers and gay pullovers, and up which peasants toil in summer, carrying small votive bovines of pottery to the shrine of the *Mare de Deu*, The Mother of God, of Nuria. They could go up the funicular if they chose, but to toil up brings more glory. This statue was buried 'when the Moors came' and found again, like many another, through a supernatural phenomenon – this time by a bull which, refusing to leave the spot, pawed the ground in ecstasy. Sterile women in quest of children queue up to put their heads into a cauldron kept there for the purpose, calling on the Mother, while their husbands violently ring a bell outside to ensure celestial attention. In Aragon we saw people shutting themselves into a chest. Does some psychological urge demand a return to the darkness of the primeval cave, symbol of the Earth Mother?

After a grilling sojourn in Barcelona the year I have been writing about, I left this way, staying at Ripoll to look at the shepherds' gear. At that time there was not a Spanish-speaking person in the inn, and the two men responsible for the museum were practically in the same linguistic condition. One was a well-off flockmaster, whose love of his own surroundings had led him to start this excellent piece of work. Today, having lost every word of their language, I cannot imagine how I was able to spend so memorable a morning in their company.

The light mountain air was delicious after weeks of city heat, but thunder rolled in the heights. The flockmaster explained how he forecast the weather for the use of his shepherds, beginning on St Lucia's Day, December 13th. The reckoning is a complicated and anxious one, continuing day by day till January 5th, Vigil of the Epiphany. It requires two days' forecast for each month to come. It is done by personal observation of the sky, direction of wind, places of cloud formation and other signs which he refrained from telling me. No observation is taken on Christmas Day. This ancient method of forecasting the weather – the most important concern in the lives of these mountain pastoral people as we saw in Aragon – is called 'The Signs' and is believed to be infallible. In particularly bad weather they fire guns, loaded with shot blessed by their priest, against the witches who are held responsible.

For branding the flocks Greek letters are used, descended perhaps from the Greek merchant venturers. If so, this shows a much longer continuity than the use of Celtic numerals by our Westmorland shepherds. The lovely designs on sheep bells and collars, on horns, wooden spoons and all their paraphernalia is *musica* to them, thus embracing more of the arts than did even the Latin use of the word.

When not long ago I was at Lérida, and had seen its Orphan Boys dancing the traditional Stick dance which, cast off by the men, has descended to them and which they force newcomers to learn directly they appear in the orphanage, we drove across the Altos de la Dehesa, miles of moorland, to visit the famous rock shelter at Cogul. Wild-flowers brightened the scrub, brilliant corncockles and several varieties of yellow daisy, as we passed lost villages whose only link to anywhere is the very third-class road on which we shuddered and bumped. I had had introductions to some kind *señores* in Lérida, one of whom arrived at our inn as we were starting, to offer his company. I was a trifle dismayed, for the friend with me – not S. B. – had no Spanish and a two-way conversation can be uncommonly exhausting. But the *caballero* was a student of English preparing for 'el Cambridge', which means the Cambridge language certificate for foreigners, to be taken under the auspices of the British Institute, and he intended putting in a little conversation practice. Afterwards we doubted whether without him we could have coped with all the peculiarities of Cogul.

The whole population eagerly attended our arrival, rushing out directly the car was sighted. The rock shelter, being a historic monument, could only be visited with its proper guardian; a ladder and bucket were necessary though we could not imagine a use for the latter. These articles were kept in the Casa Municipal. Children, let out of school when the car came in sight, ran to find the Mayor. He was out, gone to fetch a mule. Everyone was alive to what was required, for about once in three years some anthropologist, painstaking enough to study his material *in situ*, will arrive in the same way, demanding his way to the shelter in various languages. Ladder and bucket appeared; the first was hoisted on to the roof of the car by dozens of helpful hands, the man with the bucket, the Mayor and his aide all crammed inside and with a few more hanging on outside we slowly bumped out of Cogul, crossed an ancient bridge and were told the road went no further. So the little procession, ladder and all, went up an ancient packroad leading eventually over the pale sierras to Tarragona and its port. The guardian disappeared with the bucket into a stream bed where a trickle of water flowed. When he came up with it filled to the brim he pointed upwards, and there was the shelter just above our heads.

It is exactly what it is called, a shelter, the soft stone hollowed out by winds and rains of twenty thousand years until the roof overhangs in the shape of a lightly curved hand. The plane of the curving fingers holds the paintings about twelve feet above the present ground level. It has always been known. Iberian lettering forms a yet undeciphered inscription and primitive Roman lettering another. The latter tells of a votive cult. It is thus clear that this faraway spot has been venerated since Paleolithic times, through the immensely long Neolithic and Metal Ages, through that intriguing Iberian period, short but brilliant, until the people imbibed so much from Rome that they became Ibero-Roman and inscribed these Roman letters.

Travellers on the packroad throughout all ages must have sheltered beneath the out-curving rock, yet it remained for a local priest, entering to escape a sudden storm, to note *and report* the figures above his head. The black and red women, naked to the waist, with flaccid hanging breasts as in some African tribes today, and skirts to their calves, appear in couples. The long-held idea of a dancing circle of women no longer serves, for each couple is now assigned to a different period, the black superimposed on the red, showing long ages of cult use, veneration and repainting.[3] What is certain is that each pair of women is connected with the small male figure, once red, now overpainted in black, ritually dressed with knee ornaments and head feathers and stylistically drawn with exaggerated phallus – most surely denoting a male fecundity cult already in practice in the Old Stone Age.

The ladder was placed in position for us but up went the guardian first, carrying his bucket. Out came the municipal

C*

floorcloth well soaked, vigorous pattings, even rubbings, wetted the rock, and with this treatment the colour darkened and the scenes of twenty to twelve thousand years ago emerged into clarity. An outer screen of some sort has long been promised by the Barcelona prehistory authorities to safeguard these treasures from still further decay, but who shall stay the hand of the man with the bucket?

Several village notables came to meet us and on the way back I learnt that this region had seen severe fighting. 'At least', said the schoolmaster, 'it would have been severe only the Italians ran away.' Previous bombing had destroyed many houses, and homeless families were pointed out to us living in shelters not unlike the prehistoric one and no more enclosed, carrying on some sort of life like wild animals in a lair. This, on a small scale, is but one of the deplorable sights which Spain unashamedly spreads before modern eyes. A much worse one is the illicit squatters' quarter – illicit but still there – alongside the railway outside Málaga, where hovels of corrugated iron, boards, even of branches of trees, have sprung up on a no-man's land. There are no roads, no paths, no *retretes*, no floors, no light, no water. After rain the whole area is a lake of pestilential mud, in which unspeakable children attempt to play and from which the odour stinks to Heaven and the passing trains.

VALENCIA

Yo, como soy de Valencia,	*As I come from Valencia*
canto la que me da gana.	*I sing whatever I please.*

A Jota from Liria

O Valencia, Valencia de la Valenciana!

Cry of an exiled Moor

The way to Valencia takes one down the Fabled Shore so beautifully named by Miss Rose Macaulay, a shore which my perhaps prejudiced eyes interpret differently from her sharp ones, a shore crowded with barely known, passionately interesting human doings unsought by her and her over-worked car. (Small wonder it would occasionally refuse to *marchar*.)

Tarragona rises before one's eyes – literally rises, for there stands the Iberian city on its hilltop as it did when the Greeks came sailing down the coast and the heavy-handed Romans, who never could leave peaceful people alone, followed them for fabled metals. Cyclopean walls pierced by low Iberian doorways support Roman towers, while on the northern walls mediaeval masonry with renaissance windows has risen above the Roman work.

But this is nothing to Sagunto, that other Iberian city lower down the coast. Here the primitive walls bear Punic work, then Roman, then small, light Moorish crenellations – the history of the Fabled Shore in stone and brick. When the Sagunto museum was full of good things (nearly all removed) I made friends with an elderly attendant on duty there. He was always standing in front of the tablets bearing Iberian lettering – like that at the Cogul rock shelter – and one day he told me it was the greatest wish of his life to find the key to that undeciphered language.

'I believe', he said earnestly, 'that by dint of looking at it I shall one day understand it.'

The nearest that scholars have yet come to success is the interpretation of two words on a decorated vase. The scene depicts a sea fight between two ships, and an inscription across the sky reads *Gudua Deitzdea*. If this is read as though it were Euskarian, which grew into Basque, it would mean 'the Battle Cry', which precisely fits the scene and is the only Iberian inscription yet rationally read. But Basque scholars will have none of it. They await a second Rosetta stone.

Besides the Iberian gates and the Roman necropolis where a little girl was buried with her jointed doll, Tarragona owns her giants. They sally forth on festal days, greeted by proprietary grins and pats from the citizens. The feast of Corpus Christi is announced on its Eve by a trumpet call in two parts, blared from the balcony of the Municipal Palace by two heralds in the costume of the time of Philip II, and the same evening the giants come swaying out like ships in full sail. They are a Moorish King and Queen and a smaller couple, the Negrito and his spouse, she coyly fondling a parrot. The large pair are some twenty feet high, and all are led by a mounted drummer and three *gaiteros*. In this part of the country a *gaita*, unlike the Galician instrument of the same name, is a harsh pipe without a bag.

On the morning of the great day we went up the narrow street which probably follows the line of the Iberian one, up the imposing flight of steps to the Cathedral doors where the faithful giants waited, propped against thirteenth-century carvings. On the pavement was a large carpet of rich colours, a Civil Guard and a verger or two perpetually shooing people from it. A closer inspection showed one of those ephemeral carpets made of closely packed flower-heads in the true folk style, like our flower-poles in Somerset and our well-dressing in Derbyshire. This one did not stop at flowers, for shavings had been used, salt for white and cinders for a handsome black border, the whole most beautifully laid out in a bold design by young men parishioners. It was entirely remade after the morning procession had walked upon it.

When festal mass and procession were over, giants, Mayor, Councillors and the heads of the Falange, who always make a point of being seen at religious ceremonies, returned to the Municipal Palace where the giants entertained their fellow citizens with a dance. Solemnly they turned and changed sides, billowing with stately gait as though on rollers – though they had not arrived at the finesse of kissing each other as I have seen Belgian giants do. When it was over their carriers took care to raise the draperies concealing them, to make sure they got their share of the applause.

Satisfaction with their own performance was written on their scarlet faces. Giants are a city tradition rather than one of the 'folk', and have a long history behind them. The earliest record of a giant in Spain is one in the Corpus Christi procession at Barcelona in 1320; those in Belgium are recorded in the following century, and our own at Chester a little later still.

I am, as before stated, a train addict in Spain for several reasons. It is true that timetables are a trial, depending not only on hours but on days of the week, but the trains are seldom crowded in the second class, and the old fashioned broadgauge lines allow the *rapidos* to bowl along comfortably. So when another travel took me, and S.B. with me, down the coast, we had plenty of time to note the change from Catalonia to the province of Valencia, and the string of small towns lying like white pearls along the shore amidst the greenery of ilex, palm and tamarisk. They bear romantic Moorish names, Benicarlo, Benicasín, and the bluest of blue waters lap their beaches.

The *plana*, or plain, opens out between mountains and sea and on it lies Castellon de la Plana. We went there to see the famous rock paintings of the Remigia cave, and scarcely had we arrived when its custodian politely called upon us. This is Señor Porcar, the well-known artist, who finds no difficulty in combining paleolithic with modern art. His favourite modern subjects are signals and railway lines. His directions as to how to reach the cave were discouraging. Some 38 kilometres in a car, then a climb up a mountain path. How far up? Oh, half an hour or perhaps an hour. (That meant two.) A small farm where, if they are at home, the people will give you the key. And if they are not home? Then they will be out in the fields and you will not be able to find them. But this is what we had come to Castellon for.

'Well, then,' said Señor Porcar casily, 'come instead to my

studio where you will see the paintings far better than in the cave.'

This was absolutely true. There we should have been ricking our necks and straining our eyes, here we stood or sat at ease and looked our fill on the wonderful reproductions, practically replicas, drawn by the custodian of the cave. The very veins in the rock were there and the markings of damp, or thin stalagmite deposit. There were the elongated, virile archers of the eastern Spanish School, there the flights of arrows speeding towards the game, an elegant deer, a charging boar. There an enemy tribe, the warriors decked with war-feathers, a chief enlivening their spirits by a defiant dance in the face of the foe. This art is technically inferior to the great Franco-Cantabrian School whose artists produced the masterpieces in the caves of Altamira, Font de Gaume, Lascaux and the rest. Nevertheless painters of the Levante School possessed a genius for depicting movement which was never reached in the north. There the human figure is rarely seen and even so is given a ritual, not a natural, aspect. Not in the Pyrenees do we see intrepid honey-takers swinging down a cliff face on creeper ropes, angry bees buzzing round their heads, nor the single-file march of four bedizened warriors. So far as human interest goes this later School far outstrips the best Magdalenian period in the north.

One breath-taking painting after another was displayed for our eyes alone. In these somewhat isolated towns, where educated society is small, the enthusiasm with which one is greeted is humbling. The Curator of a museum, the Librarian, throws everything aside for the stranger and devotes hours to his service. In Madrid the Archeological Museum opened its stores, and my hand was invited to dip into cases to bring out the Iberian figurine I needed. Hospitality at the Valencian Prehistoric Museum lasted a week. At Córdoba a year since, the Archeological Museum, its patio filled with ferns and flowers, Roman and Iberian stones, welcomed me day after day, a guardian at my disposal, a work table in a good light.

When a troop of big girls led by their parish priest visited the museum and me, leaning against my table, breathing down my neck, my guardian hurried to my side and pocketed a tiny Ibero-Roman head while I hastily palmed the bronze figurine on which I was working. We neither of us suspected the girls of making off with the objects but they would have fingered them without shame. Throughout the visit their *Cura* gave no explanations whatsoever, neither historical, artistic nor ethnological, and it seemed as though a flock of parakeets had flown through the rooms.

Wherever there are Spanish women there is this bird-chatter. We know the Franco place for women is at home – a good place to chatter in. If her husband takes her to a restaurant she and her daughters, her sisters-in-law and both mothers-in-law sit round the table in tight black dresses shrieking as though behind zoo bars, from the *sopa* to the *flan*.

So lively were the parakeets of Castellon de la Plana that their voices are still ringing in my ears. The small hotel was run by Mama – a nice old thing in a white apron – a fat, lazy son and a pretty, senseless parakeet. When this *chica* was on duty all the *chicas* of the quarter called to see her. They swung on the chairs, sat on the arms, jumped on the seats like the gay flock of birdlings they seemed to be. A quiet, scarred man occupying one chair, a warrior from the war, listened with a patient smile. Soon their friendly curiosity led the girls to address the foreign ladies. One sweet little thing in a yellow dress approached so closely I thought she was about to whisper a confidence concerning her *novio*. Instead her red lips let out such a screech that I leapt in my seat.

'Señora! Do you live in London? Have you come from

Barcelona? Do you like Spain? Do you like Castellon? What do you do here?'

A second's pause in which I managed to say, '*Chica*, although foreigners we are not deaf.'

The little nitwit, finger on lip, turned to the others. 'They aren't deaf,' she hissed.

Presently they ran out screaming. The yellow one hopped upstairs with the daughter of the house, her shrieks growing mercifully ever fainter. The scarred guest in silence enacted one of the most expressive little mimes I have seen. With his hand turning in a spiral he indicated the turns of the stairs. 'Up, up,' his gesture said, 'up and out of my hearing.' I caught his eye as a blessed peace descended upon him and us.

I once ventured to ask my Seville Professor of Spanish if the girls were ever checked or the pitch of their voices corrected. With condescending charity he said talking was their chief pleasure. Going further in this mode of thought, a Spanish girl of English education told me her countrymen willingly look for a pretty chatterer for a wife, believing it a man's duty to care for the sweet little thing if marry he must. It is possible this may be a left-over from the Mohammedan outlook.

The screeching is not always so kindly meant as that of the yellow *chica*. Tourists, unless courier- and coach-protected, soon learn the savagery of Spanish children. Xenophobia, latent in the peninsula, appears in the raw in the children. They delight in showing it, especially to a woman wearing a hat. '*Sombrero*,' they shriek, dancing backwards in front of the wearer, '*Sombrero, sombrero!*' so that northerners are tempted to go hatless under an untempered sun. They will run at your side, fifteen, twenty children together, tug at your skirt, pull at your sleeve, yelling. The more they are bidden to go away the closer they press. No adult ever comes to the foreigner's aid, no policeman dreams of dispersing them,

I think the tamed children of fashionable Torremolinos
are one of the reasons for its being fashionable. Two or three
generations of villa-owning foreigners in that village of not
outstanding beauty have dulled the children's appetite for
victims. A pleasant surprise it is to find your little companions able to talk peaceably and to greet you with 'Good
night' at ten o'clock in the morning.

Only once or twice have I been able to get my own back
on the more fiendish sort. One recipe I can recommend is to
advance on the child who yells '*Francesa!*' (they know of no
other country but France) with the answering cry of
'*Española*'!, whereat they run. But my Castellon recipe will
remain my chef d'œuvre for I shall not dare to spoil that victory. A party of big girls, fifteen- and sixteen-year-olds, well
dressed, hair well oiled, coming out of some technical school
immediately filled the street with familiar parakeet screeches.
Mock English words could presently be distinguished. What
one can (and must) put up with from child savages cannot
be accepted from grown-up girls of some sort of education.
I turned with false, honeyed smiles.

'Listen,' said the foreign lady, 'I have something to tell
you.'

The group bent inquisitively forward, all agog to hear
what this strange person had to say, and in their own
language too.

'Girls,' said she, 'you are abominably badly brought up.
Go home and tell your Mamas so.' Turning to hide a smile
of triumph she departed, leaving silence behind her. After
that moral victory we left Castellon with its unexpectedly
lovely public gardens, where in thickest shade nightingales
sing and where syringa, growing about the statue of Ribalta,
Castellon's greatest son, scents the air.

Our first visit to Valencia, in the spring before the cata-
clysm, had brought us from the south, and dazed after a
night in the train I thought we must have taken the wrong

turning and been landed in Catalonia. Here were the Catalan place-names, Abuixech, Montsant; there the family names over the shops, Ferrer, Sert, Llops. Until then we had not known that the Catalan tongue is used in changing forms right down the Levante coast even so far south as Alicante, nor that with it goes the race and in some degree the customs. Guide books tell one that Valencia is oriental and its population of Moorish blood. They firmly believe themselves to be full-blooded Moors and glory in scrambling on to their mules over the tail, which, they say, is the Moorish way of mounting. Yet the Cid's successful campaign first brought the province under Christian rule as early as 1094. It is true that the Moors came back and many also remained after the Reconquista, especially horticulturalists in the *huerta*. Even after the final expulsion many families stayed quietly on their farms, continued the planting of their rich lands and the upkeep of their irrigation system unmolested, even pro-tected, by non-Moorish neighbours who realised better than a far-away government into what straits the province would fall without them,* while Castile went blindly on its fanatical way with the natural results.

Our hotel windows looked down a street at the end of which was a small theatre on which blazed advertisements of a regional play. Before the performances, out came a Valen-cian musician in country costume, to attract an audience with country airs on his country instrument, the *donzaina* or pipe, his boy playing the tiny drum called *tabalet*. We determined to go, but having been inculcated with the dictum that on no account must *señoras* be seen in a theatre unprotected, we consulted our elderly concierge.

'No, *señoras*, no,' he pronounced. 'But if I can leave my post in time I will accompany you myself.'

He never left his post in time, but on peeping at the photo-graphs in the foyer we came to the conclusion that even with

* Valencia has 47·3 rainy days in the year, so Baedeker informs me.

his unimpeachable escort we might not have appreciated the show. Besides the Valencian scenes were the usual cabaret ladies of Spain. One, I remember, advertised herself as *Artista Sugestiva*, posing in a pair of black corsets.

However, we saw plenty of regional life for we had timed our visit for the festival of *Las Fallas*, the bonfires to celebrate St Joseph's Day, the Patronal Feast. Valencian bonfires are not common pyramids of waste and brushwood. They are organised by each street, each with a committee, an artist-modeller, dress-makers and collectors of money and material. In rich streets large sums are raised. There is a local craft in modelled heads in papier mâché, cleverly painted. The artists inherit the craft and start work the previous year in order to fulfil their obligations. On the nights before the great night, competing streets parade their finished figures, some life-size, some gigantic, accompanied by the entire population of the street, a band and the boys with the regulation squibs. These nocturnal parades go on all night long, for Spaniards seem to harbour an antipathy for their beds. Finally the figures are set up on their platforms, the space beneath packed with straw, broken-down furniture and rubbish, with the noisiest fireworks obtainable.

That year one *falla* was a fine tableau from local history, a Valencian cavalier on a white charger rescuing a girl from raiding Moors. She was dressed in the lovely costume of the *huerta*, one of the latest of Spanish costumes to evolve and certainly unknown when Moors were about. But what is an anachronism to a *fallista*? Several *fallas* showed country scenes, one a charming view of a *barraca* with peasants drinking outside. This is the local type of dwelling, of the simplest design possible, whitewashed walls and a sharply sloping roof of thatch, a cross on the pointed gable. Other *fallas* were monstrous in size and vulgarity. One, which I unfortunately still remember, was entitled *Joyas del Teatro*. Whenever one passed it a crowd of masculine admirers were

A barraca: whitewashed walls and a sharply sloping roof

gazing their fill upon rows of life-sized dancers, *las girls*, all bending over as one girl, their frills of skirts thrown over their heads in their never-changing pose, all displaying their little papier mâché behinds in transparent panties to the busy street. It was a pleasing thought that this *exposé* was made to be burned.

From photographs of the 1955 *fallas* I see they have grown bigger still and yet more vulgar. The winning figures in the competitions before the war, housed in what was the beginnings of a folk museum, are life-size, no more, all decent types of Valencian folk, sad, comic, sentimental. Children make their own little *fallas* on doorstep or window ledge and these are some of the most charming – miniature flower and orange gardens, dolls' *barracas*, anything within their powers of portrayal.

The nearer we got to March 19th the thicker grew the crowds, the louder the squibs. At midnight on the Eve of St Joseph thousands surged into the square where is the sunken flower market, on the stone roof of which a programme of regional music and dance was to be given. There we were, wedged into the front row, the usual kind *señores* at our elbows to explain things to the *señoras de Londres*. Here the Pyrenean culture of Catalonia meets southern culture from Murcia and Andalusia, notably in the *Jota* and its music. The northern element was in the instruments – the strident *donzaina* and little *tabalet* – and in the musicians' costume, the southern element in the opposing guitarists and singers. These men wore the costume of the city, satin breeches, pumps and curious little skull caps. They played the usual stereotyped guitar prelude, repeated over and over again until the singer, having focused attention and complacently sure that everyone was awaiting his good pleasure, suddenly pierced the night with a high, forced tenor. He sings his verse, the dancers dance their thirty-two bars, cease abruptly and into the pause bursts the ear-splitting sound of *donzaina* and drum. It is followed by guitars and song, guitars and dance, until the shattering turn comes round again.

The *Jota* of Valencia is not of the bounding Aragonese type. It shows some Andalusian influence yet avoids the rigid grace of Andalusian movement. It is quieter, simpler, and the passionate facial expressions of *flamenco* dancers are entirely absent. The women's dress of delicate pastel shades with fine lace fichus helps the comparison, for the gaudy spots and frills are as absent as the frowning brow. The costume of Valencia, one of the loveliest in Spain, is not of historical interest except for the hair combs. One cannot pretend there has been continuity of style throughout the ages yet, somehow or other, the heads of Valencian women today show affinity with the heads of Iberian women living on the same coast 400 years before Christ.

The famous Lady of Elche, the bust found on the site of the ancient Ilici,* was bought for France and taken to the Louvre, to be returned to Spain as a *beau geste* by the aged Pétain to a fellow dictator. It is lodged now at the end of a great gallery in the Prado. The *Dama* wears a high cap or a comb beneath her veil and enormous ear-discs framing her

* The Iberian Elche on the hill above the present town.

Affinity: a figurine of 400 B.C., an Ibero-Roman head, and a modern Valencian

sickly, decadent, yet, people think, beautiful face, on which faint lipstick can still be descried. Sacheverell Sitwell calls her a 'sacred prostitute', but no trace of an Iberian temple for a sacred prostitute to dwell in has ever been discovered, and it is still a question to whom the wealth of votive figurines was offered. He also calls her a virgin and 'the Madonna of Elche' so his readers may choose. There is, however, no choice as to the *Dama* being 'the only work of art left by Carthage.'⁴ The Barcelona museum alone refutes this pronouncement and she has long been accepted as a flowering of Iberian, not Punic, art. Her fellow Iberian ladies, mostly of small size, wear the veil raised over cap or comb, but less exaggerated ear-pieces. Passing down the centuries we can see Ibero-Roman ladies, one for instance with the raised veil, the other with large ear-discs, both from Alcoy. And later again a small terracotta head now in the Córdoba museum, with hair waved in Roman style and an upstanding comb at the back.

The girls dancing the *Jota Valenciana* that night wore the regional metal comb at the back of their heads and on each side a narrow one curved to fit round the head. Their hair, plaited or coiled over each ear, seemed to echo the great ear-discs of the *Dama*, while for still further ornamentation silver- or gold-headed pins were stuck through the hair earphones.

There was no Chain dance on the roof of the flower-market. The northern *Farandole* type nowadays stops short in Catalonia. But it existed in what is now Valencia in Iberian times. The famous vase from Liria (*c.*400 B.C.) shows us a Chain dance made up of three men and four women headed by two musicians, one of whom plays the double pipe, the other the single. The men, wearing decorative baldricks and ornamental fringes below the knee, lead the women in a gentle amble, for all the world like *farandoleurs* who have covered much ground.

There were no Iberian costumes in the *fallas* but plenty of modern Valencian ones on the figures prepared for the flames. On the night of March 19th, as the great bells tolled out midnight, every *falla* was set alight and in a few minutes the work of weeks went up in flames. The city turned rose-red, the Cathedral and Miguelete towers seemed floodlit and even as their own *falla* blazed its makers rushed off to another street, leaving the bonfire men to crawl out from beneath the burning platform and to watch the dying of the flames.

When after that first visit I came to the conclusion that round about Valencia was the meeting-place of north and south, I worked out this theme in an article[5] on the *Jota*, supporting it by many musical illustrations. But as in all research, the last word is never written. I have found that although the roads cross at Valencia northern influence has trickled further south, to Alicante and even into Murcia. The cross-roads are at Valencia on account of the city's physical geography. Its two-named river, the Arabic Guadalaviar (the Iberian Turia), turned southern influence up the waterway away from the coast; the shore road coming down from Catalonia brought distant Pyrenean culture to the south.

ALICANTE

Muchos Moros dejan muerto.   Many Moors are left for dead.

A Castilian Romance

A few years ago I had a long stay at Alicante, first to see the processions of Holy Week and then to wait for St George's Day and the famous *Moros y Cristianos* of Alcoy. The time was filled with work of a pleasant local kind which only comes to one in an unhurried visit. A local musician came to call who, unlike most Spanish husbands, introduced me to his wife, a friendly little person unversed in foreigners. I spent several afternoons with her in her little house on the hill above the town. Our conversation, or rather hers, never paused for one moment. She felt it her duty to supply me with all she knew about local customs, but took payment in the fingering of my coat, blouse, skirt, with exclamations of admiration. The country was in a poor state that year after prolonged drought, electricity failing, industries stopping work. England, to her, was what Spain has always sought – Eldorado.

I had to listen to horrific stories of their war. She and her husband, active figures in social work of the post-war régime, were of course Franquists, therefore the perpetrators of the horrors were the 'Reds'. Yet, the front door closed, windows shut, that quick look round reminding one so uncomfortably of Mussolini's Italy, out poured tales of another colour.

My hostess was no parakeet. Her voice was gentle, her singing voice delightful, and I obtained delightful airs from her native Montaña de Mariaga, rising inland from Alicante. They were all of the simple Catalan, not the southern, type. One day she called in her sister and little niece and when they also had felt and admired every article upon me, we had a dance or two from the *niña*. Then it was I began to correct my previous notions of the north-south meeting-place of cultures.

The musician husband called so assiduously, bringing with him local pressmen, that my hotel concierge took it upon himself to deny my presence, regardless of the plate-glass windows of the dining-room behind which 'the foreign lady' could plainly be descried eating *paella*. Lives are so monotonous in these provincial towns that a little over-zealousness here, as in Castellon, is understandable.

But to make up for long visits I was taken to see the *huerta* of Alicante, and to call on the *Señor Cura* of Muchamiel. He is a well-educated young priest from Barcelona, an ardent musician who trains his choir properly and collects classical and traditional records for his gramophone. He asked eager questions as to what was being given at Barcelona concerts and about somebody called 'Vow-garn'. It took some time to recognise this as Vaughan Williams. He begged us to come again when he would take me to see a lady parishioner who not only sang regional songs but danced the local dances. I did not properly grasp parts of his rapid talk and, understanding him to say this lady was eighty-nine years of age, I wondered a little at his joking allusions to so venerable a parishioner.

Easter Day was spent on the hill above the port, watching the traditional Easter fair held on its slopes. It is a family *fiesta*, parents and children, big boys and girls – who keep a long way apart – and gypsy children, very poor but each girl with a flower in her hair. Young men brought guitars and accordions, nobody brought castanets but everybody brought the Easter *mona*. This is a loaf shaped like a fat vegetable marrow, in which is embedded a hard-boiled egg, the Paschal egg of all our egg-rolling, egg-dancing customs. The gypsy children danced to entertain the company, the elder girls singing the tune, after which pence were collected with gypsy smiles or scowls. The dances were of the same style as those of the musician's little niece – a solo or a pair dance, arms raised in *Jota* style, little stamping steps up and down obliquely before the partner. Even without castanets they brought a breath of the south to that Alicante hill.

Easter Monday, 1949, was one of those interesting, utterly exhausting days which occasionally fall to the lot of the collector. The musician and his wife conducted me to Muchamiel, the grinding tramway packed with chattering holiday people. The fingering and patting, the wonder and admiration began at once, each *Alicantina* within reaching distance stretching out an eager hand. The little lady delightedly exhibited her charge.

'Will she speak English for us?'

Hoping to be free of them the sooner, I idiotically recited 'Mary Had a Little Lamb'. They were ravished. However, being on show is not the best beginning to a day's work.

We fetched the Padre from his *presbiterio* and turned into a path beside an irrigation canal brimming with clear, gliding water. Small lock gates now and again turned the flow, which ran off into the *huerta*, into still smaller channels twisting under the orange trees. These again could be branched out by the horticulturalist's spade acting as a miniature lock gate. It was May and the corn was as green as springing corn could be, the scent of the orange flowers unbelievable. The Padre broke off a large branch to present to me as though it were mere hawthorn. We entered the garden of the local *Palacio*, a gaunt eighteenth-century mansion, the country house of the local *Marqués*. A strip of water ran down the centre; the stone edges were already baking under the May sunshine, and low hedges of box and lavender made an outer green oblong. Whiffs of orange flowers came to us over the old walls.

My hosts asked whether there were grass as green and trees as high in England, and then they sang songs for me and for their own pleasure, putting in their own parts, for they were all musicians. Entirely of the north were the melodies and word themes; flowers on the mountain, *florecitas de todos colores*, and the Pyrenean love symbols, the partridge, the paloma and the quail – not omitting our English male symbol, the nightingale. Everything I had from these friendly people, together with all notes taken in the Valencia library, were lost in a suitcase stolen in Barcelona station. And my memory had had no time to store the harvest.

A - qui dalt de la mont-an-ya-, fit lo bé de Déu hi lüio, les ros-es de quaire en quat - re, els cla-vells de cinc en cinc.

This is the type of northern tune that has travelled right down the Fabled Shore to Alicante at least

When dusk began to fall we found our way into the village street. The shops were still lit, for they do not close until the proprietor goes to bed. So the butcher's shop was open and bright, its owner behind the counter. Ranged in chairs in front of it were a very old lady, a very thin lady and the most enormous woman I have ever seen. Then I realised my misapprehension of the Cura's laughter, for instead of being eighty-nine years old Señora Torregrossa weighed 89 kilos. Mrs Great Tower! She was a youngish woman, not forty, good-looking. She had assumed a clean apron which must have measured two yards round and, a beribboned castanet in either hand, superbly sat under the joints and the hams waiting to receive.

The Padre sent a boy to fetch his guitar. Then began the most delightful performance, singer and accompanist combining in a manner born of long practice. The songs were *Alicantina* folk songs such as those I had heard in the garden. A feeling of the south crept in when we heard what they called a *Habanera*, nothing at all like Carmen's French imitation. The great lady rose majestically and opposite the thin one, castanets clacking, they danced a local *Jota*, all correct with sung verse and guitar interlude, peremptorily expecting me to join them. Unlike the *Jotas* of Valencia city this one contained a three-handed hey or reel, and vis-à-vis stations when ordinary *Jota* 3/8 steps were used. The aged lady then joined in, telling her daughter – or perhaps her grand-daughter, for the age of Spanish old ladies is deceptive – how to do it. The butcher also was requested to join in, but on his declining the ladies exclaimed :

'He's no good. He was out till four this morning serenading our Deputy.'

A political attention with favours in view, no doubt.

Now and again people came in to buy a bit of meat or a half-kilo of sausages. There is no mutton in that country, and cow for beef except the day after a bullfight. The customers understood that a reception was in progress and politely withdrew the moment their purchases were made. When we rose to catch the last tram back to Alicante, Señora Great Tower clasped me to her enormous self, exclaiming:

'Isn't it lovely? Isn't it lovely? When I sing I cry. Oh, isn't it lovely?'

Exactly so did a Somerset singer cry to Cecil Sharp, seizing the lapels of his coat in joy at her own songs, 'Isn't it beautiful? Isn't it beautiful?'

On St George's Eve I drove up past Jijona of nougat fame to Alcoy, situated in a high basin amongst arid mountains. I was going to see a *Morisca* without, so far as I knew, any ancient rite embedded in it. Yet I wanted to see it with my own eyes, fearing the usual descriptions omitted exactly what I was seeking. The day showed me an urban, quasi-historical drama on a larger scale than that of Aragonese Ainsa, founded on less doubtful history and following its own tradition amassed through several centuries. Alcoy had been freed from the Moors by James I of Aragon, but a few years afterwards came a renewed attack from the Kingdom of Granada.[6] The historian of the *festa* dryly remarks, 'They wish to represent the taking of the place by Moors from

Granada in 1276 and its reconquest in the same year. Permit me to say, with the most ridiculous additions.' Beyond telling us that the costumes of two of the companies are no older than the beginning of the eighteenth century, he gives no hint as to when the people of Alcoy first played their battle-drama, and local hearsay does no better.

I had a letter of introduction to the Mayor of the town but when I went to deliver it the great man was out, surveying arrangements. My chauffeur insisted on giving the letter to the Head of Police, whose men were filling the courtyard, and this proved an excellent move for, politely replacing the Mayor, the Head showed me the vantage spots, took me to the hotel where he saw fit I should lunch and seemed to be there whenever I needed a friend.

The *Morisca* takes two days to enact, the first occupied by the march of the armies through the town to display themselves, the second by a battle in a gully outside the town, which seems to have been the actual place of a fight and which even today is called the 'gorge of the battle'. I had chosen the first day and when I arrived a few companies were already parading, showing themselves off to their hearts' content. The square had a mock castle erected on one side, rows of chairs, already filling, went all round and a mass of people from the whole district was seething in the roadway. Round and round marched the companies, the pure *comparsas* composed of ten to twelve men fitting the breadth of the street, tightly glued together, the outer men leaning inwards as though slightly drunk – but they were not, then nor later – the march almost a dance with ridiculous, strutting steps, their Captain in front twirling, leaping like a dancer, waving sword or scimitar in vainglorious manner, eyes fixed on the balconies above. His men's eyes likewise, every head thrown back, a deadly-looking cigar in every mouth pointing skywards. The cigars are presented by their fellow citizens and never leave their lips all day.

The chosen dozen are wonderfully made up and costumed; the *accompañantes*, who march behind and at the sides to press back the audience, are not so perfectly turned out. Some are mounted and these tear up and down the streets, terrifying the crowds by backing their horses into them, rearing and curvetting. Each *comparsa* has its band playing marches or Paso Dobles, and how Alcoy can muster so many musicians is a marvel in itself. Each *comparsa* is named and has its place according to the length of its existence; for instance the Andalusians are the oldest of the Christian companies, the Llanes of the Moorish. There are now twelve Christian and thirteen Moorish *comparsas*. One of the most remarkable of the Christian companies is that of the Asturians. In an illustrated programme of 1910 there are pictures of them in pseudo-mediaeval uniform with casques on their heads and a cross on their breasts, but in 1949 they had become stage savages, naked to the waist and painted a dark brown. I wondered if this was the Fabled Shore's idea of the rough north. This free attire went to their heads, for they and their Chief surpassed themselves and every other company in their bounding and posturing.

The grand march began at last, Christian troops taking the whole morning to pass. Their slow progress, necessitated by the mincing steps, allowed every detail to be examined. Besides the *Asturianos*, the men of Navarre were remarkable, while those of Andalusia looked like the Brigands from *Carmen* and carried several 'Carmens' riding pillion behind them. When the *Labradores*, the Countrymen, appeared the crowd went mad with delight. These were local agriculturalists in full Valencian costume. They were by no means 'dressed up' like other companies, but simply came out in their own festal dress. There were scores of them accompanying their own *comparsa*, men in the finely pleated white breeches wide as skirts, mules bedecked with nets strewn with pompons, wreathed with orange and lemon boughs, plumes and

mirrors on their heads. On their backs rode women in their
lovely pastel shades, the combs which link with ancient
Iberian headdressing in their raven hair. Amongst them
went 'Mosen Torregrossa' on horseback, a tiny Moorish girl
held before him in the saddle. This personage is said to be a
priest who, hearing the attack beginning, left his mass to
rush forth to rally his townsmen. He may be historical but
who the little 'Gineta Moro' may be is not now known.

After the usual interminable pause for dinner, out came
the Moorish companies. These were more incredible, more
showy, more swaggering, with still more horsemen dashing
through the crowds in a still more dangerous fashion. They
represented the *Abencejarres*, the Moors who lost Granada at
the last, Berbers, *Mudejares*, Jews who fought with them and
a company of coal-black Africans. These had the greatest
applause of the day, so debonair, so black were they. People
round me told with pride how they could not go to bed because of their blackness, but lay on the floor for four nights.
And always there were the inward-leaning lines, the non-
chalant dance-step, always the long cigars pointing balcony-
wards. Some towering erections like those of the Nice
Carnival appeared with this army, arrayed upon them tableaux of lovely Sultanas and Moorish ladies with slaves and
eunuchs on guard. They got a good deal of admiration but
at the same time a good deal of criticism, for a *Morisca* is for
the men and only lately have women ventured to intrude. It
will be interesting to see if Carnival notions or *Morisca*
traditions carry the day.

The next morning, St George's Day, battle is locked in the
glen outside the town, the Castle is rushed by the Christians
and in the evening a flood-lit vision of St George appears on
the battlements. There is *mucho protocol*, as my friend the
waiter said, the companies meeting in their own quarters on
the Eve to feast, those which are charitably inclined visiting
hospitals, taking food and money to the poor of Alcoy, and

every night – which means about two in the morning – performing their 'classic dances' which no one has ever been able to describe to me. Then, of course, on the third and last day there are 'the bulls'.

My notebook records: 'Disappointing. No folk elements.' Yet amongst all the incredible people I have seen going about their ritualistic occasions I have never seen any less credible. That they are townspeople, that they have evolved their own ritual during the last few centuries – for we must remember that the date of their first performance did not follow the battle it depicts the next year as at Lérida – that this is founded not on any already established pre-Christian cult but on historical facts, is worthy of our attention. Here we have a fully flowering, almost modern tradition, still in evolution.

From Alcoy can be seen the stark sierras of Murcia and Murcia marches with Andalusia. So by divers routes we have come full circle and, yet with many omissions, the Singing of the Spanish Travels is done.

BIBLIOGRAPHY

1 VIOLET ALFORD, *Pyrenean Festivals* (London, 1937).
2 RAMON MENENDEZ PIDAL, *L'Epopée Castillane* (lectures read in French, 1909).
3 This latest opinion, already known in Cogul, is to be found in *Ars Hispaniae* (Madrid, 1947), Vol. I, pp. 66–8.
4 SACHEVERELL SITWELL, *Spain* (London, Batsford, 1950).
5 VIOLET ALFORD, 'The Valencian Cross-Roads', in *The Musical Quarterly* (New York, 1937), Vol. XXIII, No. 3.
6 DON JOSE LLOBET Y VALLLLOSERA, *La Ciudad de Alcoy a su Patron San Jorge* (1853).

I *It was the local 'razetaires', the cow-fighters, who gave the audience their thrills*

II *'Gardians' driving a young wild bull before them in the flat wastes of the Camargue*

III A raggle-taggle street drama at Amélie-les-Bains: Mr Charles Chaplin appearing with age-old folk characters

5

Bulls and Bears

On the bear and the bull . . . are focussed the desire of the whole people.

Jane Harrison, *Ancient Art and Ritual*

The nearest place to see a wild bull is at Chillingham in Northumbria, where the last remnant, fifteen in all, of Britain's wild cattle still roam. Not long since the lord of the herd killed a young bull which was, no doubt, endeavouring to steal a cow and push its way into leadership. But like the King of the Wood at Nemi the monarch could still defend his rights and so lives for another term.

The next place to see a wild bull is in Provence. Here we touch the bull cult of the Mediterranean, in that vast space of marsh and forest, the Camargue. The waves break on a flat and dreary shore across which the various Rhônes move sluggishly to the sea. The Camargue, baking in summer, icy in winter, is one of the strangest bits of country in France and it is hard to believe it lies not so many miles from the sophisticated Riviera. Its riches are its wild cattle and horses, both rapidly decreasing. Each *manade*, or herd, has its own brand, often of Greek letters within a shield, its own *gardians* to tend and conduct them to their inland summer pastures, also to show off their beasts and themselves at local fêtes – a curious speciality of the Camargue industry. I have never ascertained whether the owner is paid for this use of his herds nor what payment other than glory goes to the *gardians*.

Our first acquaintance with a wild bull was in the depths of the Camargue, driving across to Les Saintes, as the little place is called locally. We were looking about for horses and cattle but empty mile followed empty mile. Then in the flat distance a heifer crossed the road and nearer, on the other side of what might have been a Sedgmoor rhine, we came upon a bunch of white horses nearly buried in the reeds, swishing long, ragged tails as noon brought out the flies.

'Here they are,' said our driver, '*la manade du Marquis*.' Beyond the horses bulls appeared in a similar cache down amongst the reeds, peacefully ruminating. Making sure no cows were near which their lords would have to protect, thereby becoming excited, our driver jumped down and advanced upon the nearest beast exclaiming, 'Now look at me!' It seemed an unnecessary piece of bravado and we were pleased there proved to be nothing to see, the bull whirling round to crash into its green sanctuary, plainly implying, 'Leave me alone'.

Our second meeting with a Camargue bull was in a 'bull ring' far from its native pastures, at Jonquières, a village lying between Beaucaire and Nîmes. We got there too late for the festive *abrivado*, the entrance into the village at full gallop of bulls, cows, horses and horsemen who lash up speed half a mile away, to tear through the street in a swirl of dust and the clamour of the population. Everyone was making for the bull ring. In the villages this is made of boarding and carts closely placed round the square, but the population of Jonquières is composed of fans who have a permanent place with tiered seats.

After the wait essential to every gathering south of the Loire, be it funeral, banquet or bull fight, the *gardians* arrived in a showy cavalcade, each with his *Provençale* riding pillion behind him. (All girls wearing the costume are so called.) There were not enough *gardians* to go round, so a walking procession followed, each girl beautifully dressed in what foreigners call the 'Arles costume'. This is in reality the costume of all that part of Provence as far north as Tarascon and into the Camargue in the south. The chic little cap, with its velvet ribbon sticking out like a wing, only appeared about 1840, in fact in the days of Mistral and his *Mireille*. Before that the *Arlésiennes* and their fellow countrywomen wore wide, white lace caps attached beneath the chin. A fine sight it was to see them file into the rustic bull ring – '*Prendre à la file comme à Jonquières quand on danse*', goes the saying; and after an agitating cow fight, man versus vicious little cow, dance they did, *à la file*, in the Farandole and other regional dances – the *gardians* impatiently awaiting their turn, despising the dancers in their bull-loving hearts.

When their turn came it proved to be a display of horsemanship, lassoing and rope-spinning standing on their mounts. We thought them grave and earnest young men; it was the local *razetaires*, the cow fighters, who gave the audience their thrills. Presently a well-known character, the bull Cæsar, was led forth to thunderous applause. With age he had become too wily to use in the ring but was allowed to make his bow. The applause warmed his wicked old heart as he began a brisk trot, two men lying back nearly flat on his ropes. When he reached centre stage he pulled up, raised his great head and surveyed his worshippers with a patronising eye. 'Cæsar! Cæsar!' they yelled. Thrice his head went up, then turning of his own accord he stalked back to his stall. He was taken about to village feasts on purpose to receive homage.

The Marquis de Baroncelli – no Provençal ever dreams of giving a '*Monsieur le Marquis*' to this famous local character who, alas, has left his earthly herds and pastures now – owned just such a bull. Bandot did not need a bull ring to show himself off. If he spied people on the pasture he would detach himself from the herd and superciliously approach. They would by then have put a rhine – the Somerset word is so apt – between themselves and his ground from whence they called 'Bandot! Bandot!' The vainglorious old actor then raised his head to receive homage as did Cæsar at Jonquières.

Henry de Montherlant, in the preface to his early book *Les Bestiaires*, has given a gripping study of the passion for bulls felt not only in Spain but all over southern France. He sees its origin in Mithraic cult and practice. Unless they are pre-historians, writers are timid of plunging too deeply into their past, preferring to paddle in classic pools in search for origins; yet, from the heart of bull-loving France itself, comes evidence that the animal had a mystic hold on men long ages before Mithras and his Bull came to western Europe. The partial reclamation of the Vaccarès lagoon in the Camargue has revealed many coins of the earliest Greek colonisers, those Massilians we have already met on the Fabled Shore. Some of the pieces found in Vaccarès show well-designed bulls, usually charging with lowered head. Others from Massilia show the stag, the wild boar, the owl, designed it is supposed for inland tribes, whose sacred animal was struck in bronze for each – a good way of pro-moting friendship and better trading for the Greeks. Fur-ther south and somewhat later in date are those strange Iberian bulls in stone, the bull *couchant* of Osuna, the *toricos* standing forlorn on the plain near Guisando, Salamanca – so interesting to Lope de Vega, in whose days they were already '*sin pies ahora*', without feet now.

He visto vuesa merced	*Has your worship seen*
en aquel pradillo ameno	*In this pleasant field*
a los toros de Guisando?	*The bulls of Guisando?*

These, and others in Iberia and Celtiberia, were sculptured or cast in bronze or painted on pottery before the Roman legionaries brought their Mithraic cult to Spain; and long ages before then were conceived the svelte black bull of Boniches rock shelter (Cuenca), the lordly bulls of Lascaux (Dordogne) and the old, old bulls of the Clothilde cave

(Santander), so ancient that those first Aurignacian artists had not yet learned to apply their flint tools to their magico-artistic needs, but employed their own fingers to scratch the clay. One may confidently say that in the whole great western region men and bulls knew each other well.

Montherlant gives a delightful picture of Monsieur Doumergue, some time President of France, dropping over the barrier on to the sand at Nîmes to try his hand on a Provençal bull. Did he snatch the cockade? Montherlant does not tell us. '*Dans le Midi taurin*', writes M. Doumergue, '*la passion des taureaux a des racines plus profondes qu'en Espagne même*,' but if we are to take cave drawings as indicating the deepest roots there is nothing to choose between the two countries. The homage to Cæsar and Bandot is but another expression of the pitying adoration showered on Spanish bulls in the *toril* the night before a bull fight. 'Poor little thing, poor little thing,' followed by a flood of endearments, came from a fashionably dressed woman in Madrid, gazing down on the black satin backs of tomorrow's victims as the public loves to do. Women of every class – and men – try to pluck a hair from a bull's tail, until angrily pulled back by the *plaza* guards, for this is a talisman of great potency.

To my mind a Provençal bull fight – no killing, no blood – is more dangerous than a full-blooded *corrida* in Spain. There the man controls and directs the bull with cape or *muleta*; here his sole defence is a sharp-toothed comb with which to cut off the cockade. There he can be, should necessity arise, surrounded in an instant by his *cuadrilla* to distract the bull; here he is alone with his skill against a bull which has been in the arena several times before. I have seen a man caught between the horns, backed against the barrier, wrestling with all his strength to prevent the wicked head from turning to bore a horn into its adversary. A Gascon cow fight is almost as hair-raising. There the men are rolled over and over by vicious cows, lie motionless feigning death while the malicious beasts stand over them, use poles to jump over their backs, sometimes to miss the jump and be trampled on; there the maddened creatures break through the ramshackle barrier to rush through the street, tail up like a flag pole, a ragged pennant waving at the top. 'There,' said a cow fighter wiping dirt and sweat from his face, 'she's gone home.' But in going she knocked down two women and horned a dog.

On the other side of the Pyrenees I once saw a bull refuse to fight. Like Ferdinand of picture-book fame he preferred to sniff flowers, the flowers of his far-away pasture ground. It was in the Barcelona Plaza Monumontal, packed with *aficionados* more violent and a great deal nastier than the ballet fans of the same city who had such a good laugh over *The Three Cornered Hat* (p. 67). It was the first bull of the afternoon. Out he rushed, black, svelte, apparently brimming with courage, only to pull up short halfway across the arena, forelegs stuck straight out in front of him. Having the little knowledge that is dangerous I thought he had found a spot he fancied and had straightway gone into *querencia*. This is a curious and rather pathetic thing about a bull. Even the most courageous will suddenly have a memory of his pasture with its cool drinking-place, and will imagine that the way back through the *toril* he has just left will take him to it; will see the shadow of the awning on that *Sol y Sombra* side of the ring beginning to lie on the golden sand, which brings a vague memory of the tall eucalyptus trees under which he has been wont to shelter from the midday sun. He feels it would be well to stay where he is awhile, before making acquaintance with the strange world of ten thousand faces above and around him. At least this is a romantic explanation of 'having a *querencia*'. Then the *toreros* shrug their gilded shoulders, turn up their eyes to the ten thousand faces and throw out their hands, which mime is intended to convey, 'We can't do anything. There he is and there he will stay.' For none knows better than the bull fighters who must get him out of it how dangerous can become a bull in a *querencia*. And the ten thousand faces, stamped with the cruelty of Spain, look down with scorn to jeer at the men who, for their entertainment, risk Death in the Afternoon.

This time the whistles and jeers were for Ferdinand, the bull which would not fight. In one moment everybody had comprehended. Out came ten thousand handkerchiefs, each held by two corners, all bellying outwards like miniature sails. The great ring was surrounded with wavering, white aspen leaves; ten thousand voices chanted '*Fuera, fuera, fuera!*' Out, out, out.

The President of a bull fight must bow to public opinion. He made a sign. The trumpets blared a blare I had never before heard, the *fuera* blare. Out from their own place came two *cabestros*, the oxen kept to run with the fighting bulls to soothe and guide them. These two were of an elephant grey and so enormous that everybody laughed. They looked as though they could not possibly be brothers to the bull, nor even of the same race. They wore long bells under their chins and with a businesslike air trotted one behind the other to Ferdinand in his *querencia*. As could be plainly seen, almost heard, they demanded in their eunuchs' voices, 'Aren't you going to fight these boring men? Come out with us then.' Turning about without another glance at the ill-behaved boy they had been sent to fetch, all three trotted out in single file.

And would Ferdinand be returned to his flowery pastures? Not so. He would go to the butcher and his mother would be cut out from his ancestral herd to follow the same road, for never again could she be permitted to breed. Courage descends through the female and it is the cows which are tested for this essential quality. The Andalusian breeder invites his *aficionado* friends to a day on the pasture along the Guadalquivir. I have seen them trotting out of Seville, a party of superb horsemen with one superb horsewoman. Their seat is inimitable, the knee flexed to accommodate the

Arab stirrup; their short jackets fit like gloves – after an English tailor a Spanish one every time – and their hard, black hats are worn with an air. The girl wears the same hat and rides astride, legs clothed in wide, skirt-like trousers. The chains and bits jingle as the lovely Arabs and near-Arabs mince about, showing off to the passers-by. At the breeding establishment others will be waiting, the owner himself, a son, a grandson or two wild with excitement, sitting their horses as their fathers have done for generations; with the family, the *mayorales*, the stockmen. After the Amontillado (it is fashionable to talk about Tio Pepe; I think it must all be imported by England) out trots the company to the pastures stretching along the turgid river – close-cropped grass, scrubby bushes, and the far away shapes of the grazing herd. The cows will be the first to look up, as well they may, for one of them will be cut out and headed away to a suitable spot. There she is ruthlessly thrown by the long lances digging into her hind quarters. Outraged, she will struggle up and instantly charge. If she does not do so she is exiled from the herd and ends her days as *rosbif*.

If bulls which will not fight are to be seen in Barcelona, bulls running loose are the speciality of Pamplona. On one of the days of the great festival of their Patronal saint, St Firmin, custom demands that the bulls brought by rail for the festal fights shall be detrained at dawn and let loose to rush through the streets. The agile young men of Pamplona – and one must remember they are Basques, so more than usually agile – make it a point of honour to be there to meet them. They run before them trying, no doubt, a few passes on the way. All enter the arena together, bulls and men, even a Gypsy woman, a baby in her arms, another clutching her skirts.

A queer descendant of the cult bull is to be seen also in Basque countries. This is *Zesken Susko*, the Fire Bull. After a fête, when the dancing is over, the last *Fandango* done, out from a shed trots a dark shape, sparks glinting about it. It is a bull shape plainly enough, for wheels of coloured lights whirl high on its head illuminating two formidable horns. But there are only two legs. The bullhead is already crackling, flames begin to soar, to burst; the creature jog-trots – it is too heavy to do more – hither and thither, led by a guiding hand, for the man inside the shape can barely see. To and fro they go, in and out the shrieking crowd which breaks and flees. The fireworks go into full action; squibs explode, a fountain of light shoots upwards outlining the sinister head and again scattering the crowd. When things become too hot the beast sinks to earth; the man inside manages to free himself and appears as a human being, smoke-blackened, the sweat making white runnels down his face. Everyone begins to go home.

My first acquaintance with the Fire Bull was at a rather sophisticated fête at Cambo in the Nive valley, attended by many of the visitors who stay there for health and pleasure. How curious they were about Basque doings and how wrong they got it all. How alarmed they were when *Zesken Susko* took it into his bull-head to climb the tiered seats of the pelote court – for all the world like a real bull which, having jumped the barrier, begins to climb the seats of the ring, the shrieking occupants climbing before him for dear life, leaving fans, mantillas and cloaks scattered beneath his hooves.

The latest Fire Bull I have seen was at Biarritz of all places. But inland, away from Casino and great hotels, Biarritz is Basque. This fête was in a little suburb on the road to Spain. There were roundabouts and lollipop stalls and shooting galleries, and after the *bal* there were *Fandango* competitions in the middle of the road in a thick sea mist. Out of the grey dampness as the clock struck midnight trotted the Fire Bull, blazing and flaming amongst the screaming *Fandango* dancers. I could hardly see him for the mist and when I did I could hardly believe it – at Biarritz.

D*

In 1560 Queen Isabel of Spain was regaled with the sight of a live bull with fireworks blazing on his horns. In 1622 St Ignatius of Loyola could not be canonised without a living Fire Bull, while to amuse a passing Prince 'two or more' live bulls were most horribly set ablaze to run until they burned to death. His Highness declared himself highly gratified at the sight. In Aragon, still, amateur bull fighters play – or perhaps did until the Civil War which changed so much – with bulls which have flaming torches tied to their horns. Possibly from this sort of bravura came the man Fire Bull. Or again, for some reason we cannot now apprehend he, like men-bears and men-horses, existed alongside the live Bull, giving expression to a variant of cult ritual. We must not forget the Iberian *bicha* of Balazote with his bull's body and his sad human face, nor Minos and the Minotaur in a bull mask.

There seem to be very few human representations of the bull, far fewer than of the horse and bear. One such I saw unexpectedly, believing him dead and gone. He was at Amélie-les Bains, Roussillon, 'out', as they say, at Carnival time and in no hurry to go in, making a scene in the street, the *Bou Rouch* of Vallespir. The Red Bull, roughly made in bovine form, was covered with red cloth; underneath went a man bent double. The head was painted on cardboard with a pair of round sad eyes not at all unlike those of the *bicha*, as though both know themselves to be but half-men. With him was his lady, Trésine – the man in woman's clothes. A peasant led him, and one or two bull fighters – so near the Spanish frontier – pretending that the poor thing was *toro bravo*.

A well-known figure strutted along with them, in crinkled trousers and disgraceful bowler hat – Mr Charles Chaplin in his old guise, Charlot. This sort of appearance, tacked on to age-old folk characters, delights me for it shows there is life in the old bull yet. They trailed about Amélie, the Bull rush-ing into shops and being pushed out again, chasing Trésine

with whom he is understood to be in love.
Everyone told me this as though the fact
had some significance for them. The bull
fighters now and then kill him with their
sticks, but he comes to life again and on they
go, the spring-time Bull and his Bride,
enacting his own death and resurrection. A
raggle-taggle street drama, on its last legs,
but holding hard to essentials.

Away in Castile I know another man-bull
– or cow, for he is called *la Vaquilla*. He

La Vaquilla

comes out in the first days of spring masked in a very
peculiar fashion. A cow's face is painted on white cotton
stuff which is roughly made into a garment to hang round
the young man's neck and contain his arms. The cow face
comes across his chest, while a pair of horns is fixed in the
right place. His own head appears above this wrap-mask,
wearing a jaunty straw hat. He has the usual leader and an
attendant gang of skin-clad fellows hung with bells. (We
are getting back to the *Zorromoco* zone of Cantabria.) What is
interesting is that other attendants kill off the *Vaquilla* and,
drinking quantities of red wine, declare it is her blood.[1]

Here indeed is the *vetula* of the ecclesiastical prohibitions
which, repeated again and again for a thousand years, never
succeeded in putting an end to animal disguises. A Spanish
one, a prohibition by the Council of Toledo, states '. . . pro-
fane games among the Heathen and Pagans. They were
wont, namely on the second of January, to adopt the form
of beasts, cattle and calves and to run about hither and
thither'. Which is so exactly what 'they' still do that the Council of Toledo seems to have handed over its task to General
Franco, who likewise prohibits disguises in Carnival. I could
quote similar edicts and reports from all over Europe and
from the earliest Fathers of the Church to the eighteenth
century. It is self-evident that the spring folk drama scanda-

lised the Church more than other post-heathen practices and
that it is the most persistent.

Before moving on to bears I must try to describe a sight so
wonderful that I shall never forget it. It came to me through

Repeated again and again for a thousand years:
the man-heifer in an early form.
(After a figure on a Celt-Iberian vase
in the Museo Numantino, Soria)

the windows of the Oporto branch of the Sud Express. It is
worth while too, for the honour of British Travel Agents, to
tell how I came to be in that train. There is an English hotel
in the pine woods of Beira Alta, Portugal, high above the
Mondego river – a lovely spot. There is, or was, an arrangement to stop the Sud Express by signal at the village station
not far away, a great convenience to the hotel guests. Try as
I would, write as I did, telephone as I was driven to do, no
Lisbon or Oporto agency would send either ticket or information. So the traveller wrote home to her local Thomas
Cook and Son. By return came the through ticket with

instructions to show it to the village station master who would then signal the train. Only half believing, I warned him of day and hour, thrusting the ticket beneath his eyes.

'Coo–oo–ook', said he, assuming his national expression of melancholy, denoting that life was altogether too difficult for him, 'Coo–ook', and signalled the train, into which I stepped, to thunder away through the uplands round Guarda and to the wonderful sight to which this leads. As we passed into Spain at Villarformosa dusk began to fall. Behind us the Portuguese mountains were stamped in purple against a glorious sunset, Ciudad Rodrigo, that marvel of a walled city, to our right, and then the plains of Salamanca and the hot night. We seemed to run along a raised causeway, on either side of the track a river which shimmered in the very last of the daylight, its waters gently moving in dark undulations. I looked more attentively. The rivers were rivers of bulls, all gently streaming along, the faint afterglow reflected on their backs; accompanied by mounted stockmen, they moved across the Salmantino pastures until the fancy took them to lie down and doze.

BEARS

Bous méni l'ous Marti,   *I lead you the bear Martin,*
L'aspan do la countrado.   *The terror of the country.*

Bear trainer's speech at Arles

The ritual of the man-bear, carried out in strangely perfect form, is one of the miracles of Pyrenean survival. The bear has been to the people of the mountains what the bull was to the people of the plains. The hunters of the Old Stone Age from earliest days depicted him on cave walls. We see the great cave bear of Les Combarelles taking a walk and when, with the receding of the glaciation, he was replaced by the brown bear we see him too, stubby and determined in the main chamber at Lascaux over-painted with an enormous bull. Norbert Casteret found him realistically modelled in the Montespan cave where his real bear's head had in the course of ages fallen from the clay body, the skull lying on the cave floor.[2] And there are fearsome scorings high on the walls where the creatures, rising on their hind legs, enjoyed a good scratching.

Man-bear of Arles and cave bear of Les Combarelles

The many and wide-spread versions of the folk tale *Jean de l'Ours* point to the super-animality of the bear never attained by the bull. Jean, son of a bear and a lady he had taken to his cave where she lived in honoured seclusion waited on by her shaggy lord, grew into a folk hero. His strength was that of ten men, he was faithful to his companions and took the lead in a variety of adventures in the manner of half-divine sons of divine fathers in any barbarous mythology. These tales belong to mountainous country where bears are or were to be found, and stretch from the Alps to the Pyrenees. Pyreneans therefore both loved and feared their bears and, following the usual path from ritual to drama, when a real one could not be obtained, or because they became too valuable to play their rôle in the rite, a man dressed as a bear and took his place.

Village friends in Castillon-en-Couserans, Ariège, had taken me through mud and snow up a steep path to call on their village musician. He was an elderly man with a simple, shrewd face – a smallholder with a cow or two, sheep and a little land. He wore his shepherd's cloak of undyed wool, the cape and edges blanket-stitched with black, made with a hood to draw over his head (already well covered by his red barretina). His sabots went curving halfway up his shins in points like bowsprits, which caused him to rock as though each foot were indeed in a little boat. He and his wife were overjoyed to have company, and insisted on bringing out the garlicky sausage, bread and red wine, all of which they carry up some 600 feet from the village shop. The shepherd was prevailed upon to play us a tune on his poor old flageolet, cracked and bound up like a wounded man. Its tone left something to be desired, but he knew the *Bourrée Ariégeoise*, *La Castagne* and some charming song tunes, *Jeannetoun filabo* and *La Migo Abandounado*.

Migo oun as estach?	*Love, where have you been?*
Y'a loung temps a nou t'ei bisto	*It's long since I have seen you.*

He told us how, when 'they' came to make an inventory of Church goods (at the time of the Revolution he said, for that is an historical occurrence all know, but it was in reality at the separation of Church from State), the trainers of performing bears chained their pupils to the church doors. The inventory-makers retired and the inventories have not been made to this day.

This is the country of performing bears and when they were fashionable every family had a pupil or two, caught very young and brought up with the children. Trainers all have the same song, the traditional bear-song to which the creature thudded its pole on the ground in time. I heard it on the road from Toulouse to Narbonne.

> *Tara lara da*
> *Doundé, doundé, larida . . .*

When we asked if there were bears about nowadays the old shepherd laughed as though the idea were highly amusing.

'There's one,' he said. 'Only one,' and pointed to the forest which began a little way above his house. 'There he goes now,' he added in a matter-of-fact way, and we all rushed to the window to see the bachelor bear taking his lonely walk.

A party of dancers from the village travelled to London one winter, to dance at the Folk Dance Festival in the Albert Hall. They brought the musician down from his mountain to play for them. On the morning of the start he failed to turn up and two of the young men tore up to fetch him, as far as they could get by car, then on foot. They hardly expected to catch the train which would take them to Toulouse for Paris and London, and were in a fever of impatience. He had merely forgotten which day it was.

But the memory in my mind is of the shepherd, left behind on one pavement of Westminster Bridge, while his party stood shouting at him from the other. A policeman came to the rescue, held up the rush of traffic so that the old fellow in his white cloak and his sabots could stroll across, not even perceiving the snorting cars nor the policeman who held them in leash. The road had just become conveniently empty for him.

There used to be more bears on the Spanish side than on the French. It is wilder, there are fewer of the human kind with guns so that bear families can grow up more or less in peace. But since the Civil War, disturbed by frontier guards and fleeing refugees, they have been coming over to the French slopes again. A pastor of the Reformed Church living in the Vallée d'Aspe, whose veracity I really cannot question, told me that one day in full daylight in a lane he saw bear spoor going towards cottages outside the village of Accous. He was without his gun but went on warily. Peering round the next bend he was just in time to see two bear families crossing the lane to regain the woods, after a good meal on cabbages. Waiting there motionless he counted twelve Pyrenean bears, two mammas each with five cubs of different litters. The father bears had not accompanied the party or *le pasteur Bost* would have had to take to his legs.

When I made up my mind to see a *Chasse à l'Ours*, which I hardly believed in, we arrived one day too late. A collector's life is largely made up of arriving too late. This time it was thanks to the then landlord of the Hotel des Martinets at Amélie-les-Bains who, being a Parisian, could not believe that our questions as to local doings were of the slightest importance. So we were quietly travelling across France while the excitements were going on in Vallespir. When, on learning the irreparable fact, we remonstrated with the Parisian, he laughed in a pitying way at so ridiculous a reason for visiting Amélie. We should of course have come to drink the waters.

We were a party of four, my eldest sister, S.B.-C., myself and afterwards S.B. We each had our duties and could conveniently split into units when occasion demanded, such as the *Entrallisada* going through the streets of Arles at the same time as the *Bail de la Posta* in the fairground at Prats. In spite of missing the bear hunt there seemed an enormous amount to see and we broke new ground. We went, for instance, to call on the jailer of Céret prison. A very intelligent man he was and the leader of the local Cobla band, for French Catalonia possesses Coblas but without the tiny pipe and drum of Spanish Catalonia. Monsieur Manyach in the prison entry gave us much information and a variety of tunes, and laughed at the tambourines used by the Amélie dancers, opining that the leader had a supply in his tourists' Bazaar* for which there was no sale. Everything he suspected of being untraditional was 'contraband'. He recounted the tragedy of the girl who received no *ramaillet* – a flower spray

* The use of them is now accepted as Catalan. So is 'tradition' formed.

– from her young man before the ceremonious *Bail del Ramaillet*, so went home and hanged herself. The tale was quite circumstantial; it took place on the fête of St Jean at Serralongue. Finally he composed a *Sardana* for me, then and there, in the prison doorway.

When Carnival and the Bear Hunts came round again we set off once more, two of us this time; I returned to Vallespir, S.B. to Luz, halfway up the long valley which opens at Lourdes to end under the precipices of the Cirque de Gavarnie. I went to sunshine and yellow mimosa, she to ice and snow. The previous year we had worn out our shoes on the road between Amélie and Arles-sur-Tech, so this time I stayed at the latter place in the little hotel which had grown out of the inn. I was welcomed warmly – everyone was looking out for purveyors of song, dance and bear-lore, so that this Carnival proved to be one of the most repaying and utterly exhausting times in my life. The whole town knew about the 'lady from London' who had come to see the bear. I have never lived in London, but I have learnt how to profit from that always slightly awed description. I have asked to look out of private windows at processions, have marched into closed museums and once on to the balcony of a *Casa Municipal*, announcing I had arrived directly from London to see their drama, race, Hobby Horse or other festive animal. No such stratagem was necessary at Arles-sur-Tech. People ran out of their houses, or walked for miles, to tell me something which might interest me. One night a young man was ushered in who had walked nine miles up from Pla and was going to walk nine miles down again, after begging me to pay a visit to his bear too.

My first experience of the Bear Hunt was somewhat frightening. To begin with the creature was duplicated, so that just when one felt the danger had passed another bear appeared. Candlemas, February 2nd, brought them out, obedient to Pyrenean tradition. 'If Candlemas is warm the

bear will look out of his lair, but winter will continue for
another forty days.' So says the proverb, which is firmly
believed. Out they came, the men-bears, on the right date
and the sun shone so hot at Prats de Mollo that one searched
for shade. Not a leaf was out, so I ate my picnic lunch in the
shade of a wall until a gun suddenly boomed from the
Vauban fort on the opposite slope. From where I was I
could see intense excitement spring up at the foot of the hill,
men tearing upwards, women and packs of shrilling children
herding together at the bottom.

As I approached a little boy rushed up, exclaiming,
'*Madame! Grand danger! Il ne faut pas aller par là!*'

More alarming was the advice given by grown-ups as to
how to escape the attentions of the bears. Up in the fort they
were dressed and given five litres of red wine each to help
them sustain their rôles. Two shots were fired and instantly
a stream of men poured out of the fort and down the hill,
fleeing. Presently I made out two figures resembling at that
distance Red Indians, with towering headpieces. These two
would spring upon the fleeing men and roll them on the
ground. When this happened a shot rang out from somewhere and the bear would drop down dead. Attendant boys
with gourds (the regional skin bottle) ran to them, gave
them a drink, brushed them down and offered another gourd
holding I then knew not what.

The bear costumes consisted one of fringed black, the
other of fringed brown woollen material, lamb skins on their
heads rolled into immense caps, another lamb skin hanging
down their backs. Their faces were pitch black, their hands
blacker. Each time they caught somebody, man, woman or
child, they left black smudges on the victim's face and re-
blackened their hands in the soot and oil contained in the
proffered gourd. Men were rolled and blackened; the new
schoolmaster was rolled and blackened. He had locked the
school doors and windows but the creatures got in all the

same and out tumbled the children shrieking. By four o'clock there was not a clean face in Prats save mine. And the people, shriek as they did, the men yelling as much as the girls, at heart were pleased, for blackening is age-old ferti-lising magic which they know all about from one generation to another.

The previous year we had made friends with the highly respectable daughter of one of the innkeepers, who had given us a charming Christmas Carol in the Catalan tongue. I now descried her strolling arm-in-arm with other girls in an aban-doned manner, her blouse torn open, her face blackened. Standing inoffensively in the square a passing bear spied my clean face. Up he rushed waving frightful paws.

'Don't run. Stand still,' advised the people round me. My heart thudded. But I did manage to stand there – perhaps I was too frightened to run. Then, just in the nick of time, I bethought me of a bribe. Snatching a note from my bag I pressed it into the menacing paw. '*Merci*,' said the bear and turned his attention elsewhere.

Everyone was telling tales of what they had been known to do and what they had done this year. It is certain that in-credible licence reigns. It is Saturnalia in Vallespir. They climb balconies and crawl into upstairs windows. I saw them both at it. Inside they take immense liberties, put their hands down girls' blouses to blacken their breasts – it is Carnival, fertilising powers are about. They roll in clean beds; they get down the chimneys of the hospital to appear amongst the patients and the scandalised nuns. If anyone wants to play a trick on a girl he gives the bears a sum to catch and blacken her, and they are never too drunk to run like the wind. At length two 'barbers' arrive from somewhere (they are in reality the creature's ritual companion, the man in woman's clothes), catch the worn-out actors and chain them.

They broke away again and again so that I, with three total strangers, made a dash into a near-by café, smashed the glass door and rushed out again. The *cafetier* made no remonstrance: '*C'est le jour de l'ours.*' Finally the brutes were firmly chained, shaved with a hatchet, and broke with their ladies into a mad gallop of a dance. All was over for another year.

Determined to see the end, I had let the last train depart long before and had intended seeking the innkeeper's daughter to beg a bed, luggage-less as I was. But the sight of this young person, promenading all black and free, made me think twice. Then with my collector's luck a young man I knew appeared, having come up to Prats in a car. The car was already full of unknown tourists but he crammed me in, and late that Candlemas night I tottered into my inn, feeling there was no need to imagine the ancient Saturnalia. I had seen it.

All the week a certain little tune made itself heard about the streets of Arles. Boys whistled, girls sang it, men too, with anticipatory grins on their red, Catalan faces. When the children heard it they howled and ran to *maman*. This was the bear's signature tune, a taking little air known all along the Pyrenees and used in far western villages for doings just as intriguing as the bear's.*

One night my innkeeper looked in to announce, 'They have come to show you the heads.' At the door stood a Carnival Committee man, for at Arles a firm hand is kept on things to prevent Carnival relapsing into Saturnalia. The committee man had, however, himself taken a step in that direction and was already solemnly fuddled. He led me to the café which was the bear's HQ and up a stair. There, in

* It is also the air of the Wine Glass dance of the Basque Hobby Horse.

the loft, spread out ready for the morrow, was a goatskin robe and a bear's head – a real one with a workable jaw, bloody teeth and glassy eyes. The little girl of the café, who had followed us up, took one glance and burst into the customary howl. There was also an array of smallish casks on which were painted two human faces, one on the front, the other on the back, garnished with jutting wooden noses and long plaits of hair made of dried garlic stems. The strange beings who were to wear them also wear women's cotton skirts, and belts from which hang clanging cow bells – all the ritual paraphernalia.

The day for Arles' celebration is the Sunday after Candlemas, which keeps it within the correct season, and they usher it in by parading the bear with his 'trainer' and his lady, Rosetta – the usual young man. The company was full of attentions for the visitor 'from London', came to call upon her, presented her with sweets and one of those horrible little bouquets of artificial flowers so much admired in both the Catalonias amidst their wealth of mimosa, roses and winter flowers. Also a neatly typed copy of the trainer's speech. This was necessary, for the discourse was in the execrable Catalan of the French side of the frontier. It was an invitation to the bear's wedding addressed to the *amables habitants dal ditjous Vallespir*' (Kind inhabitants of this our Vallespir), urging them to come to dance at the *Ball dal matrimoni*. The trainer, who was a fine, big railwayman, armed with the trainer's pole, ended very politely in French, '*A l'honneur de votre présence*,' and the incredible company passed on.

Very different from the orgy up at Prats is this hunt and capture of the *grosse bastiasse* in an orchard outside the town, green with junipers, silver with runnels of water and brightly dotted with all these fantastic figures. The Arles bear is captured and brought back to the town (trying to catch Rosetta as he goes), there to enact his yearly marriage, catching the Bride, leading her to his 'cave' – a hut erected in the square – treating her to cake and wine. One can easily descry the source of the folk tale, *Jean de l'Ours* here, when the rite was no play but the real thing. His work done, his annual death must follow. He is shaved as part of a clever dance by the trainer, a shot spits out and Arles' spring dæmon falls dead. In an impressive final scene his company dances in a tight ring round his great, lifeless body.

We are not shown his revival, neither are the cask-headed men explained satisfactorily. Taking their cow bells, skirts and cask-masks into consideration, I am inclined to see in them a composite representation of winter, the ritual accompanists seen all over Spain, with possibly a relic of a two-faced local godling of the Janus–Diano sort. The winter representation has the additional, very uncertain evidence of the remarks all round me, 'They must be finished off.' (And they were. The bear himself beat their casks to pieces with his pole till garlic, noses and head dresses lay all about the road and the shavings poured out.) The hazardous 'two-faced Diano' suggestion has a little support, for this character is seen here and there, notably with the dancers of Ochagavia in Navarre as their two-faced Fool, the Bobo.[3] Apart from surmise this Arles example, although a little sophisticated, is one of the best animal-dramas I know. The ritual marriage and death are perfectly enacted.

The next consignment of bears live and die in Andorra, the once 'hidden Republic'. Ceremonies take place on December 26th or in Carnival at the queer little capital, Andorra la Vella, at Escaldes, and high up the valleys at Encamps. It is uncertain whether they now continue and although they have their folklore value I cannot imagine that anyone reading this would wish to go to Andorra through thickest snow and hardest ice.

Tourists pour into the little republic in summer now that the way is made easy by the road from Ax-les-Thermes

over the 5,000-feet pass. We ventured there when it was in
the making. Our over-crowded country bus met the great
steam rollers (made in Rochester) on the very edge of a
precipice which seemed to drop a thousand feet into the
valley of the Valira. Here we stuck while one of the monsters
churned back and forth in mud and rubble, and here we
remained two hours or three. Supper-time came and went.
We had long since eaten whatever refreshment we had with
us. A gang of Andorran lads, excited at returning home
from a period of work in France, handed round their gourds
and as the red wine poured in comforting jets down their
throats they got livelier and livelier. '*Hé, xiquets!*' was their
cry, *xiquets* meaning 'young fellow' in their Catalan dialect.
For a long time we had felt that sinking feeling, especially
as dusk crept grey over the pass and no progress was made.
An idea struck one of us. There is stimulating power in
arsenic, vitality in quinine. We produced a bottle of 'One
Day Cold Cure', each solemnly swallowed two pills – and
felt much better. The steam roller manoeuvred itself out of
the way at its own time.

Andorra is disappointing. There is nothing mysterious
about it; it is merely the last survivor of several such peasant
republics once independent in the heart of the Pyrenees. The
Vallée d'Ossau was one of these, independent of the Kingdom of Navarre and Béarn, and Henri Quatre, although
nouste Henric to the people of Béarn, was careful to address
the peasants of the valley as '*Messieurs d'Ossau*'.

Andorra, geographically, linguistically and ethnographi-
cally, is part of Catalonia and, as everybody knows, is under
the joint protection of France in the person of the Prefect of
the Department of Pyrénées Orientales and the Bishop of
Urgel for Spain. The Andorran Councillors still use their
sixteenth-century Council Chamber and duly assume their
cloaks and three-cornered hats when they meet. Their horses
and mules are stabled under the Chamber.

We heard the church bells of Ordino pealing to ward off thunderstorm and hail. The parishioners were all out in the fields so it was the obliging Señor Cura himself who ran through the downpour to ring them, a piece of prophylactic magic which may have some scientific foundation, like the Swiss firing of cannon in the vineyards, and rather more efficacious than the traditional throwing up of a shoe for the same purpose.

My next bear, first reported in all its disreputable, deeply significant details by S.B. while I viewed the Vallespir rites, was in the Gavarnie valley, far up at the village of Gèdre. I found this bear's doings probably nearer a primitive rite than those of French Catalonia. On the way up to Gèdre, which is over 3,000 feet in altitude, are other bears, alarming in their habits, which hold firmly to the essential pattern. These belong to Luz, that grey town of the fortified church, and to the hamlet of Esquièze close by. The same company as elsewhere goes forth; one lady I saw beautifully dressed in the regional costume, the scarlet capulet on her head, carrying a basket for the gifts, eggs, bacon, even an orange – so precious up there in the snow. There were several gangs round Luz and they seemed to be well received as purveyors of a far-distant spring.

As we approached Gèdre we got right into the snow and to 'bring in spring' would be a still harder task. Heavy and thick it lay on the roofs, only slithering a little under the mid-day sun. Presently a man-bear came running down the street, escorted rather than hunted by his gang. He too was welcomed although he fought a passing man, growling and wrestling with his victim. The spirit here was entirely different from the menacing atmosphere of Prats de Mollo and the showmanship of Arles. But out in the country, where S.B. had met her gang a year or so previously, some realistic fertility mime was performed by the bear. The creature, told by his trainer to '*faire comme les jeunes gens en Carnaval*', lay down in the road to enact that which is necessary to fecundate, and the accompanying 'Doctor' offered a magic bean, that well-known symbol of female fertility. 'Obscenity is good fertility magic,' says Professor Rose – not that these young men intended obscenity. They were merely carrying out the actions which had always been carried out at that season. It was an integral part of their drama.

> *Sem al temps de Carnestoltes*   *We are in Carnival time,*
> *Qu'es el temps dels aymados*   *Time for lovers*

says a Catalan folk song.

If one can believe him, La Boulinière, in 1825,[4] heard of a Bear Hunt right down in the flat of the valley where 'one of the young men dresses himself like a bear, and at dusk runs through the woods, a torch in his hand; all the others follow him and endeavour to catch him, which is rather difficult although the torch acts as guide'. Neither torch nor night hunt is now remembered, and the account sounds like one of those nineteenth-century, romanticised tales then in fashion when writing of countryfolk. I prefer the hard-headed outlook of Henry, a French-Catalan writer ten years later, to whom the local dæmon was merely ' . . . *un homme de la lie du peuple, ses camarades vêtus des haillons les plus sales et barbouillés de la façon le plus ignoble, le font danser. Nous n'aurions pas fait mention de cette dégoutante farce si ce n'était un usage d'une grande antiquité*'.[5]

Leaving what once was certainly sublime for the ridiculous, the bear drama shall end with a story from my honoured friend, the Director of the Basque Museum at Bayonne. He is not Basque, but Basques come to him all the same for explanations and advice, for they identify him with their own museum. There is, in the mountains above Sare, a large stalactite cave much frequented by tourist coaches from the coast. It has very little prehistoric interest. One day the proprietor of the cave arrived at the museum. '*Pour faire joli,'* said he, he intended placing a stuffed bear in his cave. The tourists would like it and he knew bears lived in caves. The only question was – should it be a brown bear or a white one?

BIBLIOGRAPHY

1 J. CARO BAROJA, *Los Pueblos de España* (Barcelona, 1946).
2 NORBERT CASTERET, *Ten Years Under the Earth* (London, Dent, 1940).
3 ALFORD and GALLOP, 'Traces of a Dianic Cult from Catalonia to Portugal', in *Folk-Lore* (London), Vol. XLVI, p. 350.
4 LA BOULINIÈRE, *Itinéraire déscriptif et pittoresque des Hautes Pyrénées françoises* (Paris, 1825).
5 HENRY, *Histoire de Rousillon* (Paris, 1835).

6

Basque doings

The Pyrenees are only a little less horrible than the Alps.

An eighteenth century traveller

My first introduction to the Pyrenees and the Basques led me straight back to England and to Cecil Sharp. One long-ago Shrove Tuesday in St Jean de Luz a door in a wall opened before me and out came a string of dancing Morris men. They were dressed in white like ours, they had little bells on their legs like ours, they carried sticks like ours and one of their tunes was *We won't go Home till Morning*.* So intrigued was I at this, my first glimpse at the possibilities of comparative study, that after following them about all day I sat down and wrote to Cecil Sharp, telling him of their like-ness to our Morris men. He wrote back asking me in the most matter-of-fact way to note the tunes, a thing I had never done in my life. Very oddly one of the waiters in our hotel was an elderly Basque – very oddly because this inde-pendent race rarely takes such a job. He made assignations at the salon piano when he thought the room would be empty. There he sang a few airs which, remembering the schoolroom modulator and helped by the piano keyboard, I managed to get down. One I remember was written in 2/4 with a series of neat little triplets, when it would have run easily in 6/8. They duly went to Cecil Sharp who, when we got back to England, invited me to see him in Adelaide Road, Hampstead, where he then lived. I was much flattered. He was lecturing that night, a few of his first disciples illus-trating dances and William Kimber playing his concertina for them. He too was staying the night at Adelaide Road

* Which is an English version of *Malbrouck s'en va t'en guerre.*

124

and that was my introduction to this remarkable old friend.* We had spinach soup for supper, long green streamers floating about like seaweed without any creamy *liaison* whatsoever. Afterwards we all went together to the lecture and with us went Cecil Sharp's daughter Joan, who put up her hair for the evening to look more grown-up when dancing with older girls.

I was timid with Cecil Sharp. He made me feel uncomfortably ignorant. I *was* ignorant. Moreover he continued to have this effect on me and when, a year or so afterwards, I entered for the newly-born English Folk Dance Society's examination I wished I had not done so. He sat with a girl member to put me through my paces and they did not like me at all. My dancing was different from what he wanted to see because I had been taught other sorts of dancing for years by other sorts of people. I knew my footwork to be more finished than that of many of the brand-new members of the new Society and somehow this rankled ridiculously. I was allowed to graduate but was always distrusted as a freelance. I remained one. Later again, when my modest book *English Folk Dances*[1] was published, though writing kindly Cecil Sharp certainly made me feel an upstart.

On the other hand, from being impatient of his undoubted dogmatism and perhaps dictatorship – yet who else was there to direct? – I have come to value his work far more than in the early days. There are many workers now in the field he then ploughed alone but I notice they frequently neglect to read, mark and learn from the prefaces to his dance books and other writings. Neither are his photographs studied. There, before anywhere else, is the first-hand information we still look for, fifty years older and therefore fifty years nearer the sources. His dance notation also, a miracle of concise

* Mr William Kimber was the primary source of information on the English Morris. He was a dancer in the Morris 'side' of Headington, Oxon.

direction, was practically invented by himself and has served several generations of dancers since.* It is quite true that he had not the extra-English knowledge which is now ours. He never saw a great gathering of European folk dancers, nor had he the time for field work save in England and the English-descended Appalachian villages of the U.S.A. His energies were consumed in 'giving back to the people of England their heritage'.

After my breaking the news of the existence of Basque Morris men Cecil Sharp heard of them again from an elderly lady, a folk-song enthusiast, Miss Janet Blunt – whose acquaintance I too made at her home, Adderbury Manor, a wonderful seventeenth-century Cotswold house. There she showed me a picture painted on wood of the Adderbury Morris Fool who was also the village idiot, and whose costume consisted of an ancient Oxford gown and broken mortarboard. Her method of noting a song beat even mine, for she sat her village singer down beside her at the piano and picked out the air line by line in the key in which it was sung. Her version of *Cruel Lamkin*, for instance, appears to have been sung by a baritone. The singer was in reality an old lady with an old lady's deep voice, whose version contains these exquisite lines:

> *Worried father, worried father,*
> *May it do you some good.*

Miss Blunt spent a summer in the Pays Basque and after viewing her photographs and notes Cecil Sharp ingenuously told me he 'knew all about the Basque dances now'. Half a lifetime after that I still wonder if *I* do.

My prolonged Pyrenean travels cannot be brought into the

---

* This, in its turn, served as the foundation for the notations throughout the series 'Handbooks of European National Dances', twenty-six volumes, under my editorship (London, Max Parrish, 1948–53).

compass of two or three journeys. Bayonne was my home and there I lived the best part of the year for many years, going up the long Pyrenean valleys by train, country bus, car and cart. Then I shifted my headquarters to a country house outside Pau, from there scouring lovely Béarn, the valleys of Bigorre, Luchon, Ariège and the Aude. Even now, when I see the Pic du Midi soaring on the horizon, I feel that I am going home.

My first plan had been an intensive study of the Basques on both sides of the frontier and for that Bayonne was the strategic point, but when Rodney Gallop told me how far advanced was his preparation for the same work[2] I paused and allowed my eyes to rove along the range. It was Professor Gavel, the well-known Basque language scholar, who really settled the matter for me. He did not appear to find my plan to 'do' the Pyrenees presumptuous. I can still hear his quiet voice saying, '*Vous aurez le temps. Vous n'êtes pas pressée.*'

That decided me, a daughter of the city of Merchant Venturers, to become a Venturer in custom. The results of that undertaking are largely published in my *Pyrenean Festivals*[3] and in many articles in the *Musical Quarterly* (New York)[4] and other journals. But a rich aftermath remains in my notebooks and I am able to bring earlier observations up to date through post-war travels, some of which will appear here. The much discussed Basque character will emerge as it appears to me from people I have actually met – not from books, hearsay, nor from the *Saturday Evening Post*.

My Bayonne home was an old country house at St Etienne, the first village on the Pau road. It stands high on the north bank of the Adour looking across the river to the Pays Basque. With excessive heat a sea fog would form, insidiously envelop the Biscay shore and come rolling up the river, like Alice's thunder, in great lumps. It would bring the temperature down 15° in half an hour, and the hydrangeas would lift their enfeebled heads to stand up all pink and blue under the towering trees of the garden. Up the river came also porpoises chasing the *alose*, the so-called white salmon which is really shad, the chief catch of the Adour fishermen. A few rolling, rampageous porpoises killing salmon for sport and leaving them to float, white bellies upwards, to and fro on the tide, meant ruin for the fishery. Bayonne people would line up along the Pont St Esprit (over which the Devil fled from the incorruptible Basques, forgetting as he ran which was which of the only two words he had been able to learn, *bai* and *ez*, 'yes' and 'no') to watch porpoises chasing *alose* and fishermen chasing porpoises. After the destruction of the best part of the season's catch two young fishermen went out in their boat and shot the criminals. Up and down the Adour, in Niagaras of spray, also raced our one-time Prince of Wales in his speed-boat from the *Club Nautique*.

The old house, getting more and more embedded in camellia trees and mimosa, stands on the edge of the Départment des Landes and has a Gascon name, *Le Balen* (in French *Le Vaillant*), thus called after some unusually hard-working Gascon farmer of long ago. His farm buildings still stand; his cesspit lay cheek by jowl with our well. The cuisine of that lavish house was unbelievably good in its local manner. The first cook I knew there was a *Landais* girl and the Landes are famous for cooking. The second was a Basque from Macaye, a foothill village to which one would hardly look for refined cookery. When she heard her first dinner menu she amiably remarked in her strong Basque accent:

'*Bieng. Chacung a son mauvais gout.*' Merely a little slip in her unpractised French.

She never could be taught to use the third person singular, '*Madame est servie*', after the prescribed manner. It was always *vous*. When begged to alter she replied, still amiably:

'*Nong.* We too are a noble family. We have our coat of arms – besides, my father told me not to.'

IV The resplendent Hobby horse of Soule: nowadays he makes an attempt at the forgotten raising, by himself leaping high

V The Moors and the Christians, the Bads and the Goods of a Basque Pastorale, with Sara, Abraham's wife

It is true that many ancient farmer families have their coats of arms. The whole Baztán valley, for instance, was ennobled after 1212 when, at Navas de Tolosa, their men rushed the pavilion of a Moorish ruler, tearing down the chains which enclosed it and capturing the Calif and his draughtboard. The chains now hang in the cathedral of Pamplona and are shown in the arms of Navarre, the draughtboard in those of Baztán.

However, the noble young Basque did almost as well as the Landais commoner, cooked the great *alose* to a turn with mussel sauce, gave us her own Basque *piperada*, which is scrambled eggs with tomatoes and scarlet and green pimientos as hot as chillies, and a *pâté Basque*, which is a round pasty filled with savoury meat and potato.

How many winter mornings I have been deposited by the Hendaye Rapide on Bayonne platform I cannot say. How many times I have walked up to Le Balen, my luggage following on a handcart, meeting the dustcart drawn by a pair of small cream-coloured cows which pad along, making their bell tinkle to warn people to run out with their rubbish. Chestnut leaves would be budding here, camellias in bloom, mimosa swaying its yellow chicken feathers. In spring long-stemmed, pale primroses, so fragile compared with our hardy yellow ones, grew in a delectable little wood near by, and before the hay was cut the scent of the grass called *flou* was like lilies of the valley. Just beyond the wood, whence can be seen the delicate twin spires of Bayonne cathedral, are a few cottages known as *le quartier du Basque*. This unnamed Basque chose to dwell on the wrong side of the river for reasons of his own.

My friends owned a gaunt Alsatian named Guarda, who lived in a state of being called home. 'Would you believe it?' asked the Basque confidentially. 'I always have a fright when I hear that call, "Guarda! Guarda!"' *Guarda* is the Basque name for a Customs man.

VI *In Einsiedeln there were devils with horns and long tails. One in particular dashed from custody, dragging his chain, to pursue us*

They are famous for their smuggling, are the Basques, and always seem to have been. Stories of their exploits are told with roars of laughter under the noses of the non-Basque-speaking *Douaniers*. My friends, the Director of the *Musée Basque* and Madame Boissel, live on the Basque side of the river, with a garden rising steeply from its bank. There is a broken hedge up there, through which runs a well-worn path, right across their garden. This ends abruptly at the spot almost touched by the top windows of a house, the lower floor of which is on river level. Mend the hole as they will, efface the path as they may, both reappear before many nights are out. I fancy our Basque met the goods on his shore, after they had been silently rowed across in the dead of night. The main part of the heavy goods smuggled across from Irun is rowed over the Bidassoa in that way. If fired on, the men will leap into the river to swim across, letting boat and goods drift out to sea. There is a story of how the boat, failing to drift away, was towed in and the casks opened. They were full – of sea-water.

One summer a Customs officer lived on the ground floor of the same house I lived in, in my chosen village up near the mountain frontier. In the small hours I heard running feet approaching. No espadrilles shod them. Boots. '*Douaniers*,' I said to myself and, having absorbed the local spirit, I hoped none of our men were in trouble on their frontier paths. The boots came straight to the front door. There was a knocking, a hurried opening and a low conversation.

'*Venez voir.*' And again, '*Venez vous-même.*'

Suddenly came, 'And the lady up there?'

'Pooh,' said the officer. 'She's English.' Therefore out of it and no talebearer. Presently they all went off, officer and all, but no arrests were made that night.

A rich Basque family owned a seventeenth-century house in my village, *Americanos* as they were called – returned from South America with a fortune. We used to go roaming the mountains together, picking the minute camomile flowers on Atsoulay for *tisane* and visiting the Field of the Goat, where notorious Basque witches and warlocks held Sabbaths near the village of Zugarramurdi. Coming down in the dusk one evening we were pulled up by shouts from above.

'Who are you? Where are you going?'

The Customs men had spied us from above. They were too lazy to come down to our level so the conversation was carried on at the tops of our voices. When they learned we came from our village the bawling ceased and we went on. We could well understand their suspicions. We were dropping down to an isolated farm, part of the *Americano* property, the master of which had just come out of prison for smuggling. The *Americano* boys and girls knew all about it and, far from blaming their tenant, admired and sustained him. They told me the story with glee. One or another of this man's large family was always ill or injured, always being taken to hospital at St Jean de Luz, always lying in the small milk lorry wrapped up in a blanket. The excisemen – the farm being on one side of the frontier and the milk customers on the other – perfunctorily glanced at the familiar vehicle, sympathised with the wrapped-up child. One fine day, gossip being a little prolonged, a *Douanier* leant against the lorry, whereupon a peculiar sound came to his ears. *Gluck, gluck, gluck.* He jerked the vehicle roughly. *Gluck, gluck.* Out came the child, out came the milkcans, up came the flooring – and there appeared a neatly made tin container precisely the shape of the lorry floor. It was full of Spanish alcohol. This little play had been played week by week for the fifteen years of the farmer's tenancy. No wonder he spent two in jail.

It is not thought dishonourable – a one-time Curé of St Engrace was said to be an excellent smuggler. One day I was walking up the slopes above my village when *Monsieur le Maire* overtook me. He was a substantial man, in business as in person, and very polite to the newcomer to his Commune. We walked along together till a side path appeared. Abruptly he left me, saying he had business that way. I learnt afterwards that the business was to visit his new assignment of Pyrenean ponies driven over from the Spanish side. But when I, with the curiosity of a newcomer, went in search of them the *borde* with its enclosure and shed was empty. By that time the ponies were trotting down the lanes to some horse fair.

But after the last war this sort of Basque smuggling was swamped by an uglier and more contemptible one. A flood of strangers, from as far away as Bordeaux, overflowed the trains and buses. They ignored the bridge which marks the frontier by walking through the stream, just out of sight of the guards on either side. Every morning the village bus arrived packed, every afternoon it took the 'foreigners' away again. Legitimate travellers had to defend their seats vigorously. Later, the bus-owner hired from elsewhere and presently a procession of buses would arrive – to the disgust and derision of the village people. They would stay just long enough to give the crowd time to splash through the stream into the Spanish hamlet and often left behind suspicious characters who strolled about at night, too close to the houses for comfort. The French Customs men stood about supinely while silks and wines and shoes and oranges were brought in under their very eyes. It was ridiculous and scandalous. About once a week they suddenly did their duty. On the closed day the roads would be splattered with orange pulp where the thrown-away fruit, not worth the fine, lay rotting. But the clothing and the tobacco and the rest was duly paid for and the smugglers made up for it all the rest of the week. Not only the buses brought them but vans, lorries, smart private cars, bicycles. On Sundays every road and lane was thick with them. It was no longer smuggling. It became depredation. Looking on at the sight I found a young French

guard at my side. He kindly said, 'I shouldn't go over now if
I were you. Wait till the buses have left.'

Naturally I did go over. I had always been in the habit of
'going over' long years before the plunderers came. Basque
friends of mine live in 'the last house in France' and after the
sort of conversation we like to have – lasting from three to
four hours, as interesting and animated as in any Paris salon –
a delicious tea is served in the large, cool room with its priceless *kutchak* – the carved family chests. On the walls hang pictures of amazing Virgins standing Isis-like on the horns of
the moon or sitting like the Infantina de Castilla in a tree, all
jewelled and diademed, all draped in robes so spreading that
they seem living tents – their tiny faces, rosy or black,
peeping out at the apex.

As the heat lessened my hostess would say, 'I always take
a turn towards evening. Will you come too?'

The turn takes us out of her back door into a garden of fig
trees and flowers, out again into a path running down to the
stream, across the stream on stepping-stones. We are in
Spain. That is to say, Basque Spain. The turn now takes us
to a gaunt house, the 'first in Spain', in which is the general
shop – and a few other things. We buy chocolate at one-third
of the French price. We then mysteriously leave, not by the
door but by a great, dark staircase. At the top, in the very
attics of the house, tightly shuttered against adverse eyes, lit
by the feeblest of electric lights, is a branch, no less, of a
famous draper of San Sebastian. They too are illicit, for a
Customs agreement allows no such commerce within a certain number of kilometres of the frontier. But the going is
too good to be missed. They have secretly (more or less)
established themselves there for as long as luck holds.
Nothing more incongruous can be imagined: the village
store, the staircase, the darkened attics, the elegant town
salesmen – how do they transport them there? – and a
dazzling display of the best Spanish dress materials, silk,

satin, cotton, ninon. I forgot all about clothing coupons.

We are safely back under the eyes of the tent-like Virgins. Nobody but they has seen us leave. But the purchases still have to travel the two miles to my village, and towards evening the Customs men amuse themselves by patrolling the road. One of the sweet little daughters of the house says she is going to confession. If I will take one parcel she will take the other. We do so. We separately meet a brace of Customs men with whom she chats, holding her parcel well in evidence, while I pass by carrying mine.

The farcical situation has now come to an end. Food is plentiful in France and smuggling has reverted to its legitimate practitioners, such as my friends in 'the last house in France' and their guest.

It has been the fashion – especially amongst their own writers – to depict the Basques romantically as a simple people with a deeply religious family life, their girls adorned with virtue, their sons heroic *pelote* players given to a little contraband for sport. I assure you the Basque smuggler is a redoubtable person, frequently armed, getting off his goods in the most workman-like manner by lorries to dealers in Bordeaux or Paris. Deeply religious they are, and regular at mass, coming off their secret paths in time to appear in respectable black, up in the men's galleries in church. With some friends one day I was driving along the lanes about five o'clock on a Sunday afternoon when, in the very middle of the road, we descried an elderly man sitting beside his bicycle. The men – all Basques – sprang down to his help and, getting him to his feet, found but one thing amiss. He could not stand. The old fellow, in his Sunday best, with his velvet collar and his tucked white shirt, his closely fitting béret and an affectionate smile, said, 'I have nothing contraband. Oh no. I'm coming back from mass.' No doubt he was – five hours afterwards.

This makes me think of another Basque, a fisherman, who

sat beside me in the bus which rushes between St Jean de
Luz and Bayonne. After his heavy head had nodded several
times to my shoulder I disentangled myself and changed my
seat. Up he sat.

'That isn't polite,' said he reprovingly. 'That is *not* polite.'

Their wines make a man gay, incline him to ear-splitting
irrintzinas, to dancing and love-making. Inebriation does not
last long and is seldom offensive. The unmarried girls,
especially after a fête, are allowed great liberty of conduct.
Fensterling, or window-climbing, does not here require the
ceremonious recitation of verses beneath the balcony as in
Switzerland, nor the very odd superintendence of the girl's
father to make sure the young lover's literary efforts are up
to standard; but it is an accepted fact, and *Neska Eguna*,
which means the girls' day and is a Saturday, sees the window
open. This state of affairs is accepted save by those who will
not see. These, I now perceive, are generally ultra-Catholic,
nationalist people living in towns. They love to write up a
romantic, virtuous and thoroughly boring Basque folk of
their own imagination.

When I first went to my favourite village I set myself a
little study of the subject, for I did not believe it was true. In
the village six cases of free conduct came to my notice. One
was my own maid, a girl from an out-farm, who afterwards
made a good marriage with another man, taking her baby
with her to her new home. Another of the six also married
another man, while the other four remained at home expecting marriage in their turn. In a small town, the doctor's
daughter, like the peasant girl, opened her window, but this
family insisted on a marriage between the lovers.

Two years ago I had to restudy this custom on account of
a pending attack on what I had written by one of the said
nationalists. I found things exactly the same and the attack
faded out. The young friends with whom I was staying at
Sara had no such false ideas about their own people, and

pointed out from their windows several white mountain houses in which there was an extra child.

I take this state of affairs to be an ancient social system, not unknown in other mountainous countries, which must not be confounded with immorality. House and lands still take precedence over people in the Basque lands, and each child is valued as another pair of hands. Long before the fashion for romanticising began, a Spanish Basque writer clearly exposed the primitive notion that a suitor must know whether '*la ternera hará buena vaca*'. Having proved she is a capable mother of children a girl marries with greater facility.

Very different was the custom of the Bethmale valley of Ariège. Here girls were encouraged to become mothers for the avowed purpose of leaving their babies to go to Toulouse as wet nurses. In the city their health and their rich costume were always in demand. So callous a custom brought misery to the valley race, but the decline of the Bethmale dress has practically brought it to an end. An early observer of the Basques wrote in 1808, 'immorality amongst the unmarried persons is very frequent, much more so than in Castile . . . and girls who have "fallen" find husbands without difficulty, in many cases more easily'. Immorality in married people, on the contrary, is severely judged and trespassing couples are likely not only to find their doors linked by a path of green leaves for all to see but, like the Mayor of Casterbridge, to suffer a Skimmity ride or Charivari.

THE CHARIVARI

Tobera usaia delake
prestatu ditugu.

We have prepared a Charivari
because it is the custom.

From the play *Malkus eta Malkulina*

The Charivari is a subject large enough to require a study to itself and this I have been engaged on for some time. It seems to be the result of a deep and ancient urge to exact conformity to the communal standard of behaviour, which breaks out from all sorts of mankind even where one would think it had been entirely forgotten.* Great Britain knows it well. England (where the latest I know of took place in Sussex in 1947)† has a variety of names for it: 'Rough Music' in the south, 'Riding the Stang' in the north, 'Skimmity Riding' almost everywhere. Wales has it in the south as the 'Straw Horse', in the north as the 'Wooden Horse' or 'Cwltrin'; Ireland knows it and the Lowlands of Scotland.

The word 'Charivari' went with French emigrants to Canada, to Kentucky and Louisiana, modifying itself into 'Shivaree' – under which appellation we saw the bridal party in *Oklahoma*, where the real intention must have been forgotten, indelicately shying baby dolls into the window of the newly married couple.

The whole European world has practised it (with the exception perhaps of Scandinavia) and has long since amalgamated the classical donkey-ride with it, which ride, forcibly given to an unfaithful wife, was commented upon by Plutarch. The foundations of the proceedings are identical from Rumania to the Atlantic coast, but all sorts of local specialities vary the monotony, the cruellest the *Cencerrada* of north-west Spain, the noisiest the *Katzenmusik* of Switzerland. The greatest variety is found in the provinces of France, and the punishment play of the Basques marks the apogee of the Charivari. This race has always annexed the customs of its neighbours, marked them with its own hallmark and kept them alive long after they have died elsewhere. This is the reason why foreigners with a smattering of knowledge announce that the Basques have strange and

---

* *Punch or the London Charivari* uses the word in its superficial sense of a riot of fun.

† *Evening Standard*, July 1947, and private information. The police could not ascertain the real reason for the outbreak but the men engaged in it stuck to their assertion, 'It is our right.'

E*

unique customs. One cannot, however, say this applies to the Charivari, for so far from its dying France still greatly relishes it, suiting as it does the malicious spirit towards their neighbours of French *jeunesse*. To find what must surely be the culmination of the antique custom we go to Basse Navarre.

The other Basque provinces, Labourd and La Soule, do not mince matters, the first excelling in Rough Music or *Galarrotsa* (meaning a 'night din'). This has been known to go on every night for a month, as in a famous case at Espelette in 1828. They indulged in a Rough Play also, the crudest of fare, now come to an end. But the night punishment endures and sometimes serves a more useful purpose than registering derision at a second marriage – one of the most usual causes of the din.

In the lovely village of Itxassou in the foothills of the Pyrenees, a terrible noise burst out one night. 'Up there,' said a village friend, pointing to a solitary farm on the slopes. 'A real *Galarrotsa* it was. Ooo, ooo!' and she realistically imitated the sound of their speciality, a waxed cord briskly rubbing through the cover of a deep cooking-pot. This improvised instrument is of some antiquity, for we may remark it amongst the bells, the pots and the pans used in the night serenade administered by Fauvel, the Fox.*

My friend went on to recount an ugly case of rape and how the village men, by that ferocious uproar in the night, had signalled it to the police. A year or so later the same friend told me the man concerned had come out of prison and had shown himself at Sunday mass, a characteristically Basque manner of rehabilitation.

La Soule retains the donkey-ride, everyone mounted instead of the sole culprit, the disreputable company of disguised men and boys clattering off amid clashing bells and the singing of injurious verses to the quickly shuttered house

* *Le Roman de Fauvel*, 1310–14.

of their victim. They have, too, the habit of staged plays, farces composed for the occasion, so gross that the police are bound to interfere; so they introduce them surreptitiously between the scenes of a reputable *Pastorale*. Both farce and donkey-ride are called *Asto-lastarrak* and men go out to cry a verbal invitation in macaronic verse, Basque and Béarnais, to make sure that everybody knows the treat in store for them. A messenger will arrive at a farm and announce,

Si lou boules créde	*If you will believe it,*
Aquero qu' ey bertat	*Here is the truth,*
Igantian dirôte	*On Sunday there will be*
Asto-lastarrak.	*The Ride on Donkeys.*

I have never seen a *Pastorale* veiling a punishment play. They appear, so one is told, without any explanation or connection, the audience knowing to what they refer. The true *Pastorale* characters suddenly assume punishment duties and Lot may be seen as a wife-beaten husband if the *Pastorale* is Biblical, or Charlemagne as the Doctor to castrate an elderly bridegroom if the *Pastorale* is historical. This disgusting scene seems to be greatly appreciated, for we hear of it several times and that stock folk character, the Doctor, is in constant request. He has gained his medical knowledge through his travels, exactly as our Mummers' play Doctor has done.

> *I've been to the Lowlands, Italy, France and Spain,*
> *And now I've come home to old England again,*

announces our practitioner, while his Basque brother in a translation into French declares,

> *Je me rendis dans la royaume de Hongrie,*
> *Après avoir fait le tour de la Prussie et de la Russie,*
> *De l'Angleterre et de la Turquie*
> *Je suis revenu chez-moi.*

Some of these scenes have been found in MS. ready to interpolate into a *Pastorale*. One such, *Canico eta Beltichine*, was found in the Bordeaux City Library and is now in print. The theme is that of a man beaten by his wife for having swopped a good horse for a wretched mare. Stage directions in Basque-French point out the correct production, such as '*La manière d'arriber au Triate*', while the traditional Epilogue declares, '*Vous avez écouté notre Tragérie*', although the audience has been rocking themselves and the wooden tiers with Rabelaisian laughter.

Basse Navarre improves on this with plays wittier and less coarse – or shall we say somewhat less coarse? They too practise the night din which may go on relentlessly for fifteen nights or more, and in addition the way of unfaithfulness is signalled to all by the 'sowing of greenery'. The usual 'right' to inflict the punishment is stoutly maintained here as in England, a rhymed invitation to onlookers assuring the public that,

> *Monsieur le Curé nous a dit*
> *De le faire tous les soirs.*

If the cause is particularly repugnant to village morals the night din is followed not only by sowing the greenery but by *Tobera Mustrak*, a Show. In French this is called a Cavalcade. Now a Cavalcade must have permission from the authorities, for it fills the streets and is staged in the square. So application is made through the village Mayor to the Prefect of the Department. The Mayor, being Basque, suppresses any inkling he may have as to the real intention. When Carnival is the season, as it so often is, Carnival covers a multitude of sins. When Georges Hérelle was gathering material for his *Le Théâtre Basque* (*Le Théâtre Comique*) he expressly asked the Sub-Prefect for details of permission granted for what he delicately termed *représentations charivariques*. The good gentleman replied that he had not known a single one during his ten years of office. Hérelle dryly remarks that he himself knew of eight within that period.

Permission is obtained, an improvising poet engaged, the band bespoken, the dancers warned, the neighbourhood invited – and absolved beforehand by the *Curé*, according to the invitation verse. The unhappy objects of the play are warned too, and prepare to leave the village if they can, to shutter themselves into their houses or to pay a large sum to buy off the performers. The great day arrives. In the morning some of the company ride about to attract an audience. I once walked down an empty street one windy April day, when round the corner appeared an unexpected procession, flags flying, drums beating, a broken-down comic cart conveying some of the actors. This land is fertile in surprises of this sort. Always an hour or so later than announced the horsemen ride out, the men in gala dress, white shirt and trousers, scarlet or violet waist sashes and scarlet bérets. Behind them comes the band, then the 'Pioneers' in long aprons, axes on shoulders, and two giantesses, their long white skirts covering their bearers so that each lady ends in a pair of gaily dancing feet. They are smallish, light relatives of the great Spanish giants across the way. '*Agur Andreak*,' the people say to them, 'Good day, ladies,' and they bow politely in reply. Then come Flagbearers rhythmically waving their flags and then the dancers. These ritual dancing men have arrived at a high state of efficiency towards the upper Nive – developing from the rather poor specimens on the coast, such as those I first saw coming out of the door in the wall at St Jean de Luz. Here they are of two orders, *Kaskarotak*, a name derived from the bells they wear, and *Volantak*, the Flyers, who are the higher grade. They too wear gala dress, many ribbons and little bells down the seams of their trousers. On grand occasions the Flyers are provided with headgear like mitres decorated with flashing mirrors, pendant ribbons forming a veritable cape down their backs. Now come more riders, the Lord and Lady and the Pairs, man and woman on foot – the woman, of course, a man in petticoats. Amongst the dancers are the Wild Ladies, boys with long masses of coarse, black hair and closely veiled. I have never yet satisfied myself as to what they represent. It is true that *Basa Jaun*, the Wild Lord, who follows people at night, has a Wild Wife, but these dancers have no Lord with them.

Now come the actors who play the culprits, often in a cart, and then come, or do not come, a host of hangers-on, beggars, drovers with mules, knife-grinders, even a Hobby horse which I once saw and which had not appeared for generations, and the *Huissier*. The Bailiff or *Huissier* is the Fool of the ceremony, in parti-coloured dress with a horse-tail hanging down his back, rushing about, indulging in fraudulent money transactions, pursued by mounted *gendarmes* and fired at by the Pioneers. Finally he falls dead and is borne away to a dirge. Judge and Lawyers walk about gravely with law books under their arms, and hold the Court on a trestle stage on to which all crowd – drovers and mules and all. The accusation is read, the whole story (never mind how indelicate it is) is sung in verses by a couple of *Koblak-ariak* – which simply means makers of coplas or verse – mounted messengers tear to and fro, the dancers dance numerous interludes but always the same dances, for the traditional repertoire is small in this district. There are *Volantak Marcha* or the Flyers' March, *Sauts Basques* and an ornate Chain dance with several figures.

The verdict is then pronounced, and the sentence carried out in embarrassingly realistic scenes. The show goes on for hours – with long pauses while the actors drink and the audience up on the tiered seats eat and bawl – to end with a *Saut Basque* gravely performed by Flyers, Wild Ladies, giantesses, the Lady, the hangers-on and probably the Mayor. The evening ends with a 'ball', never-quenched thirst and ringing *irrintzinas*. Altogether a satisfying display of the forces of morality.

After the first World War some softening of village standards seemed at work and the show was sometimes staged as an entertainment only, without real culprits. One of the first I saw was purely entertainment. It showed a venal old couple, their blowsy daughter – a youth of course – cuddling her baby and the seducer, a Gascon from the town. But wars have never had much effect on this little bit of country and a year or so later a real punishment show was organised near St Jean-Pied-du-Port. It was forbidden and was carried out all the same – but on the Spanish side of the Arnéguy frontier, the whole company being fined on its return to French soil. Another real performance, for a serious cause and kept very dark, was at the village of Bidarray on the Nive in Basse Navarre, where a friend of mine was able to secure valuable photographs. Outsiders and cameras are strongly objected to as a rule, so this was something of an achievement; my friend, try as he would, could not ascertain the reason for the show. Long afterwards I learnt from a local woman that the disgraceful cause was the birth of babies, almost simultaneously, to the wife and sister-in-law of the same man.

Now it is certain the dancers do not properly belong to a Charivari show, but this important fact, in spite of his careful study, was not perceived by Hérelle. To anyone familiar with ritual dancers in Europe and more especially along the slopes of the Pyrenees it is clear that *Volantak* and *Kaskarotak* belong to what we may call the Morris brotherhood – those companies of seasonal dancers who appear in England at Whitsuntide, on the Continent usually in Carnival, accompanied by the proper characters, the Man in woman's clothes, the Fool and the Hobby horse. The real duty of these Basque dancers is to come out at Carnival, that is the very beginning of spring, when they are not connected with any play whatsoever. Then they call their procession *Santibate*, Carnival, quite simply. Like others of their brotherhood they then go through the village taking the Spring or the 'Luck' to each house, versifiers singing of village doings and the weather, as we have heard them do on the Aragonese side of the mountains. Thus, from the point of view of traditional integrity, it is a vast pity that the ritual men of Basse Navarre should ever have been called upon to appear with a Charivari punishment play.

A real *tragérie* ends this not altogether pleasant subject. During a visit to a fellow folklorist, a young doctor, I happened to ask if there had been any Charivaris in his neighbourhood in the last few years. His reply rapped out like a pistol shot. 'Last night. One killed and two wounded.'

This, the latest example known to me, took place on a Saturday night in May 1950, with results so extraordinary that it seems likely to be the last for a long time to come. There had been rumours of an illicit love affair, both lovers married people. Then 'greenery' was sown, in the untraditional form of lime sprinkled between the houses, one of which was an inn. Under the shuttered windows of the inn Rough Music burst out, larded with violently injurious calls. When the uproar had run its course the group of Charivariers started home down a narrow lane. Two shots cracked through the darkness; one young man fell instantly; his brother was wounded in the thigh, a friend in the hand. The police were called, an inquiry began. The reputed lover, a natural suspect, had one of those unshakeable alibis – he had been from home that night with friends who, perhaps too eagerly, supported him. Suspicions then rested for a while on a certain Agarra, who had himself suffered the 'greenery' some time before (which had linked his farm with the same inn) and who, it was thought, might have taken later vengeance on the Charivari group of men. Nothing, of course, could be obtained from Basques by 'Gascon' police and

Agarra was released. When the town police left they cautioned the local *gendarmes*, 'You will find him in the lane where the young man was killed.' Their psychological flair – if that is what it was – proved correct. Agarra was found in a wood close to the lane, hanging from a branch of an oak. So the Charivari of Elissaberri claimed a second death.

One of the ancient customs of this country is the importance assumed by the 'first neighbour' in times of stress, a relic doubtless of a sparsely populated land. When the master of a house dies his nearest neighbour on the side of the church, though not of the family, takes over the running of the farm or business for a few days and acts as chief mourner, following the coffin in his black cloak and respectable top hat. After the death of Agarra his first neighbour was performing his duties when, in the church itself, he was seized with a fit of frenzy and was held with difficulty by friends and a doctor.

While the struggle was going on the poor man cried out in true Charivari style, 'I'm a cuckold and they are beating me!' (This cry was actually used at a Saintonge Charivari in 1417.)

The Elissaberri Charivari now claims two killed, two wounded, one mad and, to end tragedy in comedy, the eldest son of the 'first neighbour' next day just saved from death after swallowing a chicken bone.

'I might conclude this subject with an Apology; it is not of the most delicate Kind, yet in speaking of popular Antiquities, it seemed incumbent upon me to say something about it.'

John Brand, 1777

A NOTE ON THE MASQUERADES IN SOULE

A horse being taken once a year into the grove and sacrificed as an embodiment of the god.

Sir J.G.Frazer, *The Golden Bough*

Still more showy than the Show in Basse Navarre is the Carnival Masquerade in the next little province, the Soule. This is one of those dance-dramas founded on ritual which has come down the ages from long before Plutarch's woman was made to ride the donkey with her face to its tail. Not human fallibilities, but the inexorable course of the year governs this play. It is, however, an anthropological subject too complex to enter into fully in a book which must cover other regions and countries than that of the Basques. And if it cannot be entered into fully it is better to comment as little as possible and to analyse not at all. Yet its existence must assuredly be signalled with an outline of its content, for this manifestation attracts a good deal of attention on account of its swaggering costumes and showy dancing, and if foreigners have heard anything at all about Basque dancing they will have heard of the resplendent Hobby horse of these masquerades. On page 165 appear the titles of a few works in which they may be studied.[5]

They take place in Carnival time, that is on the days just before Lent, and in Soule villages only. When some of the characters are seen in what the French call *manifestations folkloriques* at Biarritz or elsewhere, they do not compose a *Masquerade* but merely show isolated dances from the *Masquerade*. It is very difficult to make sightseers believe this.

The protagonist is a man-horse in place of the man-bear we know. He undergoes a life-and-death cycle, passing like the man-bear through pursuit, catching, binding, to which is added shoeing and castration by two vets – seriously mimed without indecorum – and a joyful recovery. Some eighty years ago he was raised like a Sword dance Captain, but on eight crossed hands instead of on locked swords. Nowadays he makes an attempt at the forgotten raising, by himself leaping high. He is attended, like other yearly protagonists, by his spring Bride in the incongruous dress of a French Army *cantinière*, by a Whiffler sweeping the way with his own symbol, a horse tail, a Flagman and a character with the lazy tongs – that queer symbol of lightning, therefore of storm and rain, used for fertilising effect by many Carnival guisers. These five characters perform, amongst other things, the famous Wine Glass dance. These are the 'Beautifuls' who compose one *Masquerade*. But with them go a crowd of the same sort of rag-tag-and-bobtail as we saw in the Show and these compose a second *Masquerade*, that of the 'Dirties' or *Noirs*.

It is these noisy hangers-on who, with their comic scenes, blur the proceedings. So does the actual dancing itself, for amongst dance-loving Basques this artistic element overrides the integral ritual part.

The *Masquerades* seem to be an extraordinary survival from seventeenth- and eighteenth-century Carnival, superimposed on something mediaeval, superimposed on something pre-Christian. They can best be understood by comparison with ritual dramas already mentioned, particularly with the Bear Hunts and with our own Padstow Old Hoss rite, truncated though that be. When such comparison has been made the same pattern may be descried in all.

THE PASTORALES

Misterio admirablerik	*An admirable Mystery*
Errepresentatu akhen dugu,	*We have acted,*
Eztakigu zien goguak	*We do not know if we*
Ahal tugunez satisfatu.	*Fulfilled your desire.*

Epilogue of Roland

Beginning with something quite other than our subject, let me beg readers not to take this verse as an example of classic Basque. It is a good example of how foreign words have been taken into a language so primitive that it had no means of expressing things spiritual, abstract, collective, mental or moral, nor desire nor thought. The familiar words in the verse above came to the Basque language from Latin, from Spanish old and modern and from the *langue d'Oc* of neighbouring Pyrenean peoples.

The *Pastorales*, full of such borrowings, grew into what they are in the same way as did the *Charivari*. Such plays, known almost everywhere in western Europe, survived until almost within memory in Brittany and Catalonia. Now the conservative Basques seem the sole retainers in France, and then only in their most conservative province of Soule. The *Pastorales* have been fully described at various times during the last century – the classic study still being that by Georges Hérelle,[6] but this can now be brought up to date through my post-war observations.

These open-air dramas, performed in late spring, have strong folk elements but are chiefly descended from mediaeval Mysteries, the setting of the stage, technique and subjects all showing this plainly. They are not ritual in the meaning of pre-Christian ritual, neither are they necessarily seasonal. The time chosen is solely on account of the large cast, for which every available man is needed. So the play must be over before the shepherds depart in June to their high pastures. The subjects range from Biblical, quasi-historical to hagiographical. My first Pastorale was 'Abraham' at Alos in 1928, my most recent 'Napoleon the First' in 1953 at far-away Larrau. So when I was asked by the Editor of the *Journal of Basque Studies* to write a comparison of what I witnessed at the beginning of my work and what I saw at my first post-war Pastorale in 1951,[7] I had about twenty-three years' experience of my own and could also draw on any of the previous studies, with a few printed references back to the eighteenth century.

In most villages there lives one family which jealously preserves a copybook in which has been copied a play, and a man of that family will be ready to act as *Pastoralier* or *Instituteur* of the play. The village goes to great expense when a play is decided on. The stage is of planks laid on barrels, often built against the *pelote* wall, and towering tiers of wooden seats are built up, for the whole district attends, flooding the roads and paths – each family bringing its dinner basket with its white napkins and wine bottles, each *Jaun* with his umbrella hooked into his coat collar, hanging down his back.

The backcloth is of white linen sheets, lightly decorated in the tasteful manner of this people with small green garlands swaying in the spring air. The band sits in an arbour constructed high above the backcloth, and the village musician with his pipe sits in full view on a kitchen chair at the back. Two doors take the actors *in* to the back and *out* on to the scene, which arrangement comes directly from the 'mansions' of the Mystery plays. Over the left-hand door are blue flowers, over the right-hand one red, and the Idol or Mahoma is fixed above the red one. This is a polichinelle with horns, partaking of the Devil and the supposed God of the Moorish infidels, who greets his adherents with extravagant gestures of joy each time they enter their mansion. Mahoma comes straight from Spain and has crossed the Pyrenees with other dramatic influences, but, I must repeat, the play is rich in folk elements from both slopes. Blue is for the Good, red for the Bad (even the Good sheep dog has blue spots painted on him), and, whatever the play – Abraham and Lot, François Premier, Roland or Napoleon – the manœuvring, marching, choreographically-fighting chorus of protagonists is composed of Christians versus Turks (Moors).

The ladies, who are young men, follow the fashion and have done so at least since the seventies when they were seen in crinolines. When I saw the bride of *Robert le Diable* she wore an elegant white dress made by the village dressmaker and a wreath and veil from the *Bon Marché* at Bayonne. The men have as nearly appropriate costumes as they can manage, a young priest wearing his own Curé's *soutane*, an imposing Cardinal dressed by the Vatican – or perhaps by Bordeaux Theatre wardrobe. The armies appear, the one in blue jackets and cocked hats, the other in red with flaunting, flowery headgear, the *Koha*.* The constant movement, the marching and countermarching, the swaying of the flags, the showy dancing of the Satans, all stamped upon the white backcloth and the backcloth stamped upon the vivid green of the mountainside make an almost incredible picture, never to be forgotten once seen. When my old friend the Director of the Musée Basque and I went to see *Robert le Diable* we sat on hard kitchen chairs in a blustering wind for seven hours, never even wishing to stretch our legs, so absorbed were we.

The performers begin their day with a procession through neighbouring villages to attract an audience and to show themselves off. Turks and Christians march or ride, ecclesiastics, angels and the ladies drive in lorries or farm carts – the whole, led by the band, making so amazing a sight that one can hardly believe one's eyes. When the theatre is in sight they leave their conveyances to march on to the stage

* *Koha* comes from *corona*, the flowery crown worn by men ritual dancers all over the north of Spain, as in the Basque country.

and into their own doors. The Turks often
arrive on horseback, the Satans on foot, and
these last try to leap on to the stage, helping
each other up by the prongs they carry, as
though they came from the lowest Hell –
there is no Mouth of Hell now if ever there
was one. Royalty is always dignified, Bads
are rough and rude and bawling, Goods are
quiet and sedate; Robert le Diable as baby,
boy and man (he grew up in the course of
seven hours) was so diabolical that it was
small wonder he was said to 'come from the
devil and that to the devil he would return'.
Abraham was magisterial, Sara, with long

'Turk'

blond plaits, was coy, but Josephine, wife of Napoleon,
was tragically inclined. All three were young men of course.
A flock of sheep sometimes appears, brought on to the stage
by their shepherds' compelling Pyrenean whistles; an up-
ward whistle, 'to the left', a downward whistle, 'to the
right', a long drawn-out whistle, 'flock stand still'. All this
they obediently do – for Pyrenean flocks are highly domesticated – while their shepherds tranquilly knit up a ball of
their own sheep's wool.

The story of the play is carried out in an extraordinary
technique which may well have been that of the Mysteries,
for it appears wherever remains of these mediæval dramas
survive as folk plays. During the International Folk Music
Conference in Yugoslavia a few years since, Dr Kretzen-
bacher of Graz and I met to exchange knowledge of Styrian
and Basque plays. To illustrate what we were describing we
alternately sprang to our feet and found we were using the
selfsame stilted actions, the selfsame rigid turns as we
marched up and down the hotel corridor. We have only to
visit Christmas Mummers – provided they have not turned
into ham actors – to witness precisely the same thing in our

own English villages. This embraces traditional Marionette theatres too, as I saw to my delight in the tiny theatre at Liége, where the two-foot Charlemagne and Roland were no stiffer, no more stylised and hardly more jerky than the six-foot Basque who played François Premier at Tardets.

In the long years of my Basque studies I have seen *Pastorales* adding up to something like ten days of performance, yet not until I saw one after the lapse of the war years did a new aspect of these dramas impose itself on my mind. I became aware of the rhythmic foundation of the technique in a way never before perceived. When three or four hours had passed I was so borne up on the rhythmic presentation that I could feel very little else, and the last hours went by almost unperceived. Without rhythm these shepherds, espadrille makers, village butchers and bakers, would never succeed in playing their play. Anything approached naturalistically is a failure – and there are would-be naturalistic moments. When the village actor is taken on the rhythmic tide he launches himself on it, forgets himself and his fear of forgetting his words and his difficulty with his arms and hands. He shelters behind the rhythm which protects him, as a Greek actor sheltered behind his mask. The Prologue (which, as already said, is the opening verses and at the same time the man who sings them) swims out on the rhythm and is borne to his grandest height, marching from centre to right, from right to centre, from centre to left and back to centre, raising both hands – arms wide-spread – at the end of each of the twenty or more verses. Behind him go the flagbearers swaying their flags in gentle, beautiful rhythm, as they too cross and recross the stage. The air sung is Gregorian and worthy of a strong young Basque voice.

Two Christians appear from the blue door. They seat themselves on cane chairs (*Pastorales* are full of pleasing anachronisms; I have seen François Premier sign the treaty of Pavia with a fountain pen and Sara, Abraham's wife, flourish a fan painted with bullfight scenes), glance at each other and rise as one man to march to the front of the stage, one singing the first two lines of a quatrain, the other answering with the last two. Each man sets his own pitch so that question and answer may be in different keys. They return to their chairs and sit on the last word of the last line. More characters enter, or one should say go out, each sitting, springing up, singing his way to the front and back to his chair. Sometimes four are doing this together in conversation. Now and again a concerted movement brings twenty or more on together. In single file they describe elongated spirals across the stage and as each man reaches a corner he turns once on himself, waving sword, pastoral staff, fan or whatever he may be carrying. We thus get two or three single files crossing from opposing directions and at the same time a succession of corner twirls. Nothing could be simpler, nothing more pleasing nor more rhythmical. When the recurring battle-dance takes place, which it does until all the Turks are killed, strict time-keeping becomes a necessity, for two long lines of dancers must spring forward and back, clashing swords or sticks as they meet. So hypnotic is this rhythmical action that the hours pass unnoticed, difficulties of language seem of little importance. When, in the newest *Pastorale*, *La Grande Guerre* or *Guillaume II*, as the French-Christians were falling back before the German-Turkish onslaughts, a solitary actor appeared far across the *pelote* ground waving the Stars and Stripes, we, the non-Basques, breathed again. 'Thank God,' we said to each other. 'Here come the Americans at last.'

Thus interspersed with ensembles and the Satans' dances the *Pastorale* moves along its way – seven hours of sitting, springing up and marching to and fro; recitative in a high tenor voice repeated by a bass and re-stated nearly an octave higher by a strident alto. Here I must refer to Hérelle's classic study, for this author denies that *Pastorales* are sung.

The actors 'shout in a loud monotonous voice', he declares.*
When, primed by the study of his work, I saw *and heard* my
first Pastorale I really doubted my own ears. I have since
come to the conclusion that Georges Hérelle must have been
tone-deaf. They are sung from beginning to end. And here
is the recitative to which the dialogue is sung.

The air known as 'the Angel's Song', sung by Heavenly
characters and those about to die, is beautiful, antique and
heartrending, and when the women in the audience heard it
and saw the clean pillow prepared for the hero to die on,
they would lift up their voices in a wail as antique as the
song, 'Aye, aye, aye . . . ' That wail is, I fear, one of the
things we have lost, for I have not heard it since the war.
Even Basque women become modernised.

The finale of the performance breaks through this rigid
majesty. The actors, to increase the box-office receipts, put
up to auction the honour of dancing the first *Saut Basque*.†
Young men of an aspiring village get together and soon
their spokesman, often their Mayor, is shouting his offer,
'Amotz, five hundred francs!' Or so it used to be; now they
rise willingly to thirty-five thousand. The auctioneer, the
actor with the loudest voice, stands on a chair to yell the
offers, the whole company at his back; the ladies, having
comported themselves all day with the greatest decorum,
pick up their skirts and leap on tables and chairs. (Sara, I
remember, at this point let off a piercing *irrintzina*.) Up rush
the winners, swarm on to the stage and off they go on their
Saut, a few steps to the left, a few to the right, the circle
gradually working round, bodies stiff, only legs and feet

* A. Léon, *Une Pastorale Basque* (Paris, 1909), says they are sung on two
notes. This I heard at my first Pastorale, but never since.

† This is the generic name for a particular type of men's dance.

dancing. A final entrechat is the signal for a volley of *irrint-zinas*, the runners-up shoulder out the winners and it begins all over again. A unique ending to a unique performance.

Not to lose sight of our main theme, we must return to the *Morisca* which has perpetually infiltrated into this book and into dramas far more ancient than the *Pastorales*. We examined it doing this more particularly in Aragon, where we saw it turning the antique Sword dance into something foreign to itself. Aragon is back to back, so to speak, with the Soule across the mountains; plenty of smugglers' paths allow communication in summer; the pre-Roman and Roman road over the Summus Portus leads into the next valley. Like merchants, emigrants and refugees of all periods, the *Moriscas* found their way over the mountains; the fashion trickled into France, swept over age-old customs such as the sacred well and giant-hero cult at Martres Tolosane (p. 54) and, meeting the Mysteries, found them an excellent stage on which to implant itself. Here, in the Basque *Pastorales*, it is today, inextricably grafted.

Pyrenean flute and stringed drum

THE OTHER SIDE

Zazpiak bat.   *Seven (provinces) in one.*

The Basque device

Since the Spanish Civil War these words are forever on the lips of the thousands of Basques now living in France who cannot or will not return to their homes on 'the other side'. This influx was not welcomed by the French Basques, but they are now accepting it as they have had to do many and many a time during the long history of Spain's attempted dictatorship over the Vascongadas. I notice, however, that their incoming cousins remain 'those Spaniards'.

The country they come from begins to differ from that of the French Basques the moment one has crossed the frontier. The main geographical features on the French side are three well-defined river valleys running from the western Pyrenees into the Adour and one into the sea. Each valley communicates easily with the next by roads or lovely lanes, rising to no great height until one reaches the Col d'Osquish which links Basse Navarre with the Soule. This is already a mountain pass. On 'the other side' the Navarrese valleys are immensely long but simple in form, running down to the Ebro. Guipuzkoa, into which the Hendaye–Irun frontier conducts one, is a mass of complex valleys and wild mountains, as is the province of Biscay. Factories line the roads and railways, the deep-water ports bore into the land and, in spite of close-packed tall quayside houses giving so antique an impression, carry a large amount of sea commerce. Bayonne is the sole port on the French side. As road and railway wind through the valleys a modern industrial civilisation is revealed. Nevertheless up on the mountains the old way of life goes on, the sombre farmhouses – for they have lost the gaiety of Labourd whitewash – their great eaves almost touching the earth, still shelter that all-important unit, the Basque family. All hands work on the farm, unless indeed a son has gone to 'the Americas' to seek a fortune. All live under the spreading roof, all speak Basque. Guipuzkoa is the only province left on 'the other side' which is wholly Basque-speaking. Of course you will not believe this if your holiday ticket takes you only to San Sebastian and you spend your time on the Concha beach.

The race differs, too, once the Bidassoa is crossed. After long years of looking at them with attention I can pick out a Spanish Basque in, say, the streets of Bayonne, easily enough. San Sebastian possesses a type of its own, a town type; in the mountains they more nearly approach their French cousins, yet with a difference. In the most southern province of Alava, where the language is lost, the type maintains itself as strongly as ever.

Traditional customs are as characteristic as on the French side but with another flavour. The *irrintzina*, for instance, is less savage, less alarming and less prolonged. *Pelota* is more professional – towns possessing covered courts with seats for hundreds of 'fans' and programmes of professional matches every day. The noise from these courts is shattering. The first time I was taken to the San Sebastian court called Jai Alai, I paused outside to say to my escort:

'Had we better not go in? They're fighting.'

'That's only the bookies,' said he.

It is an enormous court with front, back and side playing walls. The right wall is filled with tiered seats and the book-makers stand in a row facing the spectators, backs to the game. How they escape being hit seems a miracle. They yell the odds for every point scored and throw the slips, encased in a wooden ball, up to the client, never ceasing their shouts. The games are *Remonte* and *Pala*, which last is played with a flat wooden bat of that name. The speed of both is terrific. I much prefer watching the form called *Blaid*, played with the bare hand in a country *trinquet*, or against a village *fron-ton*. This is what one usually sees in the French *trinquet* with its penthouse roof on one or two walls, down which the ball dribbles amidst excruciating excitement, the players standing below like cats watching a mouse.

Competitions for woodcutting are another excuse for heavy betting and wild ebullitions. Each man stands on the first of his enormous beech logs waiting to hack with all his strength and speed. Presently his second will be seen pouring a trickle of wine from a gourd down his sweltering back. When one competitor overtakes another and both are hacking the same log the excitement is terrific. 'Their inclination towards amusements is unlimited,' wrote Humboldt in 1801. One hundred and fifty years later one can repeat his words. *Palanka* or *Barre*, throwing the javelin, nearly extinct in France, finds many practitioners here. The so-called javelin weighs up to 25 lb. and sometimes demands seven spins before the thrower throws. This sport is again an excellent occasion for betting.

A feast day will open with festal mass followed by a ceremonial *Auresku* outside the church, the Mayor often taking the part of the *Auresku* or First Hand – a tail man, or Last Hand, ending the chain. This dance ceremony is an epitome of the gravity and weight of Basque tradition. The leader's partner must be sought by two young men from inside her house if necessary; when brought she stands with her eyes on the ground while her *Auresku* treats her to a solo of local steps both high and low, a veritable cascade of steps performed in an undeniably erotic pose sometimes displeasing to watch.

When I was invited to partner the First Hand I hurriedly whispered to a woman near me, 'Must I not look at my partner at all?'

'Now and then,' she replied. 'But not too much.' If a girl gives the faintest smile of acceptance it would be 'a thing much talked of although a furtive glance may convey a previous understanding'.[8]

The leader and tail man then meet and perform a dance duel with set faces, defying each other. Other young men are sent to fetch other partners, each one is presented with the end of a handkerchief and, the man taking the other end, a long, linked chain is formed. Off it sets, solemnly serpentining round the *plaza*; figures such as the Bridge are performed, which means passing under the arch made by the leading couple's raised handkerchief, till the chain breaks up into pairs and a lively *Fandango* brings the ceremony to an end. In the eighteen-seventies an *Auresku* might last three hours.

The next time I took part in the Chain dance was in the middle of the Pamplona–Bayonne high road. We were coming back from a day in the Navarrese capital, when a long string of dancers emerged from a footpath, near the village of Elvetea in Baztán. It was led by an old man full of grace and courtliness, a model for the debonair younger men who followed him. As so often in this country, there was a lack of women for only the girls take part in recreation – the married housewife stays at home. So as our car drew up to let them cross the road, the unpartnered men broke off their end of the chain to swarm round us, eagerly inviting the 'foreign ladies' to join in. In a moment one of them was taking her end of the handkerchief, being led into the serpentines about the road and footing it opposite her unknown cavalier in the final *Fandango*. Delightful it is to remember the pleasure shown by those village folk when they perceived the foreigner dancing their dance with as much enjoyment as themselves.

We have historical references to the *Auresku*, from the seventeenth century at least. In 1688 three chains tried to dance at the same time on the square of Renteria, which congestion led to serious fighting amongst dancers and partisans. Following the old custom, when the Angelus sounds every man uncovers, the musicians place themselves in front of the presiding town authorities and everybody marches round the *plaza*. This is a typical proceeding in a country where the most hotly contested *pelota* match will cease as though by magic at the sound of the Angelus bell, the players snatching off their bérets to stand frozen in their places.

The Chain dance belongs equally to Navarre, under such a beautiful name as Dance of the Threshing-floor, performed literally on the great earth roundels swept clear of hand-threshed corn. At high Leiza the first Bridge is made to a sinister roll of drums. This figure then becomes a means for popular justice to be done; badly behaved people, those who have stayed too long in the inn, girls of questionable morals, find the handkerchief brought down smartly on their necks as they pass beneath it, exactly as we 'chop off his head' in *Oranges and Lemons*. Out they have to go. It was the old Leiza musician who, having proudly given his treasures to a collector of folk music (one of the Capuchin Fathers from Lekaroz College) and being shown them reduced to black and white in a notebook, cried out desperately, 'My tunes are finished. Now they are taking them away to Pamplona!'

The regional instruments are the *txistu* and drum, the first a pipe with seven holes, larger and better made than the tiny *txirula* of the French side. The musicians are accustomed to play three together in three parts, with drums played by themselves and by a fourth man. *Txistu* music is often composed for them and here one also hears the famous *zortziko*

A Zortziko rhythm

rhythm in 5/8. This has only become famous because to foreigners it is out of the common, but it is not of any great age nor is it beautiful. One finds the same air, now a *zortziko*, written in 6/8 a century ago. It is moreover the rhythm, not the dance, which properly goes by the name, but when a 5/8 section begins the figure performed to it is also called *zort-*

ziko. This heavy, thudding rhythm is now supposed to be typically Basque, perhaps because their National Anthem, *Gernikako Arbola*, is so well known an example; but of the thousands of folk songs now collected very few indeed show this rhythm.

The Sword dances are the chief displays of traditional choreography here. There are several – that of Biscay with variants, the neglected dance of Guipuzkoa with many variants and one of pure hilt-and-point character at Lesaca in Navarre – where sticks have taken the place of swords though the name, *Ezpata Danza*, continues. Julio Caro Baroja does not mention it in his *Los Vascos* (1949), and now tells me the leader was killed in the Civil War and that the dance died with him. A visit to the village would very likely put it on foot again. There are historical references to the Sword dance much earlier here than in England. A municipal order at Vitoria in 1486 lays down fines for 'those who do the Sword dance, on account of the scandals and bloodshed caused by them'. The sixteenth and seventeenth centuries continue the story; in 1827 Iztueta, the celebrated dancing master, published his *Dances of Guipuzkoa* with some of the Sword dance tunes. The Biscay dance is seen everywhere, for during the rise of the Nationalist movement in that province it was taught to the organisation *Juventud Vasco*, Basque Youth, spread all over the Spanish Basque provinces, and now into France. It is showy, beginning with an impressive 'Dedication' by the flag which is swirled over the dancers, who on one knee bend their heads to the earth; and it ends with a remarkable hoisting of the Captain, who is raised shoulder-high in a recumbent position, instead of upright as almost everywhere. At Arrexinaga however he shoots up above the heads of his men standing on the lock of swords; these are sharply pulled apart and the Captain drops to the ground on his feet.

The dance of Guipuzkoa is more elaborate still, with

F

many figures, including a Maypole-plaiting figure. This is as unlike what English people imagine Maypole plaiting should be as an Atlantic breaker is from a lake wavelet. The men speed round full tilt, as though cutting an outside edge on skates, dangerous to meet in a clash and apt to show temper towards each other if touched, even in public. This also is entirely typical of the race, who will display their rage quite openly when getting the worst of it in a *pelota* match. Variants of this Sword dance are used at Corpus Christi in several villages and, between the wars, in San Sebastian itself. Neither of these Basque Sword dances seems at first sight to belong to the European hilt-and-point family, but at San Sebastian a figure in that formation does appear as the men process through the streets. The Guipuzkoan dance shows no hoisting of the Captain; the Biscayan dance no hilt-and-point formation. We saw the Captain hoisted at nearby Ibio, Cantabria, and just recently have I seen an example from Burgos, Old Castile, where they raised the lock of swords in our English style, so that the symbol of the man and the man himself are uplifted in the same dance. The district round Burgos possesses dances showing a strong affinity with the Sword dances of Biscay, making me wonder which influenced the other and if those of the Basques are so peculiarly Basque after all.

The Spanish Basques possess no such outstanding customs as the dance-drama of La Soule. In some sort their showy Sword dances make up for this, and their folk song and music are rich in quantity. One can wander about till note-books bulge with records of small folk customs which, when compared with others of the same kind in Europe, prove of good value. On the borders of the País Vasco one perceives links with neighbouring Spanish provinces and these bring a richer contribution than that which French provinces bring to the Pays Basque. There only old Gascony marches with the Basque Country; on 'the other side'

Navarre marches with Aragon, Alava with Castile, and Biscay with the Cantabrian mountains where is stored one of the richest deposits of folklore in Spain.

Going eastwards we find on the Navarrese–Aragon borders the Jota Navarresa with rattling castanets, just moving away from the ebullience of the Jota Aragonesa. The guitar is in common use as in Aragon, mountain life is similar in both provinces and as late as the Middle Ages Basque seems to have been spoken in parts of Alto Aragón. But the old Kingdom of Navarre, Basque as it was, ruled by Kings with such typical names as Sancho Abarca, Arista and the like, birthplace of Berengaria, our English Basque Queen, has never been one of the Basque provinces; it has stood apart in politics and loyalties, fought the Moors as though their kingdoms were a part of the Spain it repulsed, and received early Iberian, Celt-Iberian and Roman culture from up the river-way – did not Pompey leave his name in Pamplona? – in a manner wholly unknown to related Basque tribes to north and west.

When, going the latter way, we reach the Biscay–Cantabrian borders we find precisely opposite conditions. Cantabrians are not now of the Basque race in spite of both having been included under the Cantabrian name since Roman days. But their climate is the same, mountain and seafaring life is the same, and a foundation of Euskarian stock has remained beneath the incoming Celts so that a foundation of folk belief and custom is the same also. With strong differences. The terrifying *irrintzina* fades into the gentler *riflido*; the *pandereta* (tambourine) is still called *tambour de Basque* though long fallen from Basque hands; the discoidal tombstone seen all over both Basque countries is seen also in the Montañas de Santander, of greater size and much greater age than any known in Basque churchyards. These, with the lamentations of wailing women, point to common funerary rites.

It is then no surprise to the St Agatha's chorus of Biscay if, on their wassailing rounds in earliest spring, a far-off echo of their songs from Cantabrian companies of *Marzas* (p. 21) comes to them across the border. The Biscayans sing the usual compliments of the season, swinging their lanterns and thumping their poles:

> *The Master of this house*
> *Has a red-gold beard*
> *And a silver shoulder;*
> *In the whole country there is no better man.*

The *Marzas* reply in popular-religious style, swinging their lanterns and ringing a bell:

Marzo florido	*Flowery March*
seas bienvenido,	*Be welcome,*
la luna llena	*The full moon*
alta y serena;	*Is high and serene;*
si quicieren oir señores,	*If you wish to listen Sirs*
los sacramentos cantar,	*To the sung sacraments,*
asomensi a la ventana	*Sit at the window*
que los vamos cantar.	*For we are going to sing.*

The thunder of Biscayan rollers acts as a bass accompaniment for both.

BIBLIOGRAPHY

1 *English Folk Dances* (A. & C. Black, 'Peeps' series, 1923).
2 RODNEY GALLOP, *A Book of the Basques* (London, 1930), translated into Spanish as *Los Vascos.*
3 *Pyrenean Festivals* (London, Chatto & Windus, 1937).
4 'Song and Dance in two Pyrenean valleys', *Musical Quarterly*, N.Y., Vol. XVII, No. 2; 'Ceremonial Dances of the Spanish Basques', Vol. XVIII, No. 3; 'Cantabrian Calendar Customs and Music', Vol. XX, No. 4; 'The Valencian Cross-Roads', Vol. XXII, No. 3.

5 GEORGES HÉRELLE, *Le Théâtre Basque* (*Le Théâtre Comique*) (Paris, 1925); ALFORD, 'The Basque Masquerade', *Folk-Lore*, Vol. XXXIX, pp. 68–90, with photographs and music; ALFORD, *Pyrenean Festivals* (*op. cit.*); GALLOP, *A Book of the Basques* (*op. cit.*).
6 GEORGES HÉRELLE, *Le Théâtre Basque* (*Le Théâtre Tragique*) (Paris, 1923).
7 'Une Pastorale Basque en 1951', in *Eusko-Jakintza*, Vol. V, Nos. 3–6.
8 RODRIGUEZ-FERRAR, *Los Vascongadas* (1873).

7

Swiss Fools and Festivals

But some again the dreadful shape of devils on them take,
And chase such as they meete and make poore boys for feare to
quake.
Some like wilde beastes do runne abrode in skinnes that divers
bee
Arayed, and eke with lothsome shapes that dreaded are to see.

The Popish Kingdome, 1570

At the First International Folk Dance Festival, London, 1935 – how common has this title now become and how questionable the folk arts now presented – I heard Mademoiselle Louise Witzig read a paper to the Conference on Carnival in her country. It was full of surprises to me who had known only a summer Switzerland – albeit not altogether a tourist one – a Switzerland of Alpine flowers, cheese chalets, cowmen's life on the alps with a small 'a', and processions of cows sonorously clanging their way up, led by the wisest cow, by the best milker, carrying a one-legged milking stool like a third horn, and by the sire of the herd, his head garlanded with flowers.

Mademoiselle Witzig was, and is, Secretary to the Swiss National Costume Society, formed for the encouragement of the costumes of the Cantons. She understood much more than costume however and opened my eyes to my own ignorance. The next thing was to go and see for myself. It was February when I reached Zurich, snow falling thickly as the day dawned. Mademoiselle Witzig had of course been consulted as to itinerary and there she was in the half-light, waiting for me on the platform. What was more, I then heard that the Swiss Costume Society was providing a car, and sending their photographer as chauffeur, and Mademoiselle Witzig herself. Could generosity go further? This, said they, was a small return for the hospitality and pleasures the Swiss dancers and musicians had experienced in London at the Folk Dance Festival. I next learned that Switzerland indulges in Carnival twice over; first in the Catholic Cantons which follow the Gregorian Calendar, and all over again in the Protestant Cantons which do not 'hold' with Pope Gregory and his Calendar, but celebrate their Carnival according to the Old Style a week later – this is also, I was told, to demonstrate to the unreformed that the reformed are not obliged to fast in Lent. So the car, the photographer and Mademoiselle Witzig would be at my disposal twice over. I felt overcome.

The first Carnival we were to see followed the Calendar, the two days before Lent, and we were to go to the heart of the original Switzerland, Canton Schwyz. Meanwhile snow fell, my comfortable pension warmed up and I spent the intervening day or two shut up in it learning from Professor Brockmann's vast knowledge[1] what to expect on our tour.

Zug, our first port of call, showed me the Central European type of Carnival disguises which begin about there, traditional characters all of them – Fools, Horned Devils and some of the 'double Gretchen' type. (This is a bent old woman carrying on her back the long Alpine basket in which sits, at his ease, a full-grown man. But it is the man's legs which are walking through the basket, it is he who goes upright, while the bent old woman is but a stuffed guy fastened on in front. These figures, if well made, are most deceptive.) The Zug Carpenters' Guild, carrying out an ancient custom, had provided lorries filled with new loaves which the Fools busily gave away. Next year it would be the task of another Guild.

Then on to the quiet old town of Schwyz, higher and colder than Zug by its sheltered lake, and immediately we

came upon the *Nüssler*, dozens of them, all masked and belled. Here we first saw the famous *Blätzli Narren*, the Leafy Fools, whose habitat stretches from Germany and Switzerland to the other end of the Austrian Alps and who have not only a live tradition behind them but a long history, printed and pictorial. They are in reality Green Men, Wild Men, our Jack-in-the-Green, and they 'bring in spring' in their own way which is less frightening than that of bulls and bears, but no less efficacious. They must have once worn leaves like our Jack and the various Wild Men still to be seen – notably an example in the Grisons who has a spring play of his own. This is similar to our Mummers' play in essence, for the Wild Man has to be killed as the worn-out year spirit, and brought back to life as the sprightly young Spring to dance with his bride,* precisely as does the Arles' bear.

But an outside influence has affected the Leafy Fools. This is almost certainly the *Schembartlaufen* of Nuremberg. In the fifteenth century this rich Carnival show was the prerogative of the Butchers' Guild, but the custom is far older than that, for by that time the name was already misunderstood. *Schembart*, already corrupted from *scema* – an old High German word meaning both spirit and mask – is synonymous with the Latin *Larva*, which meant equally spirit or mask, and the *Larvae*, as masks, 'bore the disquieting appearance of Returned Souls'. The men taking part in the Running of the Spirits therefore represent *either* the spirits *or* the masked chasers of the spirits. The first may come back to their homes during the Twelve Days of Christmas or during what is now Carnival – in the days of classical Greece during the Anthesteria which, again like Carnival, fell at the end of February.

* For illuminating photographs of the whole play see *Heimatleben*, Journal of the Swiss Costume Society, October 1947.

The Grecian father, a sprig of buckthorn between his lips to purge away evil, would, on the last day allowed them, sweep the Souls from the house. 'Out of the doors, ye spirits, it is no longer Anthesteria.'

Folk characters often bear a dual aspect as, for instance, the 'May' in Portugal – sometimes welcomed, sometimes repulsed, according to whether he is seen as the incoming spring or the outgoing winter – and, I believe, the *Schemen* of Nuremberg and Leafy Fools today are of the same double aspect. This was so well understood that when, in 1499, a young girl of Leipzig choked a masquerader – in self-defence? – she was acquitted by the Court, her defence being that she believed him to be a spirit.[2]

Folklorists, instead of building up their evidence from long comparison and deduction as they are often obliged to do, here find historical evidence in print and picture. The Guilds, Butchers' and others, staged their Carnival more and more magnificently and employed artists to design dresses and machines. These designs exist in the Schembart books left us from 1449 to 1539, so that we know what they wore for nearly a century. The Fools representing spring had tight-fitting overalls on which were painted or appliqué leaves. One year the suit would be white, the next year particoloured or, again, a fashionable costume with slashings of green. But whatever they wore they carried bouquets of green leaves out of which sprang a club or some sort of flaming grenade.* The opposite aspect was and is represented by dry moss, twigs or furry disguises, horned, beaked or diabolical.

As the Guilds grew rich a ship appeared, the famous *Narrenschiff*, the Ship of Fools. It would carry a crew of winter demons armed with squirts and more dangerous

---

* These appear to have been used like the magical 'life wand' to strike women and girls with fertilising effect. Cf. the striking at the Roman Lupercalia.

weapons, and was drawn by a dozen men and attacked by scores. The Leafy Fools, up to one hundred or more, would scale the ship on ladders and of course always routed winter in the end. It would have been an omen of disaster – such as that when the dove fails to light the fire in the *Scoppio del Carro* in Florence – if they had not been able to do so. The study of folklore teaches that nothing is more true than the axiom '*ceci vient de cela*'; everything turns out to be founded on something else. Fortunate as we are to have the Schembart books, we are still more fortunate to know, in this case of the ship, what that something is. One of the greatest strokes of luck which ever befell a study has left us an account of the ship when it was still a pagan object and known to be so.

A monk of St Trond was an eyewitness to an extra-ordinary outbreak of paganism in the year 1133. He tells how a countryman at Inda, a village between the Meuse and the Rhine, built a wooden ship secretly in a forest and set it on wheels. Weavers of Maestricht – was it already in the hands of a Guild? – put ropes over their shoulders and dragged it to Aix, Tongres and Loos. It must have been at Tongres, that once Roman city, that the monk's horrified eyes rested on the unholy spectacle, and when I was there a year or so ago I tried to visualise the frenzied rabble coming with their ship up the slope from the river Geer. Wherever it halted there was 'shouting and dancing round it far into the night', and when it was known to be approaching 'people rushed out to meet it'. 'Under the twilight of dawn', writes the monk, 'crowds of matrons, having cast away all feminine shame, loosened their hair, leapt half-naked, some clad only in their shifts, danced two hundred round the ship shamelessly. You might see there one thousand people of both sexes celebrating into the middle of the night. When that execrable dance was broken off the people ran hither and thither making a noise as though they were drunk.'

The famous Narrenschiff, the Ship of Fools

The ship was the Ship of Nerthus, a Germanic Earth Mother, in which her image sat under a covering to be touched by a priest only. She was taken out in the spring, followed by a herd of cows. During the festive period wars were postponed, weapons put aside, all iron shut away. This last touch again shows us duality of purpose – iron, so magical when new to mankind, became inimical to the pre-iron ancient beings who perhaps preferred flint, fairies, witches and worn-out divinities. Hence our use of iron against them today, the horseshoe over the stable door or, in miniature, thrown at a bride for luck; hence the necessity for removing every nail and scrap of metal before a spell can be worked. The most extraordinary thing about this extraordinary occurrence in the twelfth century, when great cathedrals were being built, when universities were being established on church foundations, is that the ship was expected and that people knew it for what it was. So much for folk memory.

We hear no more of the ship until 1440 at Antwerp and then again in 1530, by which time its transmutation from pagan rite to Carnival show was complete. Nevertheless memory of its beginnings remained, especially in the mind of authority. Ulm Council at that date prohibits it thus: 'There shall be none by day or night (who shall) disguise himself nor put on Carnival raiment, nor go abroad with ships on pain of a fine of 1 gulden.' But they went abroad with it all the same, and in 1550 a Ship of Fools, with a boarding party of Leafy Fools, went about the same part of the country as had the one which so horrified the monk of St Trond. In fact the Ship rolled on its wheels through the centuries till, about 1868, it was remarked by the early folklorist Baring Gould at Mannheim. It still goes out, shrunken now to a children's ship just as our Guys for the Fifth of November have descended to the children. I have not yet seen a Ship on Wheels with my own eyes, but even without it it was stirring enough to see its Leafy Fools in scores, to savour their long history and their undeviating conformity to tradition.

Here, in Schwyz, they cannot boast appliqué golden leaves,* but they do their best with fluttering tags and cut fringes of cloth, and so potent is the magic of this attire that in Austria housewives tear off pieces to put under the hens to make them lay. Some carry green fir brooms with which to sweep out Winter, and the company, called a *rotte* (gang) as were the *Schembart* companies 400 years ago, moves about as a whole although each man dances individually. The effect is most peculiar, strictly ordered disorder to the still more peculiar rhythm of two drums. My companions assured me no one as yet had succeeded in notating this and I could well believe it. Try as I would I could not even count the beat with certainty. The drummers told me they could not do so either. They could only drum it. The *Nüssler*, one by one, left the jogging mass to reappear on the balcony of the great inn in front of which we were. Not before the com-

* Painted and appliqué leaves are common in German Baden however.

pany had diminished to two might the drummers leave off drumming. Then started a fusillade of sweets and oranges thrown from the balcony to the crowd below. Swiss Fools are of the generous sort. Compared to my Carnival Bear Hunts under Pyrenean snows, all was strictly proper under the Alpine ones. Swiss custom reigned, not Saturnalia.

Tearing ourselves from these peaceable traditionalists, our car thrust ever higher round the flanks of the great Mythen which Lucerne visitors view so well from their lake steamers, into ever deeper snow, the snow of the 'dark forest' in which was found the famous black Virgin of Einsiedeln. She now reigns over forest and town from her chapel in the Abbey Church, founded by the first missionary to the stubborn forest folk, who responded by murdering him in the year 816. Einsiedeln later became a celebrated pilgrimage place. Hundreds of *ex voto* pictures, often of the most naïf sort, are hung in the Virgin's chapel, many from the seventeenth and eighteenth centuries; some are modern ones, just as naïf, such as a man depicted on a motor-cycle running into a car, yet saved by the radiance from Our Lady's halo which lit up the road for him. The usual pilgrims' cake, sacred to pilgrimage places, here has a vague animal stamped on it. This is called by the pilgrims the *Bock* or goat. Today it is explained as the Lamb, the Agnus Dei, but the popular name, together with the late heathendom of the 'dark forest', raises doubts as to this.

It was dusk when we arrived at the enormous chalet inn, *Der Schwann*, so we rushed straight out into the snowy street and plunged into a stream of guisers. Some were vulgar, many were ordinary; hundreds wore homemade masks of paper pulp shaped on moulds, and we learned of a mask competition that morning. Some of these youths, wearing their handmade masks and great cowbells resting on small pillows tied to their backs, ran to greet the strangers. They danced round us in a circle, making their bells clang, bending

forward to whisper gibberish in falsetto voices. This un-
canny whispering smacks too much of the first meaning of
larvae; 'the sheeted dead did squeak and gibber in the Roman
streets.'* More agreeable is the chirping cry 'Narro?' (Fool?)
to which you must reply, 'Narro.' For at this time of the year
you are all Fools together, ready to man the Ship of Fools or
to play the part amongst the Fool sons of the Fool father in
our own Revesby Plough play.

Sharp pistol shots came to our ears. Peering cautiously
round the corner of a chalet we saw a street deserted save
for one solitary figure. This was a masked guiser indulging
in the most wonderful whip-cracking display. He had no
audience and needed none. Alone he drove out Winter with
his magical whip; the lash, some eight feet long, swirling
from side to side, occupied the entire breadth of the street,
biting the snow into miniature dust storms with every
swirl. Here was something far removed from the smooth
Nüssler of Schwyz.

After supper – we were the only guests, for the pilgrimage
season was far off yet – the clanging in the street swelled to
carillon volume, and the innkeeper rushed up to say 'they'
had come to see us, that if we did not want them he could
not stop them – in fact here they were! Up the stairs and
into the great dining-room came the belled and masked line
of men, whether our attentive friends in the street or others
we could not tell. I noticed how the little waiting maids, and
even the daughters of the inn, got together and flattened
themselves apprehensively against the walls. Spring magic
had got inside.

Our uninvited guests ranged themselves in rows in front
of us, each bent forward on account of the great bell on his
back, each dancing, that is to say throwing up each foot
behind in turn in a lumbering fashion. *Clang, clang, clang!* It
was deafening. When at last they straightened up each man
* Had Shakespeare seen a Continental Carnival?

pulled off his mask and there under the goggling, simpering false faces were the red, grinning real ones of honest Einsiedeln youth. Then they had to be entertained, beers all round. What a mercy our crippling travel allowances were then unknown to us. When finally I was able to go to bed I lay awake for most of the night, so hot was my antique white-tiled stove, so mountainous the eiderdown billowing upon me, so disturbingly exciting was the clanging of the Carnival Runners' bells, approaching, receding, as they ran from house to house across the snow.

They run, these men and boys, from the Sunday till Ash Wednesday morning, day and night, night and day, only going home to eat and sleep when they can run no more. Then up and run again. Never has the magicking in of spring been so agitating to mind and nerves, and I have experienced it many times. The more so that, with icicles long as bell-ropes hanging from the eaves, 'the Summer and the May O' seemed the forlornest of hopes.

On the morning of Shrove Tuesday the dark forest appeared to be still putting up its fight against the 'new' religion. Mass took place in the Abbey Church, and at the bottom of the curved steps waited our own affable maskers and others more redoubtable. There were Devils in black skins with goats' horns and long tails, for all the world like those who, in mediaeval paintings, usher sinners into the Mouth of Hell. One in particular, led on a chain by a second man, was alarming. He dashed from custody, dragging his chain, to pursue us. Our own gang at the moment was again dancing round us in a protective circle, so the intruder was badly received. There were some rough moments, during which we retreated. But the Devil pursued. I side-stepped, and as he could not see well through his mask he lost me but grappled with Louise Witzig. Giggling but alarmed she wrestled with Satan. Our cavalier looked on, roaring with callous Swiss laughter. Fortunately the Devil's real business was elsewhere. At that moment the congregation came pouring out of Mass and away went all the guisers, innocuous and diabolical, to meet them. It was an extraordinary sight, the pagan remains growling outside the Church's pale. The Christians withstood the onslaught pretty well, dodging if they could, wrestling when they had to, but chiefly buying off the powers of darkness with Shrove Tuesday largesse.

At midday, while the February sun was still visible above the mountain walls, the *Joheen* and *Mummerien* arrived at the inn. Together they make a society dedicated to charitable 'bread throwing', and these members certainly had not been running for three days and nights. They were spotless and superior, all black breeches and white gloves, the Mummers in Fools' dress, belled and masked. As van and rear guards came companies – how did little Einsiedeln raise all her Carnival troops? – of a mixture of Fool and Devil who, I was instructed, were *Hörnlibajass*. I could make neither head nor tail of this word for my German is forgotten since Spain gripped me, and the local brand of Swiss-German completed the rout. At last some one came to my help and expounded an interesting example of far-travelling influence. *Bajass*, said he, is *Bajazzo*, a corruption from the Italian *Pagliaccio*, the famous zany or clown character in the Commedia dell'Arte, who became Pulchinella, our English Punch. In the course of years this person had trudged over the St Gothard pass in his Italian costume, his white trousers and frills, his great hooked nose and his hump. His new country set its mark on him, added three horns to his head so that he became Pagliaccio-with-little-horns, all run together into *Hörnlibajass*.

All these personages crowded into the *Schwann*, danced before us – happily there was no time for beer – had their bread-throwing stations assigned to them and all streamed out again to their positions in the town. Each man had an attendant boy to keep him supplied with loaves from enormous sacks. Crowds gathered below the platforms, and a constant cry of '*I mier eis!*' (Me, me!) went up with a forest of outstretched hands. Loaves were soon hurtling through the air, into windows, far over the heads of the crowd to people on its outskirts. The *Joheen* would not be out of place at Lord's. People seemed really to want the bread, whether from poverty or for luck I cannot say.

We left them at it as we had left the *Nüssler* of Schwyz, to rush downwards out of the snow to the main road which follows the upper Rheinthal. Along our route guisers of the leafy kind waved and yelled, much to the surprise of my Swiss companions who were not aware that Leafy Fools lived about that part. We stopped to chat and photograph and noted one Fool with a cross of red flannel sewn on his pagan back. I was already acquainted with the state of mind which prompts this prophylactic symbol, for I have seen Basque dancers protect themselves with the sign of the cross and know of Styrian Fools who hide when church bells ring. It is frequently evident that maskers know themselves to be outside the protection of the Church; indeed certain Bulgarian mummers, if killed in one of their Carnival fights, are not allowed a churchyard burial. At the old town of Wallenstadt five ancient masks are kept by the municipality, who hire them out to decent young men. Up at Flums, to which village we turned aside in some trepidation remembering the tales we had been told, they would have had nobody in a sufficiently responsible condition for that honour.

'Don't go to Flums without a man' had been dinned into our ears, and indeed they probably ill-wished us before ever we got there, for our car stuck in the railway lines of a level crossing, the Basel express just due, and when we did get there we were glad of a male back behind which to retire. At this village live two wood-carvers who, besides their cuckoo clocks and their musical boxes, make masks of their own designing. They have diabolical imaginations. The men

who wore these *larvae* were ill-behaved and rather drunk,
they jostled our brave photographer and drove hard bargains
before their villainous portraits could be made. Besides leer-
ing demons and squinting sub-humans were a few com-
pletely appalling creatures, white bandages round heads and
limbs, showing patches of bare flesh – the temperature was
well below freezing-point – and dreadful ashen faces. I
imagined their diseased fancies aspired to depict lepers, but
a folklorist whom I met later put it down to a memory of the
influenza scourge of 1918. I cannot believe this would
account for bandages. I now think these terrifying maskers
also represent the Returned Souls, returned to Flums in the
worst of their double aspect.

To me these Alpine maskers display more strongly than
my Pyrenean Carnival friends that urge in mankind to lose
himself, which is one of the underlying reasons for the seasonal outbreak. Possibly I have this impression because it
seems more surprising in the northerner of Germanic stock
than in the Aquitanian-Gallo-Roman born under a hotter
sun. It is not only the carrying on of tradition, though that
reason weighs heavily, but a pyschological urge in the indi-
vidual and in the mass. The same urge in staid Romans and
their households found its outlet at Saturnalia, and in
mediaeval clergy and clerks in the amazing Feast of Fools.
A Hungarian gypsy may 'hide himself in song'; a stolid
Swiss manages to hide himself in Carnival Running as surely
as he hides his face behind his mask. Hidden thus from his
conscious self he can override his fear of the supernatural and
can perform with the Souls what they have returned to do,
good or bad magic, fertility or blight; he can chase the
chasers and when the season for it is passed that urge to
different behaviour, bottled up through a long year, dies
away, satisfied and assuaged. It is generally accepted that
fear, fear that the warmth of the sun may fail, fear that rain
will not fall, in fact fear of hunger, evolved the many and

various agricultural rites of which we see (and practise) relics today. This thesis denotes an agriculturally-minded era when, because their aim was to encourage vegetable growth, men dressed themselves in greenery and the progenitors of the Leafy Fool appeared. This stage is generally assigned to the late Neolithic Age when the foundations of European village life were being laid. But did not Palaeolithic man also seek to 'hide' himself? What was he about when he disguised himself in a stag's skin with horns, as we see him on the walls of the Trois Frères and other caves? He had not attained to agriculture but sought his food in meat. To the animals therefore his mind was directed; power over animals was his chief desire and in an animal disguise he sought to lose his human consciousness and 'hide'.

Another town of Fools is Altstätten on the young Rhine. Here live the Röllelibutzen, the Belled Fools, the first westerly examples of the gorgeously hatted Perchten family which stretches from here to the other end of the Austrian Alps. We missed their afternoon march and the short appearance of Chräs-ma and Blattern Butzi, Leafy Fools in leaves and branches, but arrived in time for an early evening procession. There is no real dance here, only disorderly jumping and orderly marching. Sixty or more of them took part, the first eight squiring eight young ladies, the King with his two Lieutenants mounted on horseback. They all wear something like an early nineteenth-century uniform: top boots or leggings, white breeches and gloves and a dark coat; their ritual insignia are belts with sleigh bells – the *rölleli* – and wonderful headgear covered with every imaginable fruit, flower and feather, a fall of handsome ribbons hanging from the back, a muslin cap beneath and a mask with an inappropriate artificial rose between the lips. This style of head-dress and the bells increase in size as one goes eastwards until one reaches the famous Schöner Perchten at Imst, with their attendant witches and other ritual characters.

Each man used to go out by and for himself indulging in much bad behaviour, not content to spray people with water but throwing them into the street fountains, and pelting each other and their retaliating townsmen so violently that wire masks were worn to protect the face. A series of petitions to the Municipality can be read in the archives, a typical one of 1617 begging them to stop 'the unruly custom of masquerading Bützen'. Eighteenth-century references continue complaints of 'the shameless Carnival and Fools' work'.

So at long last our Bützen reformed themselves about 1922, created the usual Society to organise, and selected the eight young girls to grace the head of the procession – where they look ridiculously out of the picture, Fools' work being men's work. However, the Bützen keep up their peculiar cry – not a yodel – still jump three times before squirting water from their syringes over women and girls, and still, at top speed, pursue them to subject them to the fertilising spring magic.

Our long night drive back to Zurich took us round the southern shore of Lake Constance, far-off lights from the German side making us wonder if the Fools and the Whipping Hansele of Baden were doing their Fools' work properly, or whether the Nazi shadow lay too black on their spirits. Our chauffeur pointed out the misty shape of a boat without lights, just visible on the leaden water. Were there fishermen out there doing a little poaching or were there Jews, non-Nazis and other quiet folk making for the Swiss shore? Sometimes the Nazi boats pursued right into Swiss waters, and if the authorities were not quick enough, would haul back these fleeing people to concentration camp or to death.

SUN MAGIC IN WINTER

I kindle the sun.

A winter solstice charm

Carnival in the Protestant Cantons called us out again on what is really the first Sunday in Lent. We were joined that morning by the folklorist, Professor Brockmann, full of friendliness and cheer though snow had fallen heavily and our chauffeur-photographer declared himself anxious. Our objective was the early spring fire festival best seen along the Rhine, not really a Carnival manifestation but a sympathetic sun magic from pre-Carnival, prehistoric times. The fires flare from the Juras to the Rhine and away into Austria and Jugoslavia.

The roads were terrible. We began to meet Protestant guisers, and arrived at our chosen village Azmoos, just off the main road, at dusk. We were led to a path more or less trodden in the snow and in we plunged. The snow was soft and falling all the time but the fire was beginning to crackle, and we could see a dozen more showing red on the tops of other eminences both on the Swiss side of the young Rhine and across it in the Duchy of Liechtenstein. Men and boys buzzed like bees about our fire, digging roughly-made torches into it and when they were alight waving them round and round their heads. Sparks flew out in beautiful circles while other fires, near and far, answered with tiny spots of circling light. When our fire blazed boys approached it with long sticks which they plunged into the red-hot mass. Watching them I noted small roundels of wood with a hole in the middle impaled on the sticks. These they carefully nursed as, one after the other, they carried them to a tee of wood placed on the steepest edge of the hillside. When the roundel burst into flame the owner hit it off for all the world like a golf ball, and down it went, a tiny meteor spinning and turning into the valley below. While preparing for their swipes little boys would recite an artless verse dedicating their discs to their mothers; when young men pushed them out and got into their own stride it was not to their mothers the discs went down. Their verses were mumbled and the names remained secret in their hearts. The usual verse, written down and translated for me, for their Swiss-German was altogether too much for me, ran,

> *Schibuu, Schibaa, Schibii!*
> *Wäm söll dia Schiba si?*
> *Dia Schiba söll am Uoli si!*
> *Er wört si wohl der rächta lu*
> *Unn sim Bäbi z'mitzt uffa Puggel schluh!*

which, though you may hardly believe it, means

> *Disc, disc, disc!*
> *Who shall it go to?*
> *The disc belongs to Uoli.*
> *Let it go straight to her*
> *And hit Bäbi in the middle of her back!*

Elegant courting indeed, but what about the young lady who has disdained Uoli?

> *Disc, disc, disc!*
> *Who shall it go to?*
> *If it goes to the right person*
> *It and the poisonous Lisi will bang together!*

A new moon was setting, stars were blazing as they never blaze in an English sky, the fires were settling into glowing masses and a bitter wind sprang up. We plunged downwards while the flaming discs still flew out, taking, one may suppose, some grains of romance with them in their flight.

We had to get back to Zurich in time for a late train to Basel, for Carnival was not yet over nor my work done. Our chauffeur became more anxious and we thought of the high, narrow road above the Wallensee which, running along a northern-looking slope, never unfroze throughout the winter. Presently he came to a decision. He would put the chains on and would try it with the Professor but would his two women passengers mind taking the train at a junction near by? The passengers complied of course, the more so as they might lose the last train from Zurich to Basel. We said *auf wiedersehen* to the two men and left them at Sargans, a small junction where the Vienna express might be signalled. Signal it we did, climbed the giant stride from the icy line and immediately were in another world. The contrast between the luxurious Paris–Vienna express, over-heated, velvet-seated, redolent of the first-rate dinner being served, and snowy Azmoos, its age-old fire rites and its Schibi boys, was overwhelming.

CARNIVAL IN TOWN

> *Roll drums,*
> *Shrill fifes,*
> *Head the way*
> *To the banks of the Rhine.*
>
>   *Swiss song*

Arriving at Basel late that night, we lay on our beds fully dressed for at 4 a.m. we must be up and out again. The Basler *Morgenstreich* (literally Morning Stroke) is a queer, comic and vulgar ebullition, an urban folk custom which embraces two arts and has a history of its own.

The first art is the fifing and drumming of the bands of a number of companies composed of sober and respectable citizens, who pay moreover a solid entrance fee into their chosen *Clique*. Every year in costume and mask they illustrate some subject, mostly local politics, often coarse enough, greeted by roars of appreciation from the crowds. Their head-dresses are transparent, painted on both sides and lit up within. Just before 4 a.m., out from their H.Q. inns they poured, to light up and to strike up. As the great bells all round tolled the hour every light in the town went out. The streets were already packed and we had hard work to squeeze along beside our selected company, the truly elegant name of which was Schnuderbeeri. Drumming and fifing have always been a speciality of Basel; every boy is taught, and drumming schools exist to teach him. The tradition has come down from the call to arms of the mediaeval *Landknechten*, but like many another custom has now got caught up in the Carnival cycle. As in the far-away Valencian *Fallas* (see p. 83)[3] the Basel transparencies are painted by professionals of this little local art and they, with the satirical scenes brought out in the afternoon, are judged and awarded prizes.

It is impossible even to pretend to describe the drumming. One must hear the traditional tunes shrilling out above the demoniac syncopation befitting the demoniac masks. Boys' bands reach the same heights as those of their fathers and they march as smartly. One men's company, as they lit up, was suddenly bestowed with Hitler's head, a hundred Hitler's heads with drooping lock and lackadaisical eye, exaggerated in size and pitilessly lit from within, all on the march together. Near-by Germans make a habit of pouring into Basel to watch the *Morgenstreich* and there they stood, ranged glumly on the pavement edge, not daring to laugh for who might not be behind them? And obliged to listen to the broadest Basel wit sharpening itself on their Führer. The other seasoned jest, the *nacht-topf*, rivalled Herr Hitler in its hundred appearances – all lit up from within. How odd to our more sophisticated taste seems the never-failing humour of this domestic object.

Every company must cross the Rhine, so much bigger than the young river we had left at Azmoos, and when one meets another on a bridge the drumming swells in tremendous crescendo and complexity, for each band is under an obligation to make the other lose step. To do so would be a disgrace not wiped out till the next year. Their Drum Majors, swollen and stuffed in Gargantuan disguises, keep their men in strictest order. The companies call at inns, which are kept open all night, but there is no perceptible drunkenness for perfect drumming is their pride and their glory. At 5 a.m. the town lights come on again and at earliest crack of chilly dawn the *Morgenstreich* ceases.

BIBLIOGRAPHY

1 PROFESSOR BROCKMANN, *Schweizer Volksleben*, 2 vols. (Zurich, 1929–33). Published also in French by Paul Budry, Neuchâtel, in 1930 under the title *La Terre Helvétique*.
2 PROFESSOR FRITZ BRÜGGEMANN, *Vom Schembartlaufen* (Leipzig, 1936).
3 VIOLET ALFORD, 'Two Urban Folk Festivals', in *Folklore*, XLVIII, p. 366.

8

Processions

Erreberenzia	*Homage*
Gorputz egunean elizan	To the *Fête-Dieu,* having
Sarturik Jaunaren aurean,	entered the church
Ezpata birekin jaudatuaz	Before God, we know how to
gure Jauna	Praise the Lord with our
Badakigu dantzatzen dana.	swords.

Sword dancers' Corpus Christi hymn

French Basques celebrate Corpus Christi on the Sunday following the festival and its Octave. In French it is the *Fête-Dieu*; Basques call it *Phesta Berria*, the New Feast, presumably because it came into the Church's calendar in 1264.

In a small tract of Basse Navarre lying between the Nive and the Joyeuse, *Phesta Berria* has a flavour all its own. The first procession I saw there was at St Esteban, a village between Hasparren and St Palais. I see them still, the National Guard as they call themselves, coming up the sunken lane edged with sweet-smelling honeysuckle, the band leading, the Voltigeurs* in the rear. The rank and file was composed of some twenty young men in white trousers and their Sunday jackets, white berets on their heads stuck all over with gold leaves standing straight upright, all armed with any sort of shot-gun or rifle, even to flintlock muskets. In front came four large Sappers, *Sapurak,* wearing some sort of uniform – the postman kindly lends his and even the gendarmes – with enormous busbies of black sheepskin topped with red feathers, decorated in front with small

* An old name for a light infantryman, but these are so called because they are light on their feet.

mirrors. They wore the old-fashioned Sappers' apron but decorated it with golden leaves, and they carried heavy axes on their right shoulders. The white-gloved left hand rested elegantly on the left hip. There was an imitation Beadle with beribboned halberd and cocked hat; there was a Drum Major who danced backwards before the band, hired from Bayonne, who bore patiently with his antic conducting. There were flagbearers with incessantly and beautifully twirling flags and there were the Voltigeurs, two boys who danced without ceasing to the church, into the church and out again to the porch, where their steps became grotesque and they turned into comic characters.

We made a long day of it, driving from one village to another, sighting a regiment as it escorted its Curé to church, joining another as it danced its way through Mass, dashing off to catch a third in the morning procession to the *reposoires*, picnicking on a lovely slope amongst young bracken, wild roses and honeysuckle before setting off on our afternoon tour. We repeated the excursion the following Sunday, the Octave of the feast, and thus were enabled to compare the proceedings in several villages. Since that introduction I have been into those hidden lanes again and again to find variations in this entirely Basque jubilation.

There will be many cars bringing onlookers to St Martin d'Arbéroue, fewer at Hélette and none at all at most of the other villages. When you pass out of the region and enquire at what hour they dance into church, the scandalised answer will be '*Danser? Non, nous faisons les petits pas.*'

Armendaritz basked under the patronage of a rich Americano family at that time. This means a family which had emigrated to South America, made a fortune and come home again. The first thing a returned Americano does is to build a new pelote wall for his village and there you will see him viewing it in his excellent suit, his tan shoes and his gold watch chain. The son-in-law of the Armendaritz family was elected Captain of the *Garde Nationale* and spent both time and money on his regiment, so everything was rather sumptuous. He enrolled young and old, which is unusual, and dressed the whole eighty of them very well indeed. Round and round the village square they marched with fixed bayonets, the tall Sappers beneath their immense busbies cutting capers of joy. As they at length approached the church door the order rang out '*Entrez. Pas ordinaire*,' at which I suffered a moment's disappointment. But the *pas ordinaire* was a dance step, right up the aisle till they filled the nave and the porch.

I have seen Sappers dance up the altar steps to station themselves immovable on either side their priest; I have seen them, instead of dropping on their knees, dancing frenetically at the moment of the Elevation while the regiment thuds its muskets on the stones. I have seen a Drum Major twirl his baton round and round his head and neck, send it hurtling up to the roof to catch it again, while a witness whose word must be accepted (Monsieur Nogaret, late Librarian of the Musée Basque) once saw a Sapper leap, feet together, on to the altar, to stand there rigid, flags waving, bugles blaring. In an out-of-the-way village the young Sappers could not afford the regulation apron so their mothers lent them their best ones, all frilled and starched. The procession there trod on long, white linen runners, specially woven in narrow lengths by long-ago housewives, to be kept in the carved oaken chests seen in every house and brought out only for *Phesta Berria*. The linen lay on sweet-smelling hay and crunching osmunda leaves strewn along the lane. I have seen a Beadle carrying a halberd covered with ruched ribbon surmounted by a red metal cock, and I have seen an enormous busby hung with mirrors in front while behind the wearer had arranged little sacred pictures in sequin frames. He had three frames and two pictures, so the third was filled with a bright advertisement of Sunlight soap. Standing outside the church door and looking up the

nave it is hard to believe one's eyes. Altar lights reflect themselves in mirrors, on axes and glittering headpieces, flags
wave with a beautiful monotony, long ribbons flutter. On
either side these bedizened figures the village women kneel,
two sober black masses, each head covered with its flat
manteleta; up in the galleries – every Basque church has two
or three tiers of galleries – are rows of men in black; behind
each head its béret hangs on a nail.

After the parochial festal procession, led always by the
Guard and the dancing Sappers, after the return to the church
and the end of the Office, the regiment awaits Monsieur le
Curé to escort him home. He is placed in his honourable
position, the ranks close round him and off they go at a
quick march. If he is elderly or stout it will be as much as he
can do to keep up with the column; if he is young he will
almost dance too. Outside his house there will be a *Saut
Basque* in his honour, and he and his housekeeper will hand
round glasses of red wine in return for the politenesses done
him. On the second Sunday, after Vespers, the regiment lets
off any effervescence still seething within by brisk marches
round and round the square, by *Sauts Basques*, by drinking
and *irrintzinas*. The sun has beaten on them all day, they have
shown off to their hearts' content, the red wine of Irouléguy
is heady. If a Sapper sways, if a Drum Major falls by the way,
you must forgive them for another year.

The actual processional dance step is worth attention. We
have seen the troops of dancing men who appear in this same
district at Carnival and for *Tobera Mustrak*, the Show. They
are *Volantak*, the Flyers, and *Kaskarotak*, headed by Sappers
or Pioneers. Their principal dance then is a processional also.
The step is made up of two smooth polka steps forwards,
four very small step-hops backwards, the free leg decorating
the hop with a cut as in Scottish Highland dancing (other-
wise a beat). When this sequence is repeated the last step-hop
changes into a complete turn, a *tour en l'air*. The effect is

alternately a smooth advance and a hopping retreat. The peculiar step of the National Guard struck me at once but after a few moments I recognised it for what it is, no more than the Flyers' step bereft of all hops, the heels turning out to fill the beat. This low, inconspicuous step is no doubt suited, in the dancers' opinion, to respectful church dancing. If asked whether it were not the Flyers' step they deny it as strongly as the village which performed the '*petit pas*' denied they were dancing at all. Considering the lively tradition of Church dancing in the Spanish Basque country and in Spain itself, this reticence seems unnecessary. It does not however appear to be the forerunner of deserting the tradition, for the Garde Nationale was out and the Sappers were leaping when I visited two villages in 1954, exactly as they had been twenty-five years previously.

The truth is that Carnival tradition has so fused with religious tradition that the young ritualists hardly know which is which. Dance has fused with march, Carnival dress with uniform. Many men wear the Flyers' fall of ribbons hanging down their backs or removed from their own backs to the back of the busby. Many have dancers' bells sewn on their Sappers' aprons. Sometimes the *Koha* is worn, that resplendent flowery head-dress seen on Pastorale Turks, the Soule Hobby horse and many a man and boy dancer all over the north of Spain.

Local surprises always await the visitor. Several years running we had by-passed Iholdy, because a stiff-necked old Curé had taken upon himself to forbid the regiment to dance or to enter the church in their brilliant array. But one day the old gentleman died and the very next year, as we chanced to drive through, there they were again, after twenty years' abstinence, all smart and clean in new uniforms, ribbons and busbies and aprons, marching their new Curé to church, he and his young men round him, all beaming with pride and zeal.

Going home towards evening we found a disbanded regiment having a last drink at a roadside inn. The Drum Major was a great fine man who had been down to Bayonne the week before, to borrow epaulettes and anything he could 'scrounge' from an army friend of mine. The plume he had acquired should have been in the front of his shako but actually stood up at the back, a huge cock's tail decorating the front. This was the man who had played such a part in the smuggling round my Bayonne home that the hamlet in which he lived had become *le quartier du Basque*. But that did not stop him taking a fervent part in his New Feast. We ended our tour that year at a large village where *Dantza Khorda*, the String dance, was beginning. This is the finale for the whole village and takes from forty to fifty men and women into its chain, the leader and last man carrying bouquets of roses with sprigs of box as their insignia of office. The string wound round and round the *pelote* ground, muskets went off 'by mistake', *irrintzinas* echoed back from the *pelote* wall, dusk fell and the band went home.

Many of the characters who appear so oddly in the Corpus Christi processions today are survivals of ambulatory scenes arranged by priests and later by guilds, to teach illiterate folk. These became an important feature in the then new Corpus Christi processions. We saw some of them at Berga in Catalonia – the Archangel Michael killing off devils, the Turks fighting with the Hobby horses, and the rest (see p. 64). We frequently come across the devil himself, bringing a touch of crude comedy to the admiring crowds and, as at the Fête-Dieu at Aix-en-Provence, all sorts of mythological persons, Mars and Venus, Bacchus covered with leaves sitting on a cask, Momus covered with bells on horseback. These are understandable as depicting classical paganism versus Christianity, but when we see a dragon as at Monção in Portugal, shouting obscene repartee to the crowd,[1] or the pages of the Three Kings (again at Aix) saluting the star with rapid

waggles of their *derrières*,* what are we to think of these?
There are no such survivals in the French Basque New Feast.
The flashing mirrors are, of course, a widely known prophy-
lactic magic to reflect and cast off evil; the twirling of the
Drum Major's baton may have taken the place of proces-
sional whiffling for the same purpose; but dancing has been
Christian usage since early days, though the leap on to the
altar may be more than an officiating priest bargains for.
Everything is done with the utmost decorum, even devotion.
I remember the young Sappers in their mothers' aprons were
pallid with fervency and I remember too a youthful guard,
when called to order, turning as pale as they.

Everything points to the regiments being the present-day
representatives of the confraternities which came into being
in the late Middle Ages, to suppress the brigandage then rife
in the south-west of France. These confraternities in their
turn became the rural militia, to which we find references in
the sixteenth and seventeenth centuries.[2] In the eighteenth
century Basse Navarre furnished 1,400 men, 900 of whom
were contributed from the precise tract of country in which
the regiments now march and dance.

This supposition is confirmed when comparison is made
with the regiments of *Marcheurs* in the country called Entre
Sambre et Meuse, in Belgium. In old uniforms of precisely
the same date, these marchers make it their duty and delight
to accompany the statue of their Patron Saint in procession.
Their descent from military companies of the seventeenth
century is established – a few were known as early as 1545
when 'refreshments and powder for salvoes' were dealt out
to them. They too wear Sappers' aprons – sometimes with

* This action to denote derision is fairly common in folk practice; I
know of a case at Nancy not long ago, when it was performed at a
window to mock a hostile crowd below, but to reverse it for salutation
is strange. It was thus used, however, to greet the sun by girls in the
French Alps.

VII Early spring fire festival at Azmoos: sympathetic sun magic from prehistoric times

lace frills – false beards to give the right touch, and cockades twice the height of their busbies, and carry axes on their shoulders. They too have Voltigeurs and the Drum Major swaggers at the head of the column.[3] Until the separation of the Church from the French State it had been the custom for the military to take part in the *Fête-Dieu* processions, which custom continues in Spain today. I suppose further that the processions, coming out again after Napoleon's Concordat with the Vatican, marked their jubilation by the dancing which is so natural to a Basque, or again took up an ancient dance tradition, and that the formation of the *Garde Nationale* under the restored Monarchy gave the participants their name and their fashions in uniform. Belgian marchers have changed their uniforms from time to time, trying to catch up with army changes, until they stopped short with the showy Zouaves, Mameluks and aproned Pioneers, whom we see today both there and in the French Basque country.

HOLY WEEK IN SPAIN

Jueves Santo, Jueves Santo,	*Holy Thursday, Holy Thursday,*
tres dias antes de Pascua;	*Three days before Easter;*
Las tinieblas de la noche	*In the dark of the night*
a Cristo le vi pasar	*I saw Christ pass by*
en una Cruz de madera.	*On a Cross of wood.*

Romance from León

A party of people from the Musée Basque at Bayonne drove over the passes to Spain very early one morning in Holy Week. The trees, already in leaf down below, were silvered with rime on the slopes and bending under snow as we neared the top of the Col de Velate, the Veiled Pass. Vciled it was in grey cloud, from which flakes floated down relentlessly. A celebrity from Paris who was with us found his heart fail him as the road snowed up. After some attempts to

VIII Armendaritz: round and round the village square the tall Sappers, beneath their immense busbies, marched with fixed bayonets

G

induce the party to turn back he applied himself to me, supposing, no doubt, a female ear would receive his apprehensions more kindly than the foolhardy gentlemen of the Musée Basque. But he, poor man, was disappointed and on we went into the deepening snow. When some years afterwards I learned that this celebrity had taken a part in preventing the transfer of the French Government to North Africa in 1940, and had joined himself to the static Marshal at Vichy, I remembered his endeavours to make others turn back because he was timid of spirit.

We were going to Pamplona to witness the last of the processions, that of Good Friday. Pamplona is in Navarre and the Navarrese are Basque. Religious devotion should therefore have been intense, but I do not remember that it was. When we emerged from the snow and entered the city the procession was just getting under way. The organisation was good, for Basques can do this well when they pay attention, the various groups well dressed and orderly. There were Jewish villagers led by Scribes and Pharisees, Roman soldiers in shining helmets and many Biblical groups on foot, but there were no *pasos* in the southern style, for the great seventeenth-century school of sculpture in wood barely touched the northern arts. The finale was typically Basque. After the statues had been re-deposited safely in the Cathedral the returning processionists, now in disorder, broke into a gay *Jota* and the military bands, which an hour before had marched at a funeral pace to a lugubrious drum-beat, as gaily played for the dancers. Lent was over. On the last page of the Holy Week order of procedure one read, 'Bulls on Sunday'.

My second Holy Week in Spain was at Alicante, where the atmosphere was very different from that of effervescent Pamplona. Every region expresses itself differently in its processions according to race, climate and history. The results are always popular-religious, embracing local tradition, often theatrical, often displaying the sceptical paganism of the Mediterranean and pre-Christian practices which were still lively in the Middle Ages and which have reached the present day in more or less attenuated form. Castile, dour as its landscape, bleak as its climate, has not forgotten the Inquisition born within it, and so maintains a sombre devotion in the pure Spanish tradition and an inclination to clericalism, especially under the immense shadow of its metropolitan Cathedral of Burgos. Aragon is not noted for its Holy Week yet Hijar, a smallish town south of the Ebro, on the last three days musters hundreds of muffled drums which never leave off day or night, until the town becomes hysterical and children and invalids have to be sent away. The drummers say this is to frighten off the Devil.

It is to Andalusia that tourists flock to see processions, and to Seville in particular. Blasco Ibañez's vivid and malicious descriptions of Holy Week in Seville in his *Blood and Sand* must have brought untold thousands into the city at that season. His confraternities, meeting in the narrow Sierpes, set down their *pasos* to fight for the honour of their own Virgin; his porters were drunken and indecent; his crowds roared with laughter at them and disported themselves as at a fair. When la Macarena, Virgin Patroness of the populous quarter of that name, is taken home at dawn, her porters cause her to 'dance', the hidden troop bending their knees alternately on either side of the platform they carry. She sways alarmingly and the crowd lays wagers as to whether she will get through the church door scatheless or no. The whole chapter is of a past Seville, brutal and incredible.

Lorca also has its peculiarities which indeed appertain more to Carnival than to Holy Week. Pagan figures are carried, Roman Emperors, Mark Antony and Cleopatra; a cavalcade of Ethiopians, who are Spanish gypsies noted for their horsemanship and trick riding, comes by, and Satan and his black-winged devils. We see, however, the later triumph of Christianity. Dr Starkie says it is 'a gigantic and collective drama in which the whole town takes part, and it shows the transformation whereby ritual becomes art'.[4]

But I am on the Levante coast, the Fabled Shore. My quarters are an eighteenth-century private *palacio* turned into a hotel. My windows overlook the quayside so that when the miraculous Christ of the Sea was carried out 'to visit His boats and His people' all I had to do was to step out on my balcony. From the fishermen's quarter came a dark throng. The confraternity responsible for the ordering of their procession and for their statue wore the high, pointed cap – *caperuza*, in French *cagoule* – with mask made in one, the eye-holes giving a sinister rather than a mysterious effect, and a crumpled black sateen gown, for they are poor men.

They have beautifully decorated the great platform, on which is erected their Christ on His Cross, with boughs and flowers, amongst which shine electric lamps, for these are cheaper than great wax candles. Carrying-poles in parallel rows of four, protruding back and front from the platform, weigh down the shoulders of the serried ranks of bearers, more than half of whom are actually under the platform, hidden by its falling draperies. Platform and statue together make the *paso*. This black mass of people, lit from above so that only heads and shoulders appear, their owners seeming to wade in dark water, moves along the quayside where the whole fishing fleet is arranged, bowsprits stabbing inwards, vague masts pointing skywards.

Those crews not processing wait on their newly washed decks. A few flowers hang here and there. The four large globes of their decoy lights are lit up – the ancient Mediterranean usage was and is to attract fish by lights, so that at night the sea is studded with yellow pinpoints. The men drop on their knees as, to the solemn beat of a drum, their Christ sways painfully by. It is a moving sight.

La Macarena, borne aloft in Holy Week processions

The other processions in Alicante were less grateful than that of the fisherfolk. The chief event began on Holy Thursday and continued far into the night. The town owns many brotherhoods, all wealthier and bigger than that of the Christ of the Sea, and on that day they all sally forth, each bearing its own statues from its own parish church. They own some lovely sculpture, often by the famous sculptor of the Levante, Salzillo – whole tableaux as well as single figures, so that the *pasos* are of terrific weight. The porters are sometimes navvies or dock labourers, paid for a heavy job, sometimes brothers who beg a place beneath the stifling draperies through penitence or devotion.

A guiding brother in charge of each *paso* can only communicate with the inside porters by hammering out his signals. A silver knocker is fixed to the front of the platform and when sufficient distance has been covered – often not more than one hundred paces – its sharp raps penetrate the bands and the drumming and the bugles, the enormous edifice sinks slowly to the ground, the draperies part, and out creep the sweating, panting bearers. As the night wears on the halts become more and more frequent, but strength is somehow maintained for the entry into their parish churches towards 3 a.m. Each *paso* with its attendant confraternity occupies a long stretch of road, and each is accompanied by its own band – generally borrowed from the multitudinous barracks of present-day Spain. Military escorts are provided too, white-gloved, goose-stepping. Gorgeous banners flap and sway; parish crosses are carried and enormous lanterns on poles, gleaming silver by day, lit within at night. As one *paso* disappears drums and bugles and band begin again at the other end of the street, and another enters.

The seventeenth-century school of sculpture in wood is a miracle of delicacy. The hands alone are worth a journey to see. Facial expressions are tortured, according to Spanish taste, but however lovely are the sculptured draperies, Spanish taste again steps in to hide all the beauty of gracious wood beneath velvet or satin robes, priceless brocade and embroidery, jewels, watches, rings, bracelets, loading the exquisite figures underneath. This is bad enough but in small places, where taste is still cruder, hair will be added and eyelashes, terrible glass eyes and more terrible glass tear-drops. Spanish religious taste cannot be trusted today, so far has it moved into excesses from the glories of the primitive Valencian school of painting and the Masters of sculpture.

That night I went in the dark towards the principal church of Alicante, hoping to see its statues carried out in a late procession. But when I reached an archway leading into the church square every inch of ground was filled by waiting brethren. It was an aristocratic confraternity if not a wealthy one. Their robes were the vermilion of mediaeval missals in colour, their *cagoules* velvety black, their white gloves immaculate; their great candles, just being lit, were held away at a slope so that no wax dropped on the freshly pressed robes, and this uniformity of pose gave a striking effect of stylised design. The Prior (a layman) and his two Sub-Priors were mounted on slender Arab steeds, red and black trappings hanging to the ground. There must have been three hundred of them waiting there but not a sound was heard. I shall not forget that picture from the Middle Ages, illumination and darkness, vermilion and black, flickering candlelight catching now and again a virile Iberian-Roman face.

It was that night that I heard my first *saeta*. In a momentary drumless quiet it wavered out, far away, unmistakeable, and the jabbering crowd ceased its jabber to listen. It was a surprise to me, for Spanish friends had been unanimous in telling me *saetas* were to be heard only in Andalusia. A *saeta* is an arrow, an arrow of song shot into the air as a favourite statue is borne past. In the old days the *paso* immediately stopped so that the singer, professional, gypsy, beggarman, thief, could send forth his greeting. Today time is considered (slightly), each *paso* being supposed to have finished its route at a fixed hour, so often it no longer comes to rest but goes swaying past the singer. *Saetas* are sung to traditional melodies, but the words are supposed to be improvised. Those of Andalusia are in the *cante jondo* style and do indeed appear to come from the deeps of the singer's heart. Those of Alicante are not *cante jondo* of course. They were sung to a simple traditional air of that near-Catalonian type which has made its way down the coast, and this air was one of the things I had stolen from me in Barcelona station. So I cannot give it here.

The next night, that of Good Friday, I heard my fill. Outside the church people were gathering; amongst them a good-looking youth, seductive in his scarlet robe, carrying his *cagoule* across his arm, was walking anxiously to and fro. I was thinking, 'He is looking for his *novia*', when he stepped up to me and said:

'Would you be kind enough to tie my cravat? My mother has not come.'

His lace-edged cravat was lying loose round his neck. A quick look at near-by brothers showed me what sort of bow was required and this I tied. Whereupon the young man clapped on his *cagoule* as though his head were a candle to be extinguished and strode off with a muffled '*Gracias*'.

The sun set, and as though it were their lights-out signal the screaming swifts ceased their flights round the church tower and disappeared. The procession set forth. It cast wide round the church, and when it came into sight again on a lower level a *saeta* shot up from a man a few paces from me. He sang as though alone in the street and his arrow went to Our Lady of Sorrows, a lovely figure in mourning robes, standing alone on her platform. Immediately the man's voice ceased an answering arrow sped from a balcony opposite. So far as I could see through the darkness one figure stood there – a girl's. She sang in that curious woman's tenor, the result of Spanish voice production; her single verse was simple and her air the same as that of the man who had just sung. It was quickly over; Our Lady of Sorrows was lifted and borne onwards; lights coming on in the room behind the balcony displayed a homely scene of a proud father hugging his little daughter. For she now showed herself as not more than twelve years old in spite of the tenor voice.

Two years ago I spent a Holy Week in Málaga, famous for its processions. There seem to be more, and more gorgeous, sodalities there than anywhere else, and they own most beautiful statues dressed in the most priceless robes and mantles I have ever seen; Our Lady of Hope, and the celebrated Christ of the brethren called *de los Mutilados*, a Christ who can set prisoners free from jail. These brotherhoods are amongst the richest and the oldest in Spain, some dating from the sixteenth century when they began to take the place of the mediaeval military guilds, in the same way as the

Basque *Garde Nationale* must have taken the place of rural militia. The oldest must be that of the Servites, Servants of the Blessed Mary, founded in 1233 and owning the most famous statue in Málaga.

Holy Week was ushered in for us by *saetas* sung by the village rag-and-bone man in the patio of the country house in which I was staying. They were most effective sung in · those lovely surroundings – white walls, panelled wooden shutters to a score of windows, an eighteenth-century well shaded by a palm tree thickly twined with jessamine, pots of ferns and flowers standing round the old stonework, and the great double doors to the street as background. One *saeta* was simple and countrified, the other in *cante jondo* style, florid and ornate.

Strong sunlight threw up the vivid colours of an afternoon procession in Málaga next day. Several sodalities were marching, each carrying its own regalia, silver maces, swords, ensigns in worked gold or silver. Parochial congregations marched too, mostly in black; a few women actually in the procession wore high combs, black mantillas and black coats, all very smart and high-heeled; these were explained as sisters who do the needlework and tend the wardrobes of the statues. A few deeply penitent penitents trod the cobbled street with bare feet; one woman, supported by two others, tried to do the same on her knees, whereat the crowds groaned in sympathy.

Now and again a slender, hooded brother stepped up to a girl onlooker to whisper gallantries into her ear. There is nothing surprising in that. This is a spring rite, popular as well as religious, and since the present régime has prohibited Carnival disguisings, doings proper to that season show signs of reappearing six weeks later. At Lorca, as we have seen, it would be difficult to say which is which. After all, the religion of today stands on the religion of yesterday, and the Mediterranean laps the same shore where the Dying

G*

God is borne through a night in early spring, then as now. Andrew Lang, one of our early folklorists, once wrote that the rites of Adonis could still be seen in Holy Week in Spain, and when one has seen it for oneself he seems to have been right. The step from age-old pagan ritual to Christian observance was taken almost unperceived by the common folk, as the famous letter from Gregory the Great shows us. How profound in her knowledge of mankind was the Church in those uncertain days when, rivalled by Mithra and his Bull, powerless to turn the people from their seasonal rites, she gently – for it was no clean sweep – substituted the New for the Old.

Gregory's often quoted letter to the missionaries in England, struggling with stiff-necked Anglo-Saxons, advised them thus:

> Do not after all pull down the fanes. Destroy the idols, purify the buildings with holy water, set relics there and let them become temples of the true God. So the people will have no need to change their places of concourse, and where of old they were wont to sacrifice cattle to demons, thither let them come on the day of the saint to whom the church is dedicated, and slay the beasts no longer as a sacrifice but for a social meal in honour of Him whom they now worship. [5]

It was mild missionary work and who can blame the ignorant peasants if they saw no difference at all in going on doing what they had always done?

In honour of Adonis as spring divinity his 'gardens' were made, a likeness to himself in vegetable form. They were baskets or pots in which quick-growing plants were sown, wheat, lettuces and flowers, tended for eight days by women, carried in procession with the images of the dead Adonis and then thrown into water, the sea or a spring. This small rite was performed all round the old Mediterranean and is still

performed. I myself have seen, with some emotion, gardens
of Adonis in Provence and in Portugal. The first were at
Aix-en-Provence, a row of flower pots filled with yellowing,
spindly wheat, standing on a window ledge. They had been
forgotten and were dying there instead of being thrown into
a near-by well. The others were in the river quarter of
Oporto on Midsummer Eve, side by side with the St John's
fountains, and these were for sale in all their green beauty.
The plants were basil – still a powerfully magical plant –
wheat and small flowers in bloom. The gardens are still made
in Sardinia too, in Sicily and on the Italian mainland, just as
they were made in Babylon and in ancient Greece. In fact
around the Mediterranean, with its superimposed civilisations, each religion with its seasonal rites adding to and
taking from their forerunners, roots have sunk so deep into
Mother Earth that they will never be pulled up.

An Anglican Bishop, home from visiting the Christian
Church in India, tells me that the statue of the Virgin is now
carried through a village on a feast day. When I asked how
long had been the interval since the statue of Buddha had
thus been carried he said, 'No interval at all. He was being
carried along the next street at the same time.'

We may suppose it was just so along the streets of Spanish
towns, through the rows of potted gardens awaiting the bier;
the Old and the New, overlapping, intermingling, until one
day, the change having never been wholly made except in
name, the New itself became Old.

Leave the Mediterranean for an instant to view a Good
Friday procession in the little Portuguese town of Cascaes.
Transformation has not gone very far yet. It was one of those
macabre skeleton figures of the dead Christ, draped in white
grave clothes, that was carried through the streets, recumbent on a black-hung bier. Beneath the bier, bent nearly
double, crept two or three ladies of the town, one, to my
astonishment, wearing a brightly coloured coat and skirt.

This is their yearly penance – self-imposed – which wipes the slate clean and puts them right for another year's similar livelihood. One's thoughts inevitably turn to the temple prostitutes in the service of the Earth Mother. What was the rôle of these women during the death rites of the young Attis?

The afternoon solemnities in Málaga over, we got back to our village in time for our own procession with its two statues and a few *saetas* at the church door. It was returning late because it had started out late, and it had started out late because the sacristan – an important figure in a village community – had neglected to warn the bearers. Not having done his duty, he decided the procession should not process. This was too much for the villagers who, taking things into their own hands, alerted the bearers, roused up Señor Cura and got their procession under way.

We were eight miles from Málaga, so that a view of the Good Friday night procession appeared to be difficult to accomplish. I made up my mind to trust to luck as in my Pyrenean days, to take the last bus in and to leave my return on the knees of the gods. Dreary visions of the railway waiting-room till dawn crossed my mind. At the last moment, however, adventure receded. An English villa-owner picked me up in her car, gave me a place on her hired balcony and brought me back at three in the morning.

Crowds filled the pavements, the street stretching between them freshly swept and empty. A *saeta* arose with no procession in sight. This came from a professional engaged by someone to sing from their balcony. Very different was her *cante jondo* style, decorated, passionate, from the touching verse of the little Alicantina. But here also was the peculiar woman's tenor, the strident forcing of the upper notes. Her arrows were shot into the darkness at intervals all the night through.

Then a beat of drums came to our ears and the first procession was in sight. Its confraternity wore white satin *cagoules* and purple velvet robes; their *pasos* glittered with banks of flowers, silver, and scores of baroque candelabra holding scores of golden lights. Other brethren wore scarlet and black, a wonderful blue, purple and blue, striking black and white, every combination of deep or vivid colours in rich materials. Many sodalities own three sets of robes and mantles, one for Good Friday, one for the previous days and a third, all pressed and clean, for Easter Sunday. The *pasos*, which here are called 'thrones', show tableaux of sumptuously dressed, beautifully carved figures, depicting the course of the first Holy Week events.

Long pauses occurred, the street quiet and empty, fringed with chattering multitudes. They behaved much better than one had been led to suppose; now and again *saetas* shot up from the pavements, chiefly from men, but the professional on the balcony seemed to over-awe them, much to my regret. The Virgen de la Esperanza wore an embroidered cloak so long that her platform was provided with a kind of apron stage behind, on which her train spread out; the Cristo de los Mutilados stayed awhile beneath our balcony while the porters emerged panting from beneath the platform. I counted one hundred and forty of them. During one long stop escorting soldiers entertained the crowd with a goose-step quadrille from side to side of the street, changing places diagonally. They gained much applause.

On and on came the processionists, the guiding brethren covering the route at least three times over as they went and returned, some with penitential bare feet showing oddly beneath velvet robes, all with running pages to scout ahead so that no block should occur. On and on they came, appearing far off at one end of the street, disappearing at the other. At midnight every city light was extinguished, leaving the route to guttering candles and illuminated thrones. The effect was mysterious but theatrical – a 'pageant of art and emotion' as a Spaniard has described it. He makes no mention of religious feeling but the indecorum of Ibañez's Holy Week in Seville had no reflections in the Málaga of 1954.

When, almost the last personage, the Archbishop of Málaga came into view, the crowd seemed touched by a wave of sympathetic respect. He is an El Greco ecclesiastic, elongated, thin, bent by the weight of six yards of magenta-red train sweeping the street behind him. His hands were raised, his fingers touched, his tired eyes seemed closed. His surrounding chaplains anxiously surveyed him. This night-long Via Dolorosa was perhaps the penance of an Archbishop.

A more than usually long pause. The empty street waits. Far away a slowly moving light appears hanging above a dark hillock. Slowly on her mound, alone, mourning in her black robes, a disc of silver lights behind her head, comes Our Lady of the Servites, the solitary Mother bereft of her Son. The crowd stirs. Now at the last moments the arrows of song shoot up again. This is what they have been waiting for. This is what touches them to their hard, Spanish hearts. A sigh runs along the street like a breath of wind, a sigh which has come down to them through past ages, when other figures, with other names, were carried out before their anxious eyes at the spring Renouveau.

A SLOVENIAN STREET PROCESSION

The chorus were at first, as an ancient writer tells us, just men and boys, tillers of the earth, who danced when they rested from sowing and ploughing.

Jane Harrison, *Ancient Art and Ritual*

One day I was walking in the streets of a small town in Jugoslavia. A few women were shopping, a few children playing, a few men lounging on the walls which enclosed a little

Leaning out of the windows to snatch at the leaves

park. Strange clamours began to rise from the bottom of
the sloping street. The people round me woke up and looked
about them. The sounds grew in volume, differentiated
themselves into the clanging of bells, the blowing of horns,
women's voices singing in loud, harsh tones, the beating of
drums and a noise like sharp pistol shots.

A gay crowd of young men and girls in loose procession
overtook us, accompanied by boys blowing home-made
horns with all their might. The tootling of these horns of
bark alternated with the singing of the girls. A small birch
tree came into view, carried by a close-packed group of men.
The birch, I soon learned, symbolised *Jurija Breze*, the Old
King of spring, and all this noise was to protect him as – so
said the song the girls were singing – the tree was set up in
front of their city gates. Later I saw the girls leaning out of
windows to snatch at the leaves as the tree was borne past
below, breaking off small branches and throwing leaves and
twigs into the street. Tree-bearers and escorting crowd then

ran away with loud laughter as fast as their legs would carry them. So the Old King is torn to pieces, done away with, dead. But 'Long live the King', for the new King of spring has taken his place; the girls break into a Kolo while the ritualists rush off with him 'into the dark forests and open plains' which are his home. So says the song. In the homely way of all such rites the ritualists must get their recompense – food, small coins and drinks of the inevitable plum brandy. This little drama is, in its simplicity, an epitome of the seasonal rites we are following across the Continent.

Up the street comes a Kolo belonging to a Weavers' guild. It winds towards us led by the guild master, who sets the pace and the figures. His leadership demands a handkerchief to wave his directions and the Kolo itself demands others representing the weavers' shuttles, to be passed incessantly under the dancers' knees. This is followed by another Kolo, the guild dance of the Shoemakers in which they mime cutting, stitching and hammering.

Here in the middle of the street procession we must pause to consider the Kolo. It is of course the Chain dance, the chain open or closed. This is the ritual and recreational dance of Middle Europe which continues into Rumania as the Hora, into Bulgaria as the Horo and into Greece, where it is supposed to have originated, as the Choros. The Choros undeniably comes from the classical Chorus circling the threshing floor at the country Dionysiac festivals of proto-historic times, which was to become the classical Chorus of the Greek theatre. Even today it is danced on the village *Chorostasi*, was once the Syrtos and has now become Kala-matianos, led by a swirling dancer with a handkerchief in his hand. But a Chain dance, open or closed, is the simplest and one of the earliest dance forms, so it is found everywhere, by no means necessarily stemming from a Greek prototype.

We see it on the well-known Iberian vase from Liria, painted about 400 B.C. This is, I believe, the earliest record of the Chain dance in the west. A thousand years afterwards, in the late Middle Ages, records multiply. There is the deploring of the habit of borrowing fine clothes 'yn Carol to go' in 1303 in England; there is the tale of the dancers of Kolbigt who carolled during mass on Christmas Eve, and for a punishment went on carolling for a year without pause. This was said to have happened in the twelfth century. There is a fresco on the wall of Orslev church on the island of Zealand showing a Chain dance, the head and tail men carrying flat bouquets or rosettes as insignia of office. This was painted about A.D. 1400, and would be the most northern record save for the living examples in the Faroe Islands. There people still meet to dance a sung Chain for company and for cheer, on long winter nights when work ceases with daylight about 3 p.m. The Lowlands, both Holland and Belgium, have their Chains, the Cramignon, the Swiss have theirs under the but slightly changed name of Coraule; we have noticed the Basque forms, the String dance, the Cord dance, the Dance of the Threshing Floor – harking back to the early Greek name – and the ceremonial Auresku. Provence of course glories in it under its best-known name, the Farandole, brought, they firmly believe, to their land by the colonising Greeks, who had it from Theseus himself when he led a serpentining Chain of rejoicing after his escape from the serpentining labyrinth of the Minotaur. But the Provençaux do not need to cling to their classical legend for the Ligurians, like the Iberians, were in all probability already winding hand in hand before ever a Greek foot trod the Massilian shore. No Etruscan pictorial record of a Chain has so far come to light – they preferred Pair dances – but Italy knows many closed ring dances and Sardinia possesses the ancient Mediterranean type in her famous Ballo Tondo. Then, where Italy touches the Jugoslavian state of Slovenia, we find it in full vigour, taking on the characteristics of its east European type.

We know that Slavs to the north danced it in ancient times; the sixteenth century gives a passing record in Czechoslovakia, where its name becomes Kolo, or the Wheel. With such a wide geographical dissemination and such a history it is no surprise to find the Kolo a vehicle for celebrations of all sorts, social, ritual, seasonal, social-religious, for weddings, for baptisms, for fairs. Men from widely scattered Rumanian villages will trudge to a fair in order to spend their time, not buying or selling, not feasting or drinking, but in dancing the Hora, hour after hour, hands grasping each other's shoulders or belts, eight thousand of them in vast circles all over the fairground and in the near fields. The Gypsy musicians play and play, faster and faster, egging their patrons on with jokes and improvisations, looking them in the face, closer and closer until dancers and players alike fall into a trance. A Hora at a Bulgarian church feast went on for three days and three nights without ceasing, so says a folk song, dancers dropping out and being replaced, Gypsy fiddlers or pipers falling to the ground and others taking up the tune and the beat. [6]

The Sloveno Kolos I stood in the street to stare at are used for all the purposes mentioned above; after those depicting work, the weaving and the shoemaking, came the Bridge, *Kolo Most*, in which the leader and his partner following him raise their arms to make a bridge under which the whole chain passes. This too came serpentining up the street, a *Vojarinka* or woman leader firmly ruling her linked followers, signalling changes of figure by a handkerchief in her hand.

The Kolo next assumes a ritual aspect and meaning. It breaks up, for ten couples to stand in an east-to-west line, each group asking the other in song for permission to cross the bridge, offering as payment a 'dark-eyed maiden'. Here a little girl dashes forth, to run through the imaginary bridge gates which guard an imaginary castle. All the dancers surge up to its equally imaginary walls and the dance ends.

I was afterwards told that this dramatic song-game is the remnant of a rite commemorating a sacrifice on behalf of a dead lord of the castle when, immediately after death, he had to cross the spirit bridge to gain the other world. This is the Slav interpretation but, although we too know the spirit bridge in folk song, if we take into account our own London Bridge game with its tradition of sacrificing a prisoner to the river ('This poor pris'ner we have got, We have got, We have got'), so that the bridge, irreverently thrown across it, may be allowed to stand, one would be inclined to give *Kolo Most* and the little running girl the same explanation.*

The noise of bells was now upon us, clanging and crashing as though we were in a belfry instead of in a street. Figures odd, sinister, terrifying, rushed up to surge round us. Children shrieked, girls ran, men laughed though compelled to wrestle hard with the attacking demons. There were *Kopjasi*, who are heralds of spring; there was *Rusa*, the Horse, whose head and neck were covered with feathers and porcupine quills, whose tail was as sharp and prickly to grasp as that of our Lincolnshire Horse, the tail of which is studded with nails. This is to punish people who try to pull out a horse hair for luck. I did not see anyone trying to do this to *Rusa*, but I fancy the porcupine quills are a good preventive. He is accompanied by a collector who receives rewards, for the Horse too has his duties in the winter-versus-spring drama and must therefore be recompensed.

Several other sorts of maskers, each in a different disguise, alternately alarmed or amused the onlookers until the *Koranti* filled the street-stage, when the children and feminine part of the audience fled without pretence. These were still more terrific figures, covered with sheepskins, with animal masks, snouted or roaring, over their human faces; from their heads large horns sprang wide, or small, wickedly

* Examples from Germany and Brittany of a child walled into a bridge are given in *Folk Lore*, Vol. LXIII, p. 232.

sharp ones sprouted. Slung round them great cowbells clashed and clamoured; bags decorated with flowers and small drums were in their paws. Their progression was made by animal-like bounds changing to sharp rushes hither and thither.

With their arrival any processional form melted away. I tried to hide behind masculine backs as I had done from the Pyrenean Bear-men, and being unacquainted with the Slovene temperament I wished I were back amongst the Swiss winter devils, or the leaping goat-skin *Zorromocos* of Cantabria. The likeness to both these maskers is remarkable; they are in fact the same characters, doing the same job, wearing the same disguises half a continent apart. Their nearest brothers are Austrian Carnival-runners, and the Alpine influence has flowed down the south-eastern slopes into Slovenia, which marches with the Austrian province of Carinthia.

Slovenia shows this influence in its mountain districts in many ways – in Pair dances, for instance, which are rare further east, in costume, which has an Alpine touch, and in whip-cracking. The Kolo of the Slavs only begins in Bela Krajina, White Krajina, the district furthest from the Alps and nearest Croatia. With the Kolo begins also another style of costume. That of the women is entirely white, full white cotton skirts, white blouses and white head-kerchiefs tied in a remarkable knot, so that each girl appears to bear a white dove on her head with upstanding wings. I am told that the district takes its name from this spotless costume.

The Comus rout left us, their noise trailing behind them, and up the momentarily quiet street came a bit of old England. The drama of the Plough passed by. The quiet was pierced by ear-splitting cracks as a Whiffler, cracking his long whip round his head, and frighteningly round other people's heads, clears off winter and evil in his manner. Six young men are dragging a plough; on it two gaily decorated pine trees are fastened. The ploughman is one of the *Koranti*

guisers, hairy and horned, and as they approach they all sing
a wassailing song:

> Plough men have come at dawn
> And ploughed up the rosemary.

Outside the houses they visit they plough furrows as
imaginary as were the gates of the song-castle; this is to
bring fertility and good luck to the farmer and his family, in
which they are kinder than our Lincolnshire Plough Stots,
who plough real furrows before the door of anyone whose
recompense does not come up to their expectations. All
these personages with their bells, their whips, their shaggy
disguises and their plough would have been at home in
northern winter-spring drama, in English mud with the
towers of Lincoln Cathedral behind them, or in Alpine snow
with a background of dazzling peaks and a middle distance
of brown chalets.

Incongruously I stood in a street shaded with palms, the
buildings bad Italianate, the background an Adriatic Sea of
blinding blue. It was that once Austrian–Italian town, the
resort of wealthy Viennese, Abbazia then, Opatija now. The
International Folk Music Congress was in session there at
the invitation of the Jugoslav government, and they it was
who brought peasant singers, dancers, musicians, improvising bards and folk actors from every state of their immense land, to lay before the Congress their treasures of
folk culture from the Alps to Macedonia, from the Albanian
borders to those of Hungary.

BIBLIOGRAPHY

1 RODNEY GALLOP, *Portugal* (London, 1936).
2 PHILIPPE VEYRIN, *Les Basques* (Bayonne, 1942).
3 DR ALBERT MARINUS, *Folklore Belge* (Brussels, 1953).
4 DR WALTER STARKIE, *In Sara's Tents* (London, Murray, 1953).
5 BEDE, *Hist. Eccl.*, I, 30 (Haddon-Stubbs), cited in Chambers, *The Medieval Stage*, I, 96.
6 RAINA KATSAROVA, *Dances of Bulgaria* (London, Max Parrish, 1951).

9

Provincia Romana

By the blue rushing of the arrowy Rhône.

Byron

L'Oratoire des Saintes. C'est là qu'on les priait et qu'on déposait des couronnes.

A. Mazel, *Notes sur la Camargue*

I must say more particularly of Provence what could have been said of every region I have written about. What appears here is but a selection from the vast treasury of custom and tradition, layer upon layer throughout the ages. What is selected seems to me more typical of the country than, for instance, the Blessing of the Mules on the day of St Eloi, or the beautiful Church offerings of a fruit stuck with silver coins, or the *Chivau Frus*, the Hobby horses known all over Europe. Yet although these of Provence have more of the elegant tourney aspect than our own low-life examples, they are of great interest for comparative study in that they reveal their original powers plainly enough. Their *coupletoun* or couplet, sung to the air called Farandole by Bizet in *L'Arlésienne*, shows them being fed with chestnuts by a mythical Madamo de Limagno, 'to make them skittish'. The horse is a male, the chestnut a female symbol.

I would like to wander into studies of La Volta[1] and the Rigaudon,[2] both historical dances, but must be content to indicate where such studies can be found; and I would like to write of ancient ways of life still being lived in old-fashioned town mansion and country farm, ways which are legacies from the Roman family.

When 'popular antiquities' first attracted students their origins, in Britain at least, were invariably sought in classical mythology. The eighteenth-century gentlemen who began the study had had the usual classical education; their ideas on the Roman occupation of Britain were the ideas of their day, exaggerating the effect of Latin culture on a scattered Celtic population. This outlook lasted right into the nineteenth century, when the brothers Grimm and Mannhardt on the Continent, and Sir James Frazer in our islands, exposed their views on indigenous seasonal cults, found their origins at home rather than in ancient Greece and Rome, and opened the way to comparative studies. Provence, however, is an exceptional country; its geographical position and immensely long history forbid the exclusion of Olympus, so when one is glibly told this comes from the festival of Flora and that from Bacchic worship, one must not smile.

Provence was the first Provincia Romana, Aix its first colony, begun in 123 B.C., and it remained under a Roman rule as close as any part of Italy until that rule was no more. Also – and this is as important – before the Romans it had imbibed a foundation of Greek culture spreading from those Phocean Greek traders mentioned many times already as planting their emporium on the Iberian coast. Celtic tomb-names inscribed in Greek characters are found inland, and a tablet of about 300 B.C. indicating the house of a teacher of Latin for Greek-speaking people was found near St Victor, Marseilles. Not until the sixth century A.D. did Latin finally overpower the Greek tongue and a Gallo-Roman language become the speech of the ordinary people.

This deep classical culture must therefore be taken into account, and folk memory reaches back to classical events, albeit in garbled form. For instance, the great defeat of the first known Teutons with the Cimbri, at the foot of Mont St Victoire over 2,000 years ago, is well known to the people of today. The Campi Putridi of the slaughter is Pourrières;

Marius' triumph erected on the stream called Arc has naturally become the Arc de Triomphe; while I myself learnt from country men ploughing there that they constantly bring to light human bones, assign them to the right battle and never fail to recall their hero-general Caius Marius. The victory, at some unknown date, personified itself as a Sainte Victoire and since this outlyer of the Alps is of an impressive shape likely to have been the seat of an Earth Mother, memories earlier even than Teutons and Cimbri clung to it. These gave occasion to a spring feast and fire. This was on April 24th, the traditional date of the battle, and was kept up by the people of Pertuis until the Revolution, with Farandoles round the fire and shouts of *Victoire! Victoire!* They then took home the 'Summer and the May O' with boughs and greenery.

Another village, Vauvenargues, after a dawn Mass, reverted to pre-Christian practice. All went together to look into the chasm called Garragai, down which their hero had hurled a hundred prisoners from the battle on the advice of his Syrian prophetess, Martha, a wise woman who accompanied the general everywhere, for his superstitious mind depended on her auguries. This chasm was evidently an ancient oracle-place and is still said to be full of spirits who answer questions. This is the sort of prehistoric-classical foundation of much Provençal folklore, of great interest to unravel; to this must be added the flood of late mediaeval output from the Courts of Love, troubadours and the never-forgotten court of King René, much of which came by various channels to the common people.

One of my travels has already been followed to the coastal part of this land, the Camargue. The object then was the wild bull; now it will be the landing of the Saints and the lore, Christian and pre-Christian, which has grown about their legend, and the ramifications following the directions taken by their fellow-passengers. A great deal has been

The boat of Les Saintes Maries – Mary Salome and Mary Jacoby

written about the Three Marys, romantic, credulous, both in French and English. The most sober writer, in spite of some wishful thinking, is in my opinion a one-time Curé of Les Saintes-Maries-de-la-Mer,[3] the little town which shelters round its fortified church into which the parishioners could run at the sight of Saracen pirate ships. In spite of all this literature I must begin at the beginning, or like the audience at the Basque Pastorale, 'later on you will understand nothing'.

The Three Marys were Mary Jacoby, the mother of St James the Less and St Jude, Mary Salome, the 'mother of Zebedee's children', and Mary Magdalene. With them came Martha, her sister, the 'hostess of Christ', their brother Lazarus, Joseph of Arimathea, the person who became St Maximin, and Sara, the handmaid to the Marys. Also Amadour, who had been *valet de chambre* to Our Lady. All these people were put into a boat (or some followed in another boat) without oars or sail, and were pushed out to sea by unbelieving Jews enraged at their missionary persistence. The boat eventually came ashore 'near the city of Marseilles in the place where the Rhône runs into the sea'.

Legend says the two Marys remained where the town now

stands, and here the Curé touches interesting ground. In the crypt a pagan altar has been found, an early Christian altar (third century), an ancient hearth and human bones. These were piously gathered into a reliquary by King René himself, and an upper chapel was made above the sanctuary arch to receive them, while Sara, the Egyptian, was left in the crypt beside the pagan and the Christian altars. There it is the gypsies keep vigil (with laughter and talk and other indecorous celebrations) during the night before the feast of Mary Jacoby, May 24th.* I say 'the Egyptian' because they do. They are persuaded, or pretend to be, that they came from Egypt, hence their name, so their saint must be an Egyptian too.

Everyone knows about their gathering at Les Saintes-Maries to do honour to Sara, their bearing the relics into the sea, a guard of honour of mounted *gardians* escorting them, and after a long, blank period they are coming again. When a BBC recording of the proceedings was made in 1948 (and broadcast in July the same year), one solitary gypsy family arrived – Spanish gypsies; their decimation as anti-social people by pitiless Germans seemed likely to put an end for ever to their fête at Les Saintes. But with the recuperative powers of their race, life goes on for those who are left. The vivid account of his visit to Sara's city by Dr Starkie⁴ tells of seven thousand gypsies camped round the church a year or two ago. It is his admirable description which must be read for I have done no more than see the first caravan arrive across the Camargue under a blazing May sun, as my way led northwards.

The ramifications of the legend spread out fan-wise, the longest spoke reaching England where came Joseph of Arimathea to found Glastonbury Abbey, and to plant his sacred thorn which grew into a hawthorn blossoming at

* That of Mary Salome is on October 22nd. This the gypsies do not attend.

Christmas. (I have often seen an off-shoot from the Glaston-bury tree in full flower in December.) The shortest spoke reached Marseilles, where Lazarus took the gospel and became the first Bishop. The first church seems to have been built above a shrine of a Mother Goddess, whose place has been taken by Notre Dame de la Confession. This black, antique Virgin sits in the crypt which was once a cave, and accepts green candles only. Her sacred cake is in the shape of the boat which brought the Three Marys, *la navette*, sold at the Cathedral doors; but the present form seems to have reverted to something nearer the crudity of the female sym-bol from which the boat shape arises. Candles and *navettes* are blessed in the crypt in which Lazarus was buried.

While Sara, their handmaid, remained with her mistresses, the *valet de chambre*, Amadour, found his way to another seat of the Earth Mother in the west, the towering precipice of Roc-Amadour. This was a pilgrim place from time immemo-rial. But the ancient occupant was displaced and another of those equivocal Black Virgins fills her rocky seat. The valet becomes a saint and the pilgrimages go on.

Martha, sister to Lazarus and Mary Magdalene, set off northwards. She got no further than Tarascon before her saintly powers were called into play. The town suffered cruelly from a monster whose lair was in the woods on the bank of the Rhône. Not content with an occasional country-man, it took to coming into the town and gobbling up citizens, letting their legs hang out of its mouth like the tails of mice out of an owl's beak. St Martha went boldly to the wood, where she discovered the monster making a good meal. She tied a loop of ribbon round its scaly neck and led it, meek as a lamb, into the town, where the men of Tarascon killed it. That is the Tarasque, the local dæmon of Tarascon, dreaded, laughed at, dearly prized, like the Pyrenean bears, the *Poulain* of Pezenas, the Cheval Bayard of Belgium and other ritual animals.

Its portraits are well known, the first a roughly sculptured stone dating from before 1267; a fourteenth-century capital in the cloisters of St Trophime, Arles, now destroyed; an account of its re-making in 1675, and thus up to its last public appearance in 1946. Tradition brings it out at Whitsuntide when it shows its popular side and rushes into the crowd, knocking people over with its tail, like the Catalan Aliga and the famous dragon of the Mons Doudou, even to breaking arms and legs. When this happens the crowd appreciatively shouts, '*A ben fa!*' (Well done!).[5] This wild behaviour was accompanied by various *Jeux* organised by trade confraternities, some of which point directly to a spring fertility festival, for instance the sprinkling – one may say the soaking – of the crowd, the rain-making magic so often the accompaniment of a Renouveau rite, and the throwing of spinach seed between the girls' breasts, analogous to their blackening by the men-bears. This day demands licence and full participation by the townspeople; the brutality of the attacks and approving shouts are part of the ritual and have their counterpart in our Padstow Old Hoss ceremony and, closer at hand, in that of L'Ane de Gignac. I wish I could give a detailed account of this creature which, with its alarming workable jaws, charges into the crowd to bite people (and bit me), followed by the extraordinary and very dull ceremony called Sinibelet. But this takes place outside our Provincia Romana and has had a little study of its own.[6]

This cherishing of the dæmon is a common psychological mass-condition: children held up to touch the Tarasque; children taken to pat the Padstow Old Hoss, girls arranging his whiskers; a woman tweaking a spike from the Tarasque and hiding it in her bag; another pulling a hair from the tail of the Lincolnshire White Horse as from a fighting bull in Spain. I could extend such examples endlessly.

On St Martha's Day, July 29th, all is changed. Here is a chastened brute led by a young St Martha; Christian legend and Church organisation have taken the place of popular turbulence. If a score of layers of custom could be removed we should probably catch a glimpse of a local animal divinity, feared, placated and revered.

The fifth spoke branching from Les Saintes Maries is the most surprising of all. Mary Magdalene, who helped to bring the boat ashore by using her veil as a sail, overcome with a sense of guilt, wandered away into the Provençal wilderness. (It was in reality a rich province served by Roman roads as well as the river-way.) She lived some time with St Maximin in the place now called after him, taking with her a tear from the eye of the Saviour. Then in ever deeper penitence she again wandered off and, finding herself in the forest behind Marseilles, took refuge in a cave and there lived for many years. This is the Sainte Baume, *baume* being a cave in the langue d'Oc. The folk song 'Mario Madaleno' says:

Sept ans souto la baumo	*Seven years in the cave*
Te pondr' ana estar.	*Thou canst go and stay.*
Au bout de sept anneios	*At the end of seven years*
Jesus-Christ l'y a passat.	*Jesus Christ passed by.*

Tradition makes her remain in the cave for twice seven years, or sometimes thirty, until her penitence had been completed, living on wild roots and often without water. But a spring of fresh water came up in the Baume to quench her thirst and there she died forgiven, sending a message to *suere Martho* at Tarascon. That is the Christian legend.

But the Sainte Baume had been a sanctuary of Isis and Adonis[7] (all gods came to Provence, from many-breasted Artemis to Mithras with his Bull), so that every sort of rite was practised and every sort of survival of these rites can be expected. Remember here that 'obscenity is good fertility magic', and that both Isis and Adonis made this magic their first concern. Into the nineteenth century local marriage contracts stipulated that husbands must take their brides to the Baume, to prevent possible sterility. Girls still go by hundreds, climbing the rocky path to demand a husband of St Mary Magdalene in the cave, and to toil up to the mountain top where is one of those stone *pilons* (this one is the Saint Pilon) thought by the country people to be shrines, but thought by archaeologists to be in reality phallic pillars. There they will collect small stones to make a *castellet*. This is done by placing three flat stones to form a triangle and setting a pointed one upright in the centre. This is also called a *mouloun de joio*, a joy-mill, and if the connotations of mills and grinding is kept in mind, the opinion of a Provençal anthropologist that *castellets* are male and female principles united seems correct. Many of the girls one sees up there come on *Patronage* or Friendly Society excursions and build their joy-mills under the sympathetic, though (one supposes) ignorant, eyes of their accompanying nuns.

The best moment for these exercises was on Midsummer morn, when the mountain top was covered with people to watch the sun rise and to gather St John's herbs, thyme, rosemary and mountain sage. Today the chief pilgrimage is on the Saint's Day, July 22nd.

The latest development of the legend is this. Having toiled up with a friend through that surprising forest, dripping with moisture, running with water-channels, dark with enormous forest trees though only some twelve miles from the droughts and the mountain fires of the Riviera, we sank down in the cave and looked about. The first thing that caught my eye was a white marble statue, in the worst nineteenth-century taste, of a young woman with masses of marble hair spread about her.

'That', said my friend with a quiet laugh, 'is the statue which has replaced the one destroyed by our Reds of the Midi in the Revolution.'

'Does its badness amuse you?' I asked.

'That', said my friend, 'is the statue of the mistress of a local millionaire. When he died there was an interregnum before his heir took possession, and during that time the village people hauled that statue up here, saying that because of the hair it must be Saint Mary Magdalene.'

THE CHRISTMAS FOLK THEATRE

Et vou tené me contenenço	*And you, when you are*
En presenço	*In the presence*
D'aqueou tant bel enfant,	*Of that lovely Child,*
Vous escupé pas su li man	*Don't spit in your hands*
Como lei gavo de Prouvenço.	*Like the country folk of Provence.*

Provençal Noël

The religious folk theatre of this country can best be examined in three stages, beginning with the popular pottery or china figures called *santons*, little saints. These range from Tom Thumb santons of thimble size to beautifully coloured figures six inches in height or more. Santon makers, *santonniers*, are so by inheritance, the local art passing from father to son. The best place to see their work is on the stalls of the Christmas fair at Marseilles, in the upper Cannebière outside the church of St Charles. Here they appear in their thousands, all prices, all sizes, awaiting buyers who, also in thousands, crush round the stalls to select the little personages they require for their household crèche. They can also be seen in the Folk Museum at Marseilles, grouped in eighteenth-century household crèches, while Mistral's museum at Arles-sur-Rhône possesses a selection placed there by the poet's own hand.

To add characters to the Biblical ones adoring at the crib must be a very old practice, beginning no doubt with such an obvious person as the Innkeeper. I once made a list of twenty-six and that was not exhaustive. One must banish all notions of an orthodox, oriental Bethlehem, for the scene

Santons: familiar figures have ousted those from the Holy Land

has been transferred to Provence, and familiar figures have
ousted those of the Holy Land. The crib is in a cave or open-
sided stable in a Provençal landscape. Behind rises a green
hill crowned by a windmill, which seems natural enough
to those who enjoy Daudet's *Lettres de mon Moulin.* Paths
lead down to the stable, and on these paths the humble folk
of the country hurry to adore the *Pichoun,* the Little One.
Outside his mill the miller looks at the animated scene, an
old woman on her donkey rides down clasping a loaf as big
as a wheel, a young mother, carrying her baby in a wooden
cradle on her head, swings down the hill with the inimitable
carriage of the peasant accustomed to head-loads. Lower
still are other people, a granny, on her head the sticks she
has gathered to warm the Child, a woman with a gift of
eggs. The village *tambourinaire,* without whom no gathering
is complete, arrives to play a tune to amuse the new-born
Babe.

> *Prends là-bas un escot,*   *Take a stick there,*
> *Et touchez tambourin pour*   *And begin to drum for dancing*
> *danser*

says a noël of 1555. The tambourinaire is sometimes sup-

IX The Tarasque, the local daemon of Tarascon, dreaded, laughed at, dearly prized

ported by a player of the *vielle*; there is a seller of the famous nougat, a knife-grinder on his rounds, an old lady with a lantern venturing out to see where all these folk are going. Most of these little people appear in eighteenth-century crèches, and judging from the noëls were known much earlier. The same 1555 noël names two idiots and a crippled man. The ostler with raised lantern to view the travellers is always there. Biblical characters begin, of course, with the shepherds who kneel near the crib, their china sheep about them. The Three Kings with their camels are there at the stable, as always in popular tradition, instead of at 'the house where the young Child was'. In old crèches the angels are often perched on the roof under which the Virgin kneels by the crib, a conventional young Virgin in blue. St Joseph stands as conventionally behind with the ox and the ass. He is always an old man with a beard –

> *Now Joseph was an old man*
> *An old man was he.* . . .

'*Ce père putative*' he is called, the jocular materialism of the Midi over-stepping decorum.

It is enlightening to note that Joseph was neither canonised nor allotted a festival until the great days of the Mystery plays were waning, and his name was inserted in the Roman Breviary at the end of the fifteenth century only. The jibing tone has now dropped out of existing Nativity plays, as we shall see, St Joseph appearing in his character of protector of the Mother and Child.

The whole scene of the crèche is intricate and variegated; a modern mind needs time to attune itself to the simplicity and to find beauty and piety in these miniature works of art. For popular-religious artistic works they are. The same naïf artistry is to be seen in the *presepio* of Portugal, which was already traditional in the sixteenth century. In a great old palace in Braga I was shown family *presepios* dating from the

X '*Pastrage*' at Les Baux: *devout parishioners become the actors* seventeenth century, now safely under glass. One contained upwards of three hundred tiny figures arranged in a miniature landscape, not without a beauty of its own. In Catalonia, so closely allied to Provence in culture, it is a Belèn (Bethlehem), and nearly approaches the Provençal type. Some good examples are on exhibition in one of the Catalan houses in the Pueblo Español and are worth a visit.

The second stage of the religious folk theatre is found in the *crèches mouvantes et parlantes*, the santons grown bigger and come to a regulated life – in fact a marionette theatre devoted to a Nativity play. I first saw these movable santons in the little museum of the once royal Aix-en-Provence. They were dusty and neglected, lying in disconsolate abandon on a shelf. They were dressed in silks and velvets, and small wheels and pulleys to assist their movements were lying with them. The characters were identical with the present-day santons, but they looked more theatrical in their rich clothes than their little clay cousins. I learnt that devout ladies and gentlemen of Aix used to manipulate them and speak their lines. In most places however they belonged to professional showmen who made money out of the play during the Christmas season. An *Adoration des Bergers* was shown at Montpellier in 1851, for instance, and Toulon, Toulouse and Marseilles each had its *crèche mouvante*. They were not peculiar to Provence. As far away as Besançon, in 1899, a notice of a Nativity puppet play on the church door announced '*tout ce qui peut amuser et édifier les fidèles*'. The famous Belgian marionette theatres naturally had their Nativity plays, with Magrite, a comic Innkeeper, sweeping out the Holy Family with a broom. Toulon introduced three gypsies amongst the Provençal characters, dark-faced and raggle-taggle, who told fortunes unabashed in the presence of the Holy Family. But even these good-for-nothings – so the Midi judges them – have a pedigree, the noël which mentions them having been inspired by Lope de Vega. One gypsy still appears in a Spanish carol, bringing a gift like a respectable person:

Yo soy un gitano	*I am a gypsy*
que vengo de Egipto aquí,	*Who comes here from Egypt,*
y al Niño de Dios le traigo	*And brings to the Son of God*
un gallo – quiquiriquí!	*A cock – cockadoodle doo!*

The third stage, leaving immovable santons and movable puppets, brings us to the moving, singing, human actors. We arrive at the Pastorals or *Pastrages* of Provence.

The history of santons may perhaps begin in the twelfth century, when an Abbé Guerricus refers to 'the Child, covered with swaddling clothes, lying in a manger before the altar'.[8] But we hear of a *presepio* at Santa Maria Maggiore in Rome long before that, wherein the consecrated Host was laid during Christmas Mass. If the Child were already in the crib in the twelfth century, adorers would surely be present also; in any case the next century saw the *presepio* constructed in the church of Greccio by St Francis of Assisi in 1224, with a live ox and ass, to which came brethren from many convents as well as townspeople carrying lights, to hear a sermon from the Saint. The mother of St Francis was a lady of Provence, and her son is traditionally said to have spread the cult of the crib into her country.

The local santons seem to have developed into marionettes during the eighteenth century, when puppet plays in churches in other parts of France came much into favour; the *Pastrages* themselves may trace an ancestry far longer, finding their beginnings in the Nativity scenes of the Mysteries. Or they may be developments from the dramatic noëls so popular all over France. Mysteries and noëls certainly worked on each other. The noëls depict, in song, scenes exactly similar to those in the Mysteries; the very names of the shepherds are the same, the artless presents they bring, the farce they introduce. When the Mysteries declined in popular favour they were withdrawn from the streets into the churches, and changed their Guild organisation for an ecclesiastic one. Devout parishioners became the actors and that is the state in which we find them in Provence. This is curious when compared with the Basque Pastorales which have remained in the street and never come under clerical supervision, yet the Basques are renowned for their churchmanship.

The *Pastrage* most overrun by visitors, most written up by the Press and therefore most to be avoided is that of Les Baux. It is both moving and interesting if the crowds allow one to see it. Through the streets of that incredible town where houses grow out of the rock and rock springs up inside the houses, the population hurries to midnight Mass. Shepherds and shepherdesses of the windswept, sun-stricken Alpilles offer a lamb, which is drawn by a ram to the altar in a little cart caged over with sticks bent to form a dome above the little creature. It is far too domesticated to dream of running away and enjoys being passed from hand to hand, from the head shepherd to the youngest shepherdess. A long noël is sung by an angel and a shepherd. It is not a folk air, though of a respectable age, having been composed before the Revolution by a doctor of Les Baux; pipes and drums play throughout and at the Elevation the Lamb is made to bleat.

At Fourques, the entry into church is to a gay Rigaudon tune played by their *tambourinaire*. The head shepherd carries the lamb which has on its head a little wheel stuck with five candles; the second shepherd – there is a hierarchy amongst shepherds – leads a ram decorated with candles and artificial flowers, accompanied by children dressed up as little St Johns. In southern Europe one must get used to seeing a little St John the Baptist with shepherdesses and sheep – a confusion apparently with the Agnus Dei.

The lights on the animals' heads reminded me of a Christmas Mass in Catalonia where rams are selected, their wool washed and painted in colours, ribbons woven about their

heads and lighted candles fixed to their horns. These sires of
the flock are made to kneel before the crib. In Béarn, too, I
know of a strange shepherds' rite, taking place on St
Michael's Day instead of at Christmas. A sheep dressed up
with the usual ribbons, a huge bell beneath its chin, was led
to Mass; at the Elevation instead of the *enfant de Choeur* it
was made to ring the Sanctus bell, after which performance
it was presented to the Curé. One hardly knows what to
make of these animal rites. Do they but spring from the
crèche? In sheep districts I am inclined to see something
more primitive in them.

The *Pastrage* of Séguret, a hill village near Vaison-la-
Romaine, was an annual event and may be still. I have not
had the good fortune to see this play but have a word-of-
mouth description as well as a written one[9] from a well-
known folklorist and broadcaster who could not be better
named – Marcel Provence.

Christmas Eve is clear. The keen air smells like snow; the
whole village, actors and audience together, is making its
way through the narrow streets to the twelfth-century
church up above. Open doors and lighted windows give
glimpses of shepherdesses arranging their fichus, of angels
having their hair crimped by their mothers while the church
bells clamour through the night. At the altar rails a crèche is
installed, set out in the traditional manner with santons. An
altar bell is rung, an Ave sung and the choir of angels bursts
out from one knows not where. Then silence. From a side
chapel a moving light is seen; St Joseph comes forth leading a
weary Virgin. Dim lights all about the building denote the
closed windows of *mas* and cottage; in front of each stands the
householder wondering who these may be who travel so
late through the wintry night. From the door of his *mas* a
farmer sends off the tired couple rudely and so at every door.
They arrive in the dimly lit nave and approach the pulpit
which is draped with curtains. The pulpit is an important

piece of scenery. It represents the inn and out from it looks
the Innkeeper. He wears his nightshirt of hand-woven linen
over his Sunday suit, and his nightcap is on his head.

According to his traditional rôle he is as crusty as an innkeeper can be. The conversation between him and St
Joseph is carried on in song, and the words they use are the
many verses of Nicholas Saboly's famous noël, *Hoù! de
l'Oustau.* Here is a version written down for me at Marseilles:

Hoù! de l'oustau! Mestre,	*Ho! You of the inn! Master,*
Mestresso,	*Mistress,*
Varlet, chambriero, ci li a res?	*Varlet, maid, is there no one?*
Ai deja pica proun de fes.	*I have knocked many times*
E res noun vèn! Quinto rudesso.	*And nobody comes! This is hard to bear.*

INNKEEPER: *I have got up three times;*
Alas, I shall hardly sleep.
Who knocks down there? Who is it?
What do you want? What do you want me to do now?

ST JOSEPH: *Nazareth is our home;*
I am not what you think.
I am Joseph the carpenter,
My wife is named Mary.

INNKEEPER: *I have too many here; no more!*
God help you. Believe me you had better ask
For lodging in the moon.

ST JOSEPH: *Do not treat us thus.*
See what weather it is!
Open to us. If nothing is done
You will find us dead at the door.

INNKEEPER: *Your wife makes me compassionate*
And a little kinder;
I will give you for charity
A wretched little stable.

So at Séguret they seek the shelter under a roof of foliage which represents the stable and becomes the birthplace of the Infant. After this, says Marcel Provence, all becomes marvellous, derived he thinks directly from the Middle Ages. Anyone who has witnessed a village drama, Christian or pre-Christian, whatever it may be, knows well that this is a sober statement. One is transported back hundreds of years and one's modern breath is taken away. When the angels' voices, shrill and soulless as boys' voices are, suddenly ring out, everyone looks upwards, every heart beats quicker; all *is* marvellous. If one could see through the midnight dimness, angels would be descried perched above the heavy door, up above the altar, in the organ loft. And from every corner of the floor a shepherd's voice replies. This heavenly-human dialogue goes on for hours, on and on and on. One knows that already from the recitative-dialogue of the Basque Pastorales. Angels, of course, sing in Latin, shepherds in Provençal. This is traditional convention. Only heavenly characters may use the language of the Church. In a Mystery of the Wise and Foolish Virgins there were three degrees of language; Christ spoke the most sacred, Latin, the Wise Virgins French, the Foolish Virgins had to content themselves with their native langue d'Oc.

The shepherds now take up their instruments to play to the '*beau Dauphin*'. Shepherds have always taken music to the crib. In carols, over and over again we hear of bagpipes, oboes, flutes and drums, '*mon flageolet*', of Colin with his '*viole et son archet*', of *sonnettes* (handbells, I take it). English shepherds did likewise: 'Lo, I bring Thee a bell. Lo, I bring Thee a flaggett.' In the Coventry play one offers the pipe on which he has been playing to the Child. Tradition makes the shepherds clownish, a legacy from the Mysteries where, like the Vices, they gave comic relief.

With their instruments and music, visitors to the crèche take other presents. Like the santons they take the best they

can find, for they are poor. The shepherds have not much
to offer for they themselves live hard, up on the hills. In the
Townely play they brought a 'bob of cherries', a bird, a ball.
Those from York brought nuts threaded on a ribbon or,
more ambitious, a brooch with a bell attached to it. Those
with more imagination, and these are generally the shepherdesses, bring a tart, a cake, or with a woman's fore-thought:

Portons-lui des langes,	*Let us take Him nappies*
Aussi des drapeaux,	*Sheets also,*
Et pour sa couchette	*And for His bed*
Un petit berceau.	*A little cradle.*

The shepherds are shy, aware of their uncouthness, so
they think over beforehand how best to introduce themselves
to this new-born King. 'What will you say, Julau, when you
see the Child?' 'I shall say "*Bonjour Monsieur*",' is the reply.
'"*Comment se porte le Bon Dieu et, là-haut, tous chez-vous?*"'
The Séguret shepherds make humorous replies, waited for
with relish by the audience who know them as well as the
actors, and away they file through the tightly-packed nave,
making their way to the crèche.

The country-women make a long reply to their angels
and as their voices die away the unexpected cry of the rag-
and-bone man is heard. The *Patiare* is an important person
in a mountain community, a travelling merchant with every
right to an angelic invitation. Then there is the Charcoal-
burner, laden with a heavy sack of his forest produce, who
listens gravely to his angel and replies in song politely.
Nowadays the Séguret shepherds are too devout to be satisfactorily comic, so the village looks elsewhere for its farce.
It is found in the Compères, old, incredulous mockers, real
esprits forts of the village. They laugh at their angel and the
enraptured audience knows all the back-chat by heart. But
the heavenly atmospheric pressure proves too strong even
for them; they relent and follow the rest.

Now a wholly local character appears. Little Janeto comes running through the midnight streets of Séguret – Bethlehem. The eager little girl tells the great news to the *dou pople de Betelen* and is joined by villagers of every description, women in the handsome dress of Arles, in the heavy mountain costume of the Gavot country, all rising up from every corner of the church; the *tambourinaire* strikes up and the whole company surges forward to the crib. By now there is very little congregation left, so many have become actors.

Among the santons the Three Kings make handsome figures. In the *crèche mouvante* they were many sizes bigger and richly dressed, but they always comprise the bearded old man, the second, younger potentate and the ebony African King of tradition. Simple folk and children are sent out to meet the Three Kings towards evening of the Epiphany, but they always arrive by some other route. At Arles their entry is through the haunted Aliscamps between the Roman tombs. Mistral tells how he too was sent out with a troop of children to meet *Li Tres Rei* and how, darkness falling, they all ran home again disappointed, only to be told the great men had arrived, and to be shown the Twelfth Night cake as proof of this. Provence, and Aix in particular, has its traditional Marche des Rois, well known to everybody through Bizet's use of it in *L'Arlésienne*. The Epiphany ceremony of its performance in the cathedral of Aix by organ, brass band and fanfare is an annual treat and it is there it should be heard. At Séguret the Kings were impersonated by three notable men of the Félibrige,* the only actors not of the village.

All are now assembled before the crib. A spokesman greets the Child, the company responding verse by verse. A final chorus salutes the Holy Family and in true mediaeval manner the actors make a vow. They solemnly undertake to

* The movement founded by Mistral for the preservation of the Provençal tongue.

H'

perform their Pastorale again in the future with an engagement to compose new verses during the interval. On the
old is grafted the new. Thus, as in the English Mummers'
play, life-giving new ingredients prevent stagnation and
presently become traditional in their turn. And with the vow
the *Nouvé* comes to its close in the dim old church with

Boun vespre, boun vespre,	*Good night, good night,*
Au revèire, boun vespre	*Au revoir, good night*

and the congregation composes itself for Midnight Mass.

DRAMATIC DANCES

So forward now my champion dancers and show me your steps.

The Odyssey

The Provincia Romana is not rich in dance-dramas. The influences which have always worked on the population have
assuredly been discouraging to the survival of true ritual
drama; too much Italian communication, too strong a cur-
rent from 'polite' sources such as the Court at Aix; too many
strangers from the earliest times to the last hundred years
of fashionable life on the Côte d'Azur. The Morisca influence
also, which undermines ancient ritual, is strong, not so much
from the Reconquest of Moorish Spain as from raids and
occupation of various places by Moors turned pirates.

There were several ceremonies called Mauresques, all now
obsolete, in which, as in our English Morris, the name
appears to have been the main Moorish ingredient. The best
remembered is perhaps that at Istres on the Etang de Berre,
where one man, with bells on his legs, danced between two
women, presenting each in turn with an orange. At Riez, a
fight between Moors and Christians took the usual form.
Although quite in the Spanish Morisca style this was called
a Bravade. This name embraces all sorts of festivities in

which the endless firing of guns is the chief feature, for the Provençaux love noise almost as much as the Spaniards. Friends of mine, in their regional costume, attended the famous Bravade at St Tropez. Their visit so delighted the companies of *bravadeurs* that they received volleys fired between their feet as a mark of appreciation. Another Bravade, at Fréjus, consists of a scene between St François de Paul and a man enacting an old woman; while at Orange it was a ceremonial march of bowmen, who later became musketeers and 'let off thousands of blank cartridges'. Even the great Corpus Christi procession at Aix, with its scenes, has been called a Bravade.

Four dances of the ritual sort must be examined. The first is a Church dance founded possibly on a long-ago wine festival, Bacchic they say. This is La Danse de la Souche, the vine-stump dance. I saw it at a hill village perched above the Var, done by one of those 'groups' which have sprung up everywhere, instead of by the village people themselves who had to look on. It was the village fête, and after High Mass everyone poured out into the minute *place*, where an open-air altar had been built and where a small fire of wood was already burning. The dancers' foreman waved his flag cere-monially over the fire, some sophisticated steps in dancing-school manner were done, the Prière de la Souche was sung in macaronic verse, Provençal and French, the leading dancer (inappropriately a girl) laid the stump on the fire, and the junior priest lit it. A Farandole then started round

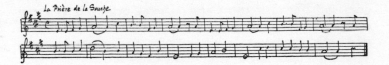

La Prière de la Souche.

fire and *place*. It was impressive but would have been more so if the dancers had been sons and daughters of the village.

The Cocos is performed by ten or twelve men, half of whom are dressed as women. These at one time – for the costume has varied – wore long dark skirts, white blouses, and crowns with points on their heads; the men in reverse, wore white trousers, dark shirts and the same sort of crowns. This seems a sophisticated idea of costume and could have been of no great age. But they all have blackened faces and wore on thighs and breasts half coconuts, carrying others in the palm of each hand. They stand in an open ring and clap their hand-coconuts on the others in rhythm, like little cymbals. Now this might almost be a description of our Bacup, Lancashire, Coconut dancers, who wear little skirts and whose Whiffler with his whip, a ritual character the Cocos cannot boast, keeps up a monotonous, hypnotic whipping throughout their long dance.

Les Fieloi (Fileuses) is certainly a ritual dance and a seasonal one with dramatic elements; its intention, equally certainly, is to bring in the spring. Its means for so doing are not very understandable now. It is a single file of men in women's white dresses worn over white trousers, with a few bells and large turned-up paper hats. Each carries a distaff on a bamboo stick with wool at the top, and a lantern in the wool. Over these goes a coloured paper shade which is lit up from within. They sally forth on a Carnival night or on Palm Sunday; a singer sings verses composed for the night and full of local allusions, as they stop outside houses to 'wassail' the inmates. The dance is of the Chain type and occasionally a Fool called Harlequin, with a blackened face, goes with them. If this Carnival *sortie* belonged to sheep country where wool means abundance, one could under-stand the spinning.* It is, however, widely spread from Toulon on the coast to Apt on the Coulon.

One Palm Sunday all was arranged for a drive to Apt. The mistral sprang up. Shutters slammed, palms creaked and

* Spinning, however, is often connected with sexual rites.

swayed, their leaves rattling like a machine-gun volley. The temperature dropped lower and lower, as did my spirits. Then my driver telephoned to announce that nothing would make him drive some hundred kilometres through the night in the teeth of that stupendous blast. So, Palm Sunday and Fieloi not waiting for the wind to drop – it blows for three days or three weeks – I had to write off this expedition as one of my collector's disappointments.* The mistral is the Gallo-Roman god of the wind, Circius, enthroned on Mont Ventoux as he should be. A find of terra-cotta trumpets, on which you may 'whistle for a wind', has been excavated on the mountain top, dating from Gallo-Roman times. Similar trumpets of green glazed pottery are sold to this day at fairs, more particularly at Marseilles and Aubagne, where children may be seen blowing for a wind with all their breath. Rhône valley heirs to the cult still adore their wind god – who drives a foreigner crazy. 'It's healthy,' they say with satisfaction. '*Cela dégage.*' God made rain and mistral, the devil hail and tempest, is their proverb. The father of the poet Mistral felt himself particularly akin to this divinity whose name he bore. He would invoke him during winnowing to blow away the chaff. '*Souffle, mon mignon,*' he would say. When the first gusts came bellowing down from Mont Ventoux he cried 'Bravo!' and if they blew too strongly he would restrain them with an '*Assez, assez*'.

The third dance – and this contains strong elements of drama – is the famous Olivettes. It is always said to be connected with the olive harvest, but except for its name I find no such connection. There are several variants and some historical evidence, in all but one case written by observers who held to the classical theory, and so of little value. For a long time I had to be content with a performance kindly given me by school children of Draguignan. It is unsatis-

* However I had the report of an eye-witness who could sing me the tune used for the dance, and a very poor one it is,

factory to observe a men's dance by children and was especially so here, the school teachers having introduced girls into the maypole figure. Some time after I again went to Draguignan (hoping my presence would not become known to the kind schoolmarms) to consult a transcription from a pamphlet of 1887. This was as satisfactory as the children's performance had been the reverse, but why their teachers had not consulted an excellent source in their own town library one cannot imagine. This dance is for sixteen young men, themselves sometimes called Olivettes. The costume is supposed to have been invented by Good King René – an advance on earlier writers who announced it as 'Roman'. They open with some simple figures, then in runs the Fool (who, so close to Italy, must needs be Harlequin) carrying a small maypole hung with sixteen ribbons. Now comes the Courdello, the plaiting of the pole by the men dancers, who have no need of intruding girls. At last comes the hilt-and-point formation, the test of this type of European Sword dance, the figure both badly observed and misconstrued by travellers whose knowledge goes no further than what they suppose to be 'the Pyrrhic'. Harlequin runs into the middle of the circle, the swords are built up into a lock on his shoulders, lowered for him to step on to it and, flag in hand, be raised shoulder high. Throning it in the air he declaims a horrid little verse, announcing himself as

> . . . *Arlequin,*
> *Monté sur des épées*
> *Comme un second Pompée*

which is taken as proof positive of the Roman origin of the dance. In his *La Chèvre d'Or* Paul Arène gives a rollicking account of it as performed in the hill village to which the golden goat led him. It too was a Bravade, announced by salvoes of gunfire, and took place at night by torchlight. Not only did a dozen men dance the 'Pyr-

rhique' with its maypole figure, which was 'brought to
Provence by Greek sailors', but they performed it before a
Turk in full eastern garb. Other writers note an Emperor, a
Prince, a Consul, a Herald. The variant from Toulon,
brought to light at my earnest request and specially learned
for a performance in England, is strongly tainted by
Morisca intrusion. Provençal girls are defended from Saracens in a hand-to-hand fight; nevertheless the hilt-and-point
formation brings it back to its true category, as does the
hoisting of the Fool.

In the old province of Dauphiné to the north lives one of
the least distorted examples of the Sword dance I have seen.
Pont de Cerbières, the hamlet 4,000 feet in altitude to which
it belongs, is so remote that no Morisca battle has reached it.
This was one of my fruitful expeditions and a more than
usually pleasant one, sharing a friend's car to bowl up from
her house at Mougins across the lavender uplands behind
Grasse, staying a night en route at Gap for a talk with the
Keeper of the Archives des Hautes Alpes who was making
a study of the Baccubert, and arriving at Briançon in the
exciting uproar of its Patronal fête.

Pont de Cerbières lies close by in its high cornland, the
mountains of the Franco-Italian frontier towering above,
the young Durance rushing below on its way to join the
Rhône. The three minuscule dancing places – for there is
but little space in the village – were already marked by small
fir trees which, by tradition, must be stolen at night from
the neighbouring forest by the dancers. I was fortunate
enough to see a rehearsal in progress without a single onlooker but myself, and to make friends with the cafetier
who is head of *Les Amis du Baccubert*. The *amis* keep the
swords and watch over tradition as closely as any Basque
grandfather over the steps of the Auresku. He told me
excitedly that a Monsieur from Scotland had written to
announce his coming 'because he did not believe Sword

dances existed outside Scotland'. The Monsieur did not appear but I have my suspicions as to his identity, and can picture his dismay at a Sword dance which does not in the least resemble any he knows.

In the afternoon the feast of St Roch began. The dance was first performed outside the church, the nine young men now appearing in their gala dress, the white shirt and trousers, the red sash of all southern France, which surprisingly reaches into this Alpine country. At one time they wore gold head-bands, a classic touch one supposes, because in local opinion their dance of course 'comes from the Romans'. They carry steel swords with gilt handles and guards, must be unmarried and may number nine, eleven or thirteen. The figures chosen depend on the number of men.

Now came a charming surprise. Five girls (who must also be unmarried), beautifully dressed in the costume of the Briançonnais region, appeared, seated themselves on a bench like a row of gay birds on a branch and began their 'mouth music'. They never slackened the tempo nor dropped the fraction of a tone; the pace was breathless, the effort prolonged, for each figure demands many repeats of the tune. About 1910 a fiddler was introduced, whose instrumental version became very different from the sung version; there is also one with a sharpened 7th in Millin's Atlas,[10] but what the girls now sing is almost identical with that noted by Tiersot[11] from the old women singers who preceded them. The Baccubert has no words but a series of ordered syllables:

Et tra la da, laderatanla, lader a ta . . .

These the girls were inclined to blur, but when one made a real mistake the others looked sharply at her, so the unmeaning syllables have their importance. The tune, claimed to be 'ancient Greek music', is a gay Rigaudon air in this, the country of Rigaudons.

The first part of the dance is called La Lève, the Lift, but the actual hoisting is forgotten. The formation is hilt-and-point with a lock, which not being woven cannot be held aloft for display. The smallest man, going into the centre, has a second lock formed on his shoulders, but instead of lifting him they all bend one knee to a nearly kneeling posture, eight times running. So the apogee of the drama is lacking; there is no death, no resurrection.

The second part of the dance is called simply Les Figures and consists of the forming of triangles, squares and stars with the swords, never however relinquishing the hilt-and-point chain. The pace, in spite of the breathless tune, is so deliberate as to become tiresome and because of this the dance should not be shown as entertainment. Highly interesting as it is to specialists it has been received with boos from an impatient French audience, which rudeness wounded the dancers to the heart.

The first printed reference to this ceremony is no earlier than 1731, when young men of Pont de Cerbières were summoned for maltreating young men of Briançon. No wonder. These last had stolen the stolen fir trees prepared for planting outside the church of St Roch, so naturally the dancers retaliated 'avant d'aller danser au Pont de Cerbières'. Sporadic references through the nineteenth century bring us to the valuable technical description published by a local doctor in 1913,[12] which is still consulted when the dancers are in doubt, thus linking living tradition with folklore study in a useful way. But the doctor's deductions take one into the realm of fantasy. 'It is a Sword dance which is celebrated in one single spot on earth,' says he. Unfortunately for the doctor's peace of mind he got to know of Brueghel's picture of the Village Fête with Sword dancers in the foreground. This was really awkward. However, Brueghel was known to have travelled in the Alps. Therefore he must have come to Pont de Cerbières and he must have come on the right day to witness the dance, and he must have remembered the Single-Under figure sufficiently to draw it accurately into a Flemish village scene. All was well. Yet this was written (and written so carefully) in 1913, when our English Sword dance books were being published and the well-known pictures of the Nuremberg and Dit-marschen dances could hardly, one would have thought, have been avoided.

The story is not finished yet. In 1952 some enthusiasts of Namur, Belgium, wished to reconstruct their own extinct Sword dance, one among many in the Lowlands. Where should they turn for technical instructions? To the Baccu-bert, which had so conveniently been transferred from Dauphiné to Flanders. And through Dr Blanchard's precise description the dance was in reality transferred to Namur as 'the' Sword dance and can there occasionally be seen in performance.

BIBLIOGRAPHY

1 'Notes on Three Provençale Dances', in *Journal of the English Folk Dance and Song Society*, Dec. 1941.
2 'The Rigaudon', in *The Musical Quarterly* (New York), July 1944.
3 A. MAZEL, *Notes sur la Camargue et les Saintes Maries-de-la-Mer* (Marseilles, Editions Publiroc, 1935).
4 DR WALTER STARKIE, *In Sara's Tents* (London, Murray, 1953).
5 LOUIS DUMONT, *La Tarasque* (Paris, 1951).
6 VIOLET ALFORD, 'Ceremonial Animals of Languedoc and the Sinibelet', in *Folk-Lore*, Vol. LIX, Dec. 1948.
7 *Revue des Traditions Populaires*, Vol. XV, p. 457.
8 J. R. H. SMIDT, *Les Noëls et la Tradition Populaire* (1932).
9 MARCEL PROVENCE, *La Pastorale de Séguret* (Aix-en-Provence, Editions du Feu, 1935).
10 A. L. MILLIN, *Atlas pour servir au Voyage dans les départements du midi de la France* (1807).
11 J. TIERSOT, *Chansons Populaires des Alpes Françaises* (Paris, 1903).
12 RAPHAEL BLANCHARD, *Le Bacuber* (1913).

Epilogue

The Basque Pastorales end their long-drawn-out course with an Epilogue. As with the Prologue, the verses and the man who sings them go by the same name.

Gente hounac aperenki	*Good people, apparently*
Debeieraci çutiegu,	*You have found us dull.*
Bena pharkamentu unmilki	*We humbly beg you*
Galthatcen deiciegu.	*To forgive us.*

If you have found me dull my Epilogue humbly begs the same forgiveness. It also informs the 'good people' who have read so far as this that since my work began the whole corpus of European folk custom is in course of changing.

Wars seem to leave an aftermath of nationalism which expresses itself in renewed attention to traditional custom – something with which the enemy has had no concern. This applies particularly to countries which have been occupied by an enemy. After 1918 the Belgian Government made grants to towns for the express purpose of remaking or re-dressing their giants. I do not know if these grants were repeated in 1945; if not, local determination not to be deprived of self-expression in giants is setting them rapidly on their feet again and adding new personages to the company. No superior outside hand is laid on local ideas and the result is good.*

In Jugoslavia the result of this surge of feeling is mixed. Custom, music, dance, in a state of active preservation unknown to western countries, were far less in need of a reviving spirit. Nevertheless a great gathering such as the

* We have remade Gog and Magog and brought the Salisbury Giant out for the Coronation.

International Folk Music Congress at Opatija in 1951 when, as has been said, the Government with lavish hospitality sent for folk artists from every province, did useful work. In one instance the country wedding feast from Montenegro, with its communal table-napkin, its nuptial *kolos*, its moves from the home of the bride to the home of the bridegroom, shown to the delegates, led to Slovenes who were present shortly afterwards reviving wedding customs in their own province; the invitation to this Congress caused hundreds of new costumes to be correctly made, amongst them again the Slovene White Krajina dress, nearly extinct. Now there is a fresh supply throughout the land calculated to last their wearers a lifetime. There is however a less beneficial side to this resurgence. Again through Government action, a company of National dancers has been formed to give displays of Jugoslav dance and music in and out of their country. It is in fact cultural propaganda. Stage arrangements, as I think unwisely, are shown in place of pure traditional art. Well done or no, such arrangements of the dramatic folk art of this land are unnecessary and deceptive; for instance a crowd of men fighting the battle for a dancing bride, when the real dance is a duel between two suitors, with the girl, far from dancing, standing by immovable. So much for the superior outside hand.

All Europe seems to be acting in the same way as regards dance. Now one is constrained to enquire cautiously, 'Is this a group?' when dancing begins, whereas before the resurgence such a question would have had no meaning. French dance and costume is in the hands – clutches one might say – of groups and the groups in the hands of some local leader who delights in proclaiming himself a *folcloriste*, but who is too frequently concerned only with outings where he may show off his people. No notion of reintroducing their dances to the village people at local fêtes enters his mind. I was told in Rousillon of people who were boycotted because they danced the village dances at their fête without reference to the group.

'They don't belong to the group so they had no business to do it,' said my informants.

This perverted notion largely spoils the work of the Fédération Française des Danses Populaires, for it actually prevents progress in what they were formed to revive. Groups whose activities are mentioned in their *Bulletin* report, '20 public appearances' or 'We made 14 journeys'. No reports on widening their efforts appear.

The Basques, long celebrated for their agility as for the anthropological value of their dance-dramas, because of this fame have suffered worse than many a part of France. After the Spanish civil war hundreds of Basques from 'the other side' came into France, burning in defeat with racialism and frustrated nationalism.* They began to teach French Basques, not their own but Spanish Basque cultural possessions. Soon groups sprang up, became theatre groups, even with theatre subsidies, seized upon French Basque dances to swell their repertories and have now pretty well ruined their own inheritance. Lack of wisdom, ignorance of ethnology and of course a spice of nationalism – 'all Basques are one' – has led to a potpourri of local traditions so complete that a new, composite tradition is in formation. Today one sees the Soule Hobby horse aped in a village of Labourd, the Biscayan Sword dance taught in all the provinces, the Spanish Basque *txistu* ousting the French Basque *txirula* and stringed drum. This composite tradition has been so inculcated that young Spanish Basques appeared at the Llangollen International Eisteddfod dressed in the Soule Masquerade costumes, Hobby horse and all, about to complacently present these French Basque dances in competitions which demand 'traditional dances of the teams' own country'. It was fortunate for adjudicators and competitors

* Before the war they had almost achieved their political aims.

that they arrived too late to compete. What is a real mis-
fortune is a composed, fancy dress for the girls. This dress
has a history of its own in the País Vasco and came into the
Pays Basque with the civil war emigrés. It was founded on
the local costume of the valley of Arratia in the province of
Biscay, to foster the surge of nationalism fathered by Arana
Goiri during the last half of the nineteenth century. When
the boys were set to learn the Biscayan Sword dance, the
girls had to be provided with something to keep pace with
their brothers. They were taught a Hoop dance, in the style
of the old Garland dances which exist along the coast right
into Cantabria. Dress and dance ran like wildfire through
nationalistic circles. I saw the dress myself in 1933, one day
of ebullition in Bilbao, made ridiculous even then by plaits
of flaxen tow pinned to the dark heads of the girls. When it
crossed the frontier with the emigrés about 1938, no one
dreamed of a visit of verification to the Musée Basque at
Bayonne, to consult lay figures and pictures which show
French Basque costumes. Instead the Spanish Basque
nationalist dress was swallowed whole, and there it is today,
worn by hundreds of French Basque girls, all practising the
same figure of a composed Spanish Basque nationalist
dance. Thus is tradition made.

The influence of the theatre groups has now reached professional dancers. Paris and London acclaim the Suite Basque
manufactured by the famous Antonio, in which he sees
nothing odd in dressing a girl as a man dressed as a girl, to
perform the Wine Glass dance, nor in displaying a row of
men showing Auresku steps, with no partner to honour
and no chain into which to lead the absent lady; nor in
appearing himself solo in a figure of the Biscayan Sword
dance which requires a small company.

I have already touched on the changes going on in Spain.
The conservation of the treasury of Spanish folk art after
the civil war became political social service, directed not by

folklorists but by Franquist social workers. Some of the far-away men's ritual dances, such as those in the Rioja, the Stick dances in León and Castile and the Sword dances already mentioned,* have not so far been tampered with, but, ironically, because they have not been 'discovered' lack of interest is telling upon them. Costumes get shabbier and shabbier, more and more figures are forgotten, ritual characters are lost. Then a new group from the town will learn the ancient dance and the village retires abashed.

Of the present state of folk song I can say but little, for the singing of folk song was already dying when my work began. I have noted lovely songs in Portugal from girls working in the vines, and had a French version of 'William and Margaret' sung to me in a weaver's cottage high above the valley of the Lez in the Pyrenees, while plenty of songs for dancing have come my way. Croatian women and those on the islands of the Adriatic still send forth their piercing harmony in seconds; the bards of Jugoslavia have never ceased their improvisations to *gusle* accompaniment, neither do the Basque improvisors appear to be losing their art though now using a few tunes only. Welsh Penillion impro-visors now often compose their verses beforehand and sing them from written copies, and when one hears Swiss people, rowing on a lake or climbing a green alp, singing folk airs in polyphony (and very well) it is certain they learnt them during their school days or at their yodel club. Their tradi-tional crafts too are not learnt now from father to son but from teachers sent for the purpose. Collectors do still find songs to record and are doing so with excellent results in our islands, but the main body of the work seems to be coming to an end on the Continent, for most of the European countries began long before we did.

The multiplication of bodies for the study of folklore in its many branches, ranging from the Unesco-sponsored

* See Andalusia, p. 38, and Aragon, p. 57.

Commission Internationale des Arts Populaires and the International Folk Music Council to the village folklore class held by the Vicar, has so re-directed the spirit of the study that that too has changed. Savants gathered in council may succeed in defining folk song, in classifying folk tales, in getting already gathered material into print. Essential as such work is it does nothing to preserve the living performance of customs. At the 8th Basque Congress, 1954, a paper of mine on their own drama was presented. During the discussion which followed a museum-trained lady laid down that there was no interest in keeping alive the Pastorales once they had been filmed and recorded. The Congress repudiated so deadening a proposal, led by three *Pastoraliers** who passionately declared themselves followers of living tradition. This was an astonishing thing, for such Pastorale producers are peasants and farmers never before seen at a Congress. Here then, meeting in a remarkable way, are two divergent lines of thought, that of the dead recording and docketing spirit and that of the re-awaking spirit of living performers.

What really stirs a traditional performer is personal interest in his inheritance. Peter Kennedy of the BBC recording team tells me his visits are often followed by a renewed taste in the performer; a singer will begin again to sing, a fiddler to fiddle, while his wish to record the extinct Symondsbury, Dorset, Mummers' play resulted in its rebirth in a young generation, and in the making of the sound film in colour 'Walk in St George'.

In the same way my visit to the little Aragonese village of Sena led to the 'coming out' of their dramatic Sword dance though it had lapsed for four years; and after a visit from Miss Maud Karpeles to Royton in Lancashire in the hope that she might note a dance which was dead and gone, the foreman was so flattered that he got his men together again

* For the rôle of these men see p. 149.

and Royton Morris has been going strongly ever since.

Enthusiastic teams of students sent into the field seem to me a pernicious method. They seem irritating and odd to their informants who, like the Irishman 'to pleasure your honour', will tell them anything and walk off. It is still the freelance, with ample time to listen to *everything* his singer or storyteller has to tell, who has the best chance of hearing something worth while. The man who begins with 'Oh What a Beautiful Morning' may end with an unknown variant of 'The Bitter Withy' and, having sung and warmly pressed your hand, will say like the Epilogue,

Eguin ahala eguin dugu	*We have done our best*
Cien diberti eraciteco.	*To please you.*
Desplazer dugu ez paguira içan	*We are vexed if we have*
Cien contentutaco.	*Not been able to content you.*

Index